Den of Spies

Also by Craig Unger

American Kompromat: How the KGB Cultivated Donald Trump, and Related Tales of Sex, Greed, Power, and Treachery

House of Trump, House of Putin: The Untold Story of Donald Trump and the Russian Mafia

When Women Win: EMILY's List and the Rise of Women in American Politics (by Ellen Malcolm and Craig Unger)

Boss Rove: Inside Karl Rove's Secret Kingdom of Power

The Fall of the House of Bush: The Untold Story of How a Band of True Believers Seized the Executive Branch, Started the Iraq War, and Still Imperils America's Future (published in paperback as *American Armageddon*)

House of Bush, House of Saud: The Secret Relationship Between the World's Two Most Powerful Dynasties

Blue Blood

Den of Spies

Reagan, Carter, and the Secret History of the Treason That Stole the White House

Craig Unger

MARINER BOOKS

BOSTON NEW YORK

 For information, address HarperCollins Publishers, 195 Broadway, New York, NY 10007.

HarperCollins books may be purchased for educational, business, or sales promotional use. For information, please email the Special Markets Department at SPsales@harpercollins.com.

FIRST EDITION

Designed by Jen Overstreet

Library of Congress Cataloging-in-Publication Data has been applied for.

ISBN 978-0-06-333060-3

24 25 26 27 28 LBC 5 4 3 2 1

To Kim

and

for Bob Parry and those who fight for the truth

The obscure we see eventually. The completely obvious, it seems, takes longer.

—Edward R. Murrow

Contents

Author's Note

THIS BOOK IS THE PRODUCT OF HUNDREDS OF INTERVIEWS AND research that took place on and off over a period of more than thirty-three years. However, it would not exist in its present form without the landmark work of Bob Parry, whom I came to regard as a friend and colleague until his death in 2018. Bob did more than any other journalist to make sure the October Surprise was not lost to history, and his widow, Diane Duston, was enormously generous in providing me access to Bob's archives, which are such an important part of this book.

Prologue

Some years ago, a new acquaintance asked me how it was that I had been consumed by the October Surprise for such a long time. He was referring to a story that, for years, I'd been unable to get out of my head about a covert operation in which the Reagan-Bush campaign made a secret deal with Iran that sabotaged the 1980 presidential election. It was a great story involving spies, coverups, and an act of treason that took place at the highest levels of government. It had also never been proven—at least not in the minds of most Americans.

As a journalist, one tends to move from one story on to the next. But this was different. I had started investigating it in 1991, and to be honest, I had been on and off it ever since. It became the background noise to my life as a journalist—something between a hobby and a part-time obsession.

I've long thought that much of what we see on the news is merely spectacle and theater, and that we rarely get a glimpse of the unseen ways in which power *really* works. Behind the curtain. In that regard, the October Surprise was a master class. There were double agents, betrayals, covert operations, cutouts, illegal arms deals, and mysterious deaths. A hall of mirrors designed to obscure the truth, it was a case study in how to hijack American foreign policy, steal the presidency, and get away with it.

All with no fingerprints.

The specific allegations dated back to the 1980 presidential election between the Republican ticket of Ronald Reagan and George H. W. Bush versus Jimmy Carter and Walter Mondale. At the time, Iran held fifty-two American hostages who had been incarcerated at the American embassy in Tehran during Iran's Islamic Revolution. The fate of those hostages became a national obsession and arguably the most important issue of the 1980 election, a crisis unfolding in real time, the resolution of which would determine who held the most powerful office in the world.

The accusations were jaw-dropping. As the 1980 presidential campaign neared the end, Republican operatives did something extraordinary to make sure the hostage crisis played out in their favor: they made a secret deal to send weapons worth millions of dollars to Iran. At the time, of course, the Republicans were not even in power, so they had no governmental or legal authority to make any agreement whatsoever with Iran. Even if they'd had that right, the Carter administration had imposed an arms embargo against Iran as a terrorist state, making the deal illegal on multiple grounds. But even worse than the illegal arms deal itself was that, in return for these weapons, the Republicans had supposedly demanded a quid pro quo from the mullahs of Iran. They would get the arms to Iran, but in return the Americans would remain in Iranian custody even longer. That's right. The Republicans were bribing Iran to *prolong* the captivity of the hostages.

If the hostages were released before the election, the thinking went, the ensuing patriotic fervor would give President Jimmy Carter such a big bounce in the polls that he would beat Reagan. But if the hostages were still incarcerated, voters would see Carter as a weak and impotent president who allowed America to be humiliated. As a result, Reagan-Bush campaign manager William Casey engineered a secret deal whereby Iran agreed to release the hostages, but only after the November elections had taken place.

When I first read about the accusation, the alleged crime was so over the top, it was literally unimaginable. Who could possibly believe that the Republicans—historically, the tough guys in American foreign policy, in the Cold War, in Vietnam, and now, rhetorically at least, in Iran—would secretly arm the Islamic fundamentalists chanting "Death to America!" in return for Khomeini's people *prolonging* the incarceration of fifty-two Americans?

If these charges were true, the entire Reagan-Bush era—indeed, modern conservatism in the United States—had been born out of a treasonous covert operation.

That was the October Surprise.

I first wrote about it in 1991, for *Esquire*, when it was being talked about all over the country. At the time, President George H. W. Bush, who was preparing to run for reelection, had sky-high approval ratings that made a second term look inevitable. But as Reagan's vice presidential candidate in 1980, Bush's name was front and center in the scandal, and the political implications were explosive. Dozens of investigative reporters at ABC News, PBS's *Frontline*, the *New York Times*, *Newsweek*, and more jumped on the story. And why not? An incumbent president who was up for reelection was tied up in a treasonous spy scandal. It was the kind of story on which a journalist could make his or her career. It wasn't just that the presidency hung in the balance. The basic premise of the story called into question the legitimacy of the entire Reagan era.

But then, suddenly, the whole story was discredited. Not just once, but repeatedly. About six months after I started investigating it, *Newsweek* ran three major stories saying the October Surprise never happened. Maybe you need to be a journalist to appreciate how bizarre and unusual that is. This was a period during which magazines like *Time* and *Newsweek* were still powerful forces shaping the national conversation. Normally, they reported what *did* happen. That's what news is. But when nothing happened, when events *didn't* take place—that's *not* news.

That was just the start, though. *The New Republic*, the *Washington Post*, and other organs of the mainstream press suddenly piled on as well, switching from intrepid journalists to a skeptical chorus. All the sources were con men and criminals—or so critics said. How could anyone have fallen for these sleazy arms dealers? Anyone who interviewed them—*me*, for example—was a gullible dupe. A conspiratorialist.

I had never seen anything like it. I had done my reporting. I knew there was something there. But suddenly the hottest story in the country, one with true historic significance, had been downgraded to a wacky conspiracy theory dreamt up by the tinfoil-hat brigade. Two congressional investigations fizzled. The whole subject was whitewashed. The October Surprise had been reported, and then it was unreported. It was news, and then it was fake news. Government officials who pursued it were ostracized as conspiracy nuts. Reporters who were on the story—like me—were discredited or marginalized. I was sued for $10 million. Long time friends and editors alike stopped returning our calls. We were toxic. *I* was toxic.

Following Bush's loss to Bill Clinton in the 1992 election, the story was mostly forgotten. Relegated to the dustbin of history. And for most Americans, the October Surprise of 1980—if they even heard about it—never happened.

Yet for decades—thirty-three years, at this writing—I kept trying to get to the bottom of it. To be clear, I did many other things over the years. I was an editor and writer for *New York* magazine. I covered national security for *Vanity Fair* for fifteen years. I contributed to *Esquire*, *The New Republic*, *The New Yorker*, the *Washington Post*, the *New York Times*, and other publications. I wrote seven books. But I kept coming back to the October Surprise.

So, when my new friend asked what kind of person would spend decades on the October Surprise, I had to pause for a moment. The answer was that I wouldn't let go because I had a front-row seat at a significant event in American history, and I could not unsee the hidden mechanisms of power that were really orchestrating these events. A vitally important chapter in contemporary American history had been erased and discredited at the time in which it was still politically relevant and actionable. And for the most part, America bought the lies. In fact, almost entirely.

So over the years, I went back to it again and again, a scab that had never healed. In 1992, I went to Israel to interview high-level

Israeli intelligence operatives whose agents had secretly facilitated arms shipments to Iran. In 1998, I went to St. Charles, Michigan, population 1,981, where a former congressman gave me reams of documents. In 2014, I finally got a visa that allowed me to travel to Iran where I interviewed the founder of the Revolutionary Guard and chief arms procurement officer during the Revolution. In 2016, when I was in Paris, I made a side trip to Versailles to interview former Iranian president Abolhassan Bani-Sadr, and later, his aides.

After all these years, this is not a mystery to solve—at least not in a traditional sense. Rather it is an attempt to square the circle between something that is both obvious and shrouded, self-evident and lost in the shadows. It is like trying to understand how a master illusionist works.

Indeed, mere minutes into his presidency, Reagan announced the release of the hostages almost as if it were a magic trick or one of the most fantastical coincidences in modern politics. He had no authority to negotiate with Iran before he took the oath of office, and Iran would not have released the hostages without some communication with team Reagan. But they did release the hostages. And yet despite the self-evident nature of that anomaly, Americans still responded like an audience of young children who had been bewitched and bewildered by a magician's sleight of hand, and reflexively rejected a conspiracy that took place in full view of the general public. In plain sight. As the *Onion* later wrote in its end-of-the-century book lampooning the great events of the twentieth century, "Hostages Released; Reagan Urges American People Not to Put Two and Two Together."

Throughout the 1990s, 2000s, and the 2010s, I was not the only reporter quietly chasing the October Surprise. Investigative reporter Robert Parry tracked down the facts, punctured numerous phony alibis, and got it right again and again. He published books, newspaper articles, and online pieces, but somehow the fruits of his labor never really became deeply rooted as part of America's shared past. Parry died in 2018, leaving me as one of the last journalists working on the three-decade-old story.

But if we are to survive as a democracy, it's vital to understand what happened all those years ago. Even if we don't like this part of our past—rather, *especially* if we don't like it—we must come to terms with it, acknowledge it, and understand how and why it happened.

So I've undertaken the task of telling what happened, how, and why—a spy story from real life that played an enormous role in contemporary American history. It's the story of how master spy William Casey and his associates put together a secret network of arms dealers, corrupt bankers, and rogue intelligence operatives for a covert operation that sabotaged the presidential election, how it was kept a secret for so long even when the facts were staring us in the face, how journalists at *Newsweek*, *The New Republic*, and other publications, unwittingly or otherwise, in effect disseminated disinformation to cover up the October Surprise, and finally, how, like a master illusionist employing a vast arsenal of trickery and deception, Casey was able to execute a magnificently successful sleight of hand that fooled the entire country.

To understand what really happened, let's go back to 1980.

Part I
Crimes and Coverups

Chapter One
Blood in the Water

No matter who you talked to in President Jimmy Carter's administration, April 24, 1980, was one of the worst days in history. "The President looked as if someone had stabbed him," National Security Adviser Zbigniew Brzezinski wrote soon after. "Pain was evident all over his face."[1]

When Chief of Staff Hamilton Jordan heard the horrifying news, he "ducked into the President's private bathroom and vomited [his] guts out."[2] As a member of Carter's Georgia retinue, Jordan had a reputation as a high-spirited good ole boy from the South, but, like it or not, he was getting an immersive education in the ugliest part of politics.

Earlier that day, eight Sikorsky RH-53D Sea Stallion helicopters had taken off from the aircraft carrier *Nimitz* in the Gulf of Oman in the Persian Gulf. They had begun a journey of nearly six hundred nautical miles at night and in unfamiliar territory to a refueling site code-named Desert One, in an Iranian desert.[3] Their mission was to rescue fifty-two Americans who had been taken hostage by militant protesters in Tehran on November 4, 1979, amid Iran's Islamic Revolution.

The fate of the hostages had galvanized the entire country. Even as America was beset by double-digit inflation, resolving the hostage crisis instantly became the most decisive issue in the upcoming presidential election. A source of immense political opportunity and peril for the Carter White House, the rescue attempt felt dangerously close to a mission of last resort after months of failed diplomatic efforts to free the hostages.

The Iranian Revolution had started more than a year earlier, in 1978. At that time Iran's leader, Mohammed Reza Pahlavi, the Shah, had extremely close ties to the United States, but he had also ruled the country through brutality, incarcerating as many as 300,000 political prisoners, killing as many as 100,000,[4] and eventually provoking millions of Iranians—from secular leftists to Islamic fundamentalists—to protest his repressive regime. On September 2, 1978, the National Intelligence Estimate—the US intelligence community's most authoritative written assessment of national security issues—painted a gloomy appraisal of the growing conflict, reporting that the Shah's regime might not survive the next several months without major concessions.[5] That assessment, however, was an anomaly among many more reports that were overly optimistic, asserting that the Shah's regime was "an island of stability," as Carter[6] had put it in late 1977, or that a new regime, once it took power, could come to terms with Washington, or that it would collapse, and, one way or another, things would go back to normal.

Throughout 1978, as one popular uprising after another took place against him, the Shah responded by imposing martial law, leading his forces to kill hundreds of Iranian protesters when they marched in the streets.[7] When President Carter urged the Shah to liberalize his policies, the Shah merely paid him lip service.[8] Without meaningful change, the protests continued to grow.

On January 1 and 2, 1979, about two hundred protesters against the Shah were killed in demonstrations. Carter refused to support more repressive measures needed to keep the Shah in power. Finally, on January 16, the Shah left Iran for Aswan, Egypt. Officially, he was just going on vacation, he claimed, but that fooled no one. At the same time, other members of his family—three of his children and his mother-in-law—were flying via an Iranian Air Force jet to Texas.[9] This was his endgame: permanent exile. In Tehran, hundreds of thousands of people celebrated his departure, cheering in the streets.[10]

On February 1, Ayatollah Ruhollah Khomeini, a charismatic anti-Shah cleric, returned from exile to be greeted by millions of people in the streets of Tehran. He quickly began to form a new revolutionary Islamic state. As opposing factions jostled for power in a new provisional government, protestors of all stripes called for the Shah to return to Iran and face trial for his crimes. But the Shah sought refuge in the United States.

That, however, was the last thing the Carter administration wanted. As he tried to forge ties to whatever new government rose out of the ashes in Tehran, Carter, a strong advocate for human rights, sought as much distance as possible between America and the Shah's brutal repression. For decades under the Shah, the regime's violent security forces known as SAVAK—forces that had been formed and trained by the CIA—had tortured Shia clerics to death. They had used electric cattle prods. Acid was dripped into nostrils. There were fingernail extractions. Prisoners were raped and urinated upon.[11] Novelists, professors, directors, and more were jailed for criticizing the regime. SAVAK's cruelty was legendary, and in this precarious moment, Iranians had not forgotten that SAVAK was a CIA creation.

Given his aversion to the Shah's brutality, not to mention his fear of further alienating the Iranian people, Carter had been loath to offer the Shah safe haven in the United States. To Carter, the Shah was a liability, and his presence in America could irrevocably alienate the new regime. The US embassy in Tehran was already a potent symbol to anti-Shah protesters. After all, the embassy was the notorious spy nest—referred to as the "Den of Spies" by Iranians—where the 1953 US-backed Iranian coup had been hatched, bringing the Shah to power. In the early days of the Islamic Revolution, the embassy was overrun three times by protesters.[12] The Carter administration knew the risks of admitting the Shah.

But the Shah's longtime backers in the State Department and the CIA pressed the matter repeatedly with the president. In addition to his close relationship with current and former members of the foreign policy establishment, the Shah had made a longtime practice of writing large checks to American powerbrokers who helped secure Iran's fate.[13] Among the most notable beneficiaries was Chase Bank and its CEO, David Rockefeller. Chase had profited mightily from joint ventures with the Iranian state bank and from advising Iran's national oil company. In 1979 alone, the bank had syndicated more than $1.7 billion in loans for Iranian public projects ($7.7 billion in 2024 dollars).[14] According to Mark Hulbert's *Interlock*, another frequent recipient of the Shah's lavish gifts was Henry Kissinger, who, in addition to having forged ties with the Shah as secretary of state, was chairman of Chase Manhattan Bank's International Advisory Committee.[15]

With Iran in flux, billions of dollars were at stake for Chase,[16] and from the moment the Shah fled Iran on January 16, 1979, a group led by Rockefeller and Kissinger began aggressively lobbying Jimmy Carter to admit the Shah to the United States, an effort that became known as Project Alpha. Unknown at the time, this story was not fully told until it was reported forty years later in a 2019 *New York Times* article by David Kirkpatrick.[17] Sometimes referred to as the Rockefeller Group, the team included a mix of political bluebloods, former CIA agents, and financial luminaries—among them cousins Archibald Roosevelt Jr. and Kermit Roosevelt Jr., grandsons of Theodore Roosevelt who were both key figures in the 1953 Iranian coup. These men were titans of the Eastern Establishment, global powerbrokers who had remade the world after the Second World War. Carter was a peanut farmer from Plains, Georgia. They came from different worlds.

Initially, Carter rebuffed their attempts to admit the Shah and tried to get both Kissinger and David Rockefeller to dissuade the Shah from coming to the United States. Both men "refused with some indignation," as Kissinger put it,[18] and instead, Project Alpha went on the offensive. Kissinger accused Carter of forcing America's loyal ally to search all over the world for a refuge "like a flying Dutchman looking for a port of call."[19] On April 7, 1979, he called Zbigniew Brzezinski and criticized the administration "in rather sharp terms" for its refusal to admit the Shah.[20] Then, with Brzezinski's encouragement, Kissinger called President Carter and let him have it. Two days later, David Rockefeller visited the White House and did the same.

"We can't get away from Iran," First Lady Rosalynn Carter noted in her diary.[21] "Many people—Kissinger, David Rockefeller, Howard Baker, John McCloy, Gerald Ford—all are after Jimmy to bring the shah to the United States, but Jimmy says it's been so long, and anti-American and anti-shah sentiments have escalated so that he doesn't want to. Jimmy said he explained to all of them that the Iranians might kidnap our Americans who are still there." Acutely aware that admitting the Shah posed a grave danger to Americans at the embassy in Tehran, Carter was exasperated. "Fuck the Shah," he said.[22] "I'm not going to welcome him here when he has other places to go where he'll be safe."

But then the Shah, who had secretly been battling lymphoma for years, became seriously ill. In October 1979, a doctor friend of David Rockefeller's who was *not* an oncologist examined the Shah, and a bogus declaration was made.[23] President Carter was told the Shah was "at the point of death" and that New York had the only medical facility that was capable of possibly saving his life, according to the *New York Times*.[24]

It was a lie, but Carter fell for it and made the worst decision of his presidency. On October 22, 1979, the Shah entered the United States, and was admitted to New York Hospital under the alias David Newsome [*sic*]. It was an inside joke, an apparent reference to Undersecretary of State David Newsom, who had repeatedly warned that if the Shah were admitted to the US, "the American Embassy would be taken, and it would be a threat to American lives."[25]

But Newsom *had* been prescient. Less than two weeks after the Shah's arrival in the United States, on November 4, 1979, hundreds of Iranians stormed the American embassy in Tehran and took seventy hostages as they demanded the extradition of the Shah from the United States. (Most of the female and African American hostages were later released, leaving fifty-two Americans in captivity.) The hostages had been seized by militant students and other protesters—apparently without consultation with or the authorization of Khomeini. But Khomeini soon gave his blessing to the takeover and issued a statement of support. Iran canceled all military treaties with the United States.

Meanwhile, Carter swiftly took punitive measures of his own. He froze all Iranian assets in the United States and banks overseas—some $12 billion (more than $50 billion in 2024 dollars).[26] Iranian oil exports to the United States came to a full stop, a move that caused oil prices to double over the following eighteen months, further exacerbating the double-digit inflation.[27] Carter also immediately imposed an arms embargo on Iran's military, which was comprised largely of weaponry America had sold to the Shah. But such measures took time before they had enough impact to force Iran's hand.

Triggered by the Shah's arrival, the hostage crisis had begun.

THE CRISIS INSTANTLY CAPTURED THE ATTENTION OF THE ENtire country. Yellow ribbons—the iconic symbol of hope for the safe return of the hostages—were festooned on trees and telephone poles everywhere. Millions of people tuned in nightly to ABC News' new show, *Nightline* with Ted Koppel, a news show created specifically to cover the ongoing drama as it unfolded. In the immediate aftermath, Americans rallied around the president. Carter's previously low approval rating soared.

Once the presidential season got underway in early 1980, however, the outcome of the hostage crisis instantly became the tipping point issue—one that was fluid, unresolved, that could go either way, and in doing so become the most decisive factor in the upcoming presidential election. As the weeks passed, and the hostages remained incarcerated, Carter's poll numbers suffered accordingly. Increasingly, he appeared to be helpless and weak. His political future depended on whether he could bring home the hostages. Day after day, America was being held hostage. Even Carter's eighty-one-year-old mother, Miss Lillian, had discomfited her son by telling the press what she would do about Ayatollah Khomeini. "If I had a million dollars to spare," she said, "I'd look for someone to kill him."[28]

But Carter had few options. According to Stuart Eizenstat, the White House domestic affairs adviser under Carter, the administration was crippled by "the absence of good intelligence by the CIA on what was happening internally with Iran." Eizenstat was speaking in a filmed discussion about the failed mission to free the hostages.[29]

In the end, there were only two choices when it came to trying to force Iran's hand—military intervention or some kind of negotiations. As for the former, Carter thought any military operation, no matter what form it took, was certain to put the hostages' lives in jeopardy, and that was out of the question for him. "I am not going to take any military action that would cause bloodshed or arouse the unstable captors of our hostages to attack them or punish them," said Carter, in a meeting with State Department personnel.[30] Consequently, he was reluctant to let US aircraft carriers patrol the Persian Gulf lest their presence lead to an unintended escalation that could endanger the hostages.[31]

As for negotiations, on November 7, three days after the hostage takeover, the president decided to send Ramsey Clark, the former attorney general under Lyndon Johnson, and Bill Miller, staff director for the Senate Select Committee on Intelligence, as emissaries to Iran to negotiate. But Khomeini refused even to allow them into the country, so that overture went nowhere.

Further complicating diplomacy was the fact that it wasn't entirely clear with whom the White House should be negotiating.

Leftists, secular activists, and Islamic fundamentalists had all united to overthrow the Shah, but now, with the nascent Islamic theocracy still in flux, warring factions were fighting among themselves, which paralyzed diplomatic initiatives. Moreover, the hostages were being held by nongovernmental actors. That meant the White House didn't know which levers to push, making communications with the Iranian government difficult and of little use.[32]

In addition, there were deeper problems with the hostage crisis that were largely unseen by the American public. Iran was not just another pawn on the geopolitical chessboard; for decades it had played a pivotal role in US foreign interests. Under the Shah, Iran had been one of the "Twin Pillars" of American policy in the Middle East along with Saudi Arabia, defending both Western oil interests and Israel. After all, the Iranian port of Bandar Abbas opened out into the Strait of Hormuz. This narrow passage between the Persian Gulf and the Gulf of Oman is the world's most important oil transit chokepoint,[33] through which more than 20 percent of the world's oil flows each day.[34] Assuring the continuous flow was vital to America's national security, the security of its allies, and the global economy.

Meanwhile Iran needed arms. Even though the Shah was gone, the Iranian military still relied almost entirely on its aging inventory of US weapons, which had to be supplemented by spare parts, tires, and other light armaments. Prior to the overthrow of the embassy, Iran had been a vital counterweight to Israel's newly feared enemy, Iraq's Saddam Hussein, who had come to power in 1979 and posed an increasingly serious threat to Israeli security. But until Iran and the United States resolved their discord, Israel couldn't arm Iran without violating the American embargo.

And yet the most obvious solution to this dilemma—an arms-for-hostages deal—was unacceptable. The age of Islamic fundamentalist terror had just been born. Ayatollah Ruhollah Khomeini had instantly provided America with a terrifying new villain. President

Carter saw such a proposal as tantamount to paying a bribe to terrorists and rejected it as immoral. Besides, to have openly discussed sending weapons to Khomeini—America's enemy—would have been political suicide.

The end result was that a diplomatic solution was politically and morally untenable for the Carter White House. There were multiple back-channel overtures through early 1980, but nothing was producing results.

And that void, in turn, created an opening for various unscrupulous parties to exploit the situation.

As it happened, the hostage crisis came at a pivotal moment in the history of American intelligence. In the years immediately before Carter took office, the CIA's deepest and darkest secrets had been spilling out one after another.

It started with the 1974 exposé of the CIA's "Family Jewels" report by Seymour Hersh in the *New York Times*,[35] which revealed that the Agency had conducted massive, illegal domestic intelligence operations against the antiwar movement and other activists during the Vietnam War. Soon after, investigations by the Church Committee in the Senate, launched by Sen. Frank Church (D-ID), and the Pike Committee, chaired by Otis Pike (D-NY) in the House of Representatives, followed and exposed the full range of the CIA's dirty little secrets for all to see.[36] Among them were a quarter century of overseas assassination attempts, illegal wiretaps, human experimentation, spying for Richard Nixon in Watergate, and more. The CIA had staged coup d'états in Syria in 1949, in Iran in 1953, in Guatemala in 1954, in the Congo in 1960, in the Dominican Republic in 1963, in South Vietnam in 1963, in Brazil in 1964, and in Chile in 1973.[37] There were CIA plots to assassinate foreign leaders in the Dominican Republic, Cuba, Chile, Vietnam, and more.

In the aftermath of the Church Committee and the Pike Committee investigations, for the first time, Congress began to rein in the power of the intelligence community. In 1976, President Gerald Ford issued Executive Order 11905 banning political assassinations.[38] The Senate also created the United States Senate Select Committee on Intelligence to provide oversight. And in 1978, Congress enacted the Foreign Intelligence Surveillance Act, which for the first time imposed significant legal limits on the ability of the CIA, the FBI, and the NSA to wiretap and spy on American citizens.[39]

To further restrain the Agency, President Carter appointed his former Naval Academy classmate, Stansfield Turner, as CIA director. In October 1977, in what became known as the Halloween Massacre, Turner purged 820 CIA operatives from the Agency, many of whom had been special or "black" operations executives and counterintelligence officers. In early 1979, another 250 people put in for retirement. At the time, an article in the *Washington Post* said, "American intelligence is dying,"[40] and placed the onus on Turner. In *Newsweek*, George Will called for Turner's resignation.[41]

Out at Langley, the conventional relationship in which the CIA reported directly to the president had been destroyed. The sanctity of the CIA had been violated. "The traditional CIA answering to the president was an empty vessel having little more than technical capability," said James Angleton, the longtime chief of counterintelligence at the CIA, according to Joe Trento's *Prelude to Terror: The Rogue CIA and the Legacy of America's Private Intelligence Network*.[42]

Back in the good old days, before the Church Committee and various intelligence reforms, covert operatives working for the CIA almost certainly would have done whatever was necessary to shore up the Shah's power, whether that meant letting SAVAK run amok or bribing mobs to demonstrate in his favor, as the CIA had done in Iran in 1953. But increasingly, specialists in black ops operations were forced to find work off-the-books and outside regular channels. Way outside.

As a result, when the hostage crisis began, the intelligence community, much of which had already been deeply alienated, was appalled by Carter's fumbling efforts in Iran. They saw it as further proof of his incompetence, and these disaffected elements regarded the president as ruinous to America's overall security. "You can't imagine the tremendous anger against the Carter administration in the military and intelligence apparatus," said Susan Clough, President Carter's personal secretary.[43] "And not just in the CIA. Emotions had been boiling for years."

Clough served as a gatekeeper to the president, a last line of access for those who wished to plead a point to Carter. From that insider perch, she saw the profoundly demoralized military and intelligence communities. By the last year of the Carter administration, she says fistfights would break out in the Pentagon about the president, and the military was politicized to a point where its allegiance to the commander in chief was in question.

For much of Carter's term, Clough tried to explain the depth of the problem to the president in private meetings. She enjoyed little success. By early 1979, knowing Carter didn't want to hear any more criticism of Stansfield Turner, Clough was so disturbed she resorted to laying out in confidential memos the dangers Carter faced.

"I told him the problem with Stansfield Turner was so serious that it would not go away or be resolved without his guidance," Clough said.[44] "It had to be dealt with, directly or indirectly, by the president. In the CIA, disloyalty was potentially far more destructive than in any other department. It was a problem that could get out of control and leave a legacy other presidents would have to deal with."

After years of working with Carter, Clough knew that the president had a routine way of dealing with the countless memos that crossed his desk. If he read the memo, and wanted to acknowledge that he read it and appreciated it, she said, he would initial it, *JC*. Sometimes, he would put the *JC* at the bottom to let you know he read the whole thing.[45]

But if he didn't like it, Clough told me, he would simply put one initial: *C*.

In this case, Carter had put a big *C* at the bottom—not *JC*. "That let me know he was not happy with it, but he had read the whole thing," she said.[46]

And he didn't want to hear another word about it.

FOR MANY CURRENT AND FORMER AGENTS WITHIN THE CIA, IT wasn't just Carter's handling of the hostage crisis that upset them; it was the fact that there was a crisis at all. In their eyes, the CIA of old could have prevented the instability in Iran from getting out of hand. Instead, on Carter's watch the United States had lost Iran—a relationship of great strategic importance, of course, but also an immense source of pride and symbolism for the CIA.

In a way, it all went back to 1953. At the time, the Anglo-Iranian Oil Company, the predecessor to British Petroleum (now BP), had been taking home more than 80 percent[47] of Iran's oil revenues; the CIA, working with its British counterparts in MI6, had decided that they would do whatever it took to keep that arrangement intact even if it meant ousting Iranian prime minister Mohammad Mossadegh. A secular social democrat, Mossadegh had been a principal figure in bringing about the end of 150 years of British interference and plundering of Iran's national resources. To achieve that goal, he first tried to renegotiate a new agreement with the Anglo-Iranian Oil Company. When that hit a dead end, Mossadegh then resolved that he had no choice but to commit the unpardonable sin of nationalizing Iran's vast oil industry. "This was the first time that anyone in the Middle East had ever done anything against imperial powers, colonial powers," said Barry Rosen, a press attaché at the US embassy in the seventies, and later one of the hostages, in the PBS documentary, *Taken Hostage: The Making of an American Enemy*.[48]

Under Mossadegh, the Shah had been reduced to a mere figurehead, but thanks to Operation Ajax, as the 1953 coup was known in the CIA, the Shah returned to rule with almost dictatorial powers, as an American proxy. So dependent was the Shah on his CIA sponsors that his loyalty, a precious commodity in the tumultuous Middle East, was never in question. As the Shah himself told Kermit Roosevelt Jr., his close friend and the CIA architect of the coup, "I owe my throne to God, my people, my army—and to you!"[49]

The coup had the support of President Dwight D. Eisenhower and Prime Minister Winston Churchill, not to mention CIA Director Allen Dulles. To ensure the Shah's ability to enforce his new powers, the CIA created, trained, and funded SAVAK, the brutal security force with which he ruled an intelligence state through surveillance, political and religious repression, imprisonment, torture, and thousands of executions. The planning for Operation Ajax took place in the American embassy in Tehran, the same spy nest Iranian protesters seized a generation later to ignite the hostage crisis, and which came to symbolize the degree to which Iran had become a proxy for American interests.

But most Americans didn't have a clue that the CIA was behind it. As *Time* declared, "This was no military coup, but a spontaneous popular uprising."[50] The fact that no American troops were involved in the coup gave the US government license to deny any role in it whatsoever. When Americans finally learned a highly sanitized version about what happened, a year later, it was via a press corps that was largely in the CIA's pocket. By this point in the Cold War, as Carl Bernstein reported in *Rolling Stone*, the CIA had infiltrated or established "friendly" relations with many of the major organs in the American press including CBS News, *Time* magazine, the *New York Times*, ABC, NBC, and the wire services.[51] One of the first to write about the coup was the *Saturday Evening Post*, which did so with the aid of CIA Director Allen Dulles, who gave the writers copious input, reviewed the articles prior to publication, and, according to Peter

Grose's Dulles biography, *Gentleman Spy*, made "a few corrections or suggestions here and there."[52]

Meanwhile, the United States had reaped immense profits from the coup, at a cost said to be less than $20 million in bribes and other expenses. It was a pittance in return for what it secured: a plentiful source of cheap oil for the entire Western world for the next generation.[53] In addition, the US got a powerful new ally in the Middle East to join Saudi Arabia. And it gained a new client state rich enough to spend some $20 billion in arms, ammunition, and military hardware (about $120 billion in 2024 dollars), in what was said to be the "most rapid build-up of military power under peacetime conditions of any nation in the history of the world."[54]

The CIA's *real* role in the coup only emerged in bits and pieces much later. It was mentioned in passing in the Final Report of the Church Committee in April 1976.[55] In 1979, just as the Shah was being ousted, Kermit Roosevelt Jr., one of the principals in the coup, published *Countercoup: The Struggle for the Control of Iran*, a highly questionable and self-serving account that was heavily edited by the CIA and focused on how he led the overthrow of former prime minister Mossadegh and brought the Shah back to the fully restored glory of the Pahlavi dynasty.[56]

Twenty years later, in 2000, James Risen obtained a previously secret account of the coup written by Donald Wilber, another one of the CIA agents who planned it, and published it in the *New York Times*.[57] But it was not until August 2013 that the US government officially acknowledged its role by releasing previously classified documents showing that it helped in both planning and executing the coup—including bribing of Iranian politicians, security, and high-ranking army officials, and releasing pro-coup propaganda.[58]

The long-term secrecy regarding Ajax only added to its mystique. Ajax was one of the first times the CIA, then only six years old, implemented a covert regime change operation.[59] More than any CIA operation, Ajax came to embody the conspiratorialist cult of clandestine operations and its *Mission: Impossible*-like secret stratagems. The coup in Iran was a proof of concept for what a fully operational CIA could achieve. It was one of the CIA's greatest and most memorable triumphs, a dazzlingly successful gambit on the world chessboard that secured a steadfast ally who would protect the strategic resources of the West—namely, oil—for decades to come.

Over time, however, blowback from the coup and its consequences became glaringly apparent. After all, the United States, supposedly the beacon of democracy, had effectively destroyed the possibility of democracy being the dominant form of government in the Middle East. America had empowered a dictatorial monarch who became increasingly extravagant in his personal behavior over the years and ruled his people with alarmingly repressive measures. Ironically, it was on the watch of Jimmy Carter, a stalwart supporter of human rights, that the chickens came home to roost.

CARTER HAD KNOWN FROM THE EARLIEST DAYS OF THE HOStage crisis that if diplomacy failed, he would need other options. A rescue would be risky, difficult, and take time to plan. Immediately after the crisis began, Carter had assented to Brzezinski's request to plan a rescue mission for the hostages, but he thought of it merely as judicious preparation for an unlikely contingency.[60] By spring 1980, however, the hostages had been incarcerated for five months with no change in sight.

As the presidential race heated up, their fate became an inescapable issue. At the start of 1980, Ronald Reagan had been the odds-on favorite to be the Republican nominee for president, with former CIA director George H. W. Bush his most serious rival. Reagan, who had barely lost the nomination to Gerald Ford in 1976, possessed such a commanding lead in the polls that his campaign manager, John Sears, had opted for an above-the-fray strategy. Iowa was the first test for the Republican candidates on January 21, but Reagan didn't even bother to participate in the televised Iowa debate.[61]

But the decision backfired; that year, the Iowa caucuses included an unofficial "straw poll" that Bush won by two thousand votes, and suddenly Reagan didn't seem like such a shoo-in. Shortly afterward, Reagan brought on William J. Casey to replace Sears and run his campaign.

The former head of the Security Exchange Commission under Richard Nixon, Casey had an eclectic résumé that included writing bestselling tax books, a successful stint as a venture capitalist, a lucrative legal practice, service in the State Department, and running the Export-Import Bank. During the Nixon years, he had become close associates with Richard Allen, Reagan's top foreign policy adviser, who had helped bring him into the campaign.[62]

Reagan, who remained very much the frontrunner for the Republican nomination, told supporters at a campaign stop in North Carolina that the hostages "shouldn't have been there six days, let alone six months." He added that Carter's actions—or rather inaction—was "bordering on appeasement."[63]

From the White House's point of view, however, too many of their initiatives had gone nowhere. Outreaches to Iran by former attorney general Ramsey Clark and Treasury Secretary G. William Miller had struck out, as had overtures through the Palestinian Liberation Organization. Cutting off imports of Iranian oil and freezing Iranian assets in the United States had little effect. Nothing seemed to work in terms of getting Iran to negotiate.

Carter repeatedly tried to cultivate a discourse with President Bani-Sadr who was more than open to releasing the hostages, but it became increasingly clear that Bani-Sadr was relatively powerless. That meant Carter was back to square one, and there was no other choice but to go ahead with the rescue mission.

Carter was petrified that any military action he took would lead to the execution of the hostages, but the news from inside Iran made it clear that things were not about to change for the better. The president had already been told that the CIA had successfully conducted reconnaissance of the landing site in a remote location in Iran's South Khorasan province.[64] So, at a National Security Council meeting on April 11, Carter gave the go-ahead to the high-risk mission to rescue the hostages in Tehran via a daring helicopter raid on the American embassy in Tehran and bring them back to America. It was called Operation Eagle Claw, and in the White House, its existence was known to only a handful of people.

The Pentagon had been working on the operation for five months, but still it was riddled with difficult challenges. The Sikorsky RH-53D Sea Stallions were heavy-lifting workhorses, but, like all helicopters, could be temperamental in desert conditions. Given such concerns, eight choppers—two more than then the six necessary to complete the mission—were to take off from the USS *Nimitz*, the enormous nuclear-powered aircraft carrier, when it was just off the south coast of Iran and fly more than six hundred miles at a low altitude to refuel at Desert One, a dry lakebed in Iran's Dasht-e Kavir salt desert.[65]

Because of their limited range, the helicopters were to be joined at Desert One by six C-130 cargo planes carrying the 118 members of the rescue team, plus gasoline to refuel the choppers, and supplies. Once they arrived at Desert One, the rescue team was to head off to a second staging area closer to Tehran.[66] Meanwhile, the CIA was to have secured trucks to pick up the troops and take them to the embassy, where the C-130s were to be circling overhead as the American forces freed the hostages. Because the Iranians guarding the embassy were student radicals—not trained soldiers—little resistance was anticipated.[67]

Security, of course, was paramount. The tight secrecy surrounding the planning was such that not even Bobby Ray Inman, the director of the National Security Agency, was in the loop.[68] Sometime in late March, about a month before the operation took place and before it had even been formally authorized, National Security Adviser Zbigniew Brzezinski dropped by the desk of Susan Clough, President Carter's personal secretary and de facto administrative chief of staff for the National Security Council. Brzezinski put some papers in the inbox and asked her if she could keep his papers with the president's.

"I wasn't quite sure what he was talking about," Clough told me.[69] "But I could tell by the people who were coming and going that something military was underway. When Brzezinski told the president what he had done, President Carter was *really* upset. The number of people who knew that we were working on a rescue operation was very small. No one was supposed to know."

Including her.

Nor was that the only security breach. "The Republicans knew about the rescue attempt," one senior Carter adviser told me in 1991. "And that raises the questions about whether there was an attempt to sabotage the military rescue effort. And I consider that to be as bad as anything I can think of."

Even under the best of circumstances Operation Eagle Claw was an enormously complicated and dangerous mission—so risky that it was a major source of contention within the administration. Secretary of State Cyrus Vance was very much against moving forward with it and turned in his resignation as a result.[70]

Nevertheless, Carter went ahead. On April 16, he and a host of senior administration officials went out to Fort Myer, Virginia, the US Army post at Arlington National Cemetery, to receive briefings from the officers overseeing Eagle Claw. When it was over, the president went over to Col. Charlie Beckwith, Delta Force's ground commander for the operation, and said he wanted to have a private word.

"I want to ask you to do two things for me," Carter told Beckwith. "I want you, before you leave Iran, to assemble all of your forces and when you think it's appropriate give them a message from me. Tell them that in the event this operation fails, for whatever reason, the fault will not be theirs, it will be mine.

"The second thing is, if any American is killed, hostage or Delta Force, and if it is possible, as long as it doesn't jeopardize the life of someone else, you bring the body back."[71]

On April 24, at 10:35 a.m. Washington time, 6:05 p.m. Iran time, the eight Sikorsky RH-53D Sea Stallion helicopters entered Iranian air space. At the time, Carter was meeting in the White House with National Security Adviser Zbigniew Brzezinski, Press Secretary Jody Powell, and Chief of Staff Hamilton Jordan to discuss the operation.[72]

At 11:48, the president called Ham Jordan back into the Oval Office. "I got a disturbing call that a couple of our helicopters are down," Carter said.[73]

Actually, it was worse than that. About two hours into the mission, one of the eight helicopters that set out from the *Nimitz* returned to the carrier because it received indications of imminent rotor blade failure.[74] They landed, verified the malfunction, and abandoned the aircraft. The crew was picked up by another chopper, but they were down to seven helicopters.

There was more trouble ahead. Risky as Operation Eagle Claw was, rigorous operational security was essential in order to avoid detection by Iranian forces. As a result, the helicopter pilots had been given strict orders to fly under radio silence. That meant no communications whatsoever even though they were flying long distances at low altitude in unfamiliar territory, much of it in the dark of night under extraordinarily difficult conditions. That proved to be a problem early on: a second chopper got lost in a blinding "dust cloud of unknown size and density," as a State Department report later put it, experienced a failure of critical navigation and flight instruments, and turned back to the *Nimitz* three hours or so into the mission.[75]

Now, they were down to just six helicopters—the bare minimum. They could not afford another mishap. But before long, a busload of more than forty Iranian pilgrims happened to be driving by. They were stopped at gunpoint and detained. Meanwhile, an Army Ranger spotted a fuel tanker speeding by, and blew it up with an antitank missile. The blinding explosion lit up the night sky.[76]

So much for operational security.

But now that they had finally refueled at Desert One and were preparing to take off, a third chopper suddenly had problems with its hydraulic system.[77] That meant just five helicopters were left—not enough to bring back all the hostages and the commandos. The mission was no longer viable. Operation Eagle Claw was aborted.

Carter's rescue attempt had failed.

But the worst was yet to come. As the helicopters started to leave Desert One and return to the *Nimitz*, one of them crashed into a C-130, setting off an enormous explosion. Eight men died in the collision.

Carter later described what took place as one of "the worst days of my life."[78] In addition to the loss of life, the repercussions in terms of trying to resolve the hostage crisis were devastating. Carter officials entertained the idea of a second rescue attempt, but after Eagle Claw, the Iranians scattered the hostages to multiple new locations, making another one nearly impossible. And now that American troops had breached Iranian territory, Iranian radicals were strengthened and could argue that moderates seeking a resolution with the United States were not to be trusted. As a result, no Iranian politician would dare openly support negotiations over the hostages. And in the United States, the enduring stench of humiliation remained and lingered right up through the November elections. "The failure was the worst day in the memory of virtually everyone involved," wrote White House domestic affairs adviser Stuart E. Eizenstat in his memoir, *President Carter: The White House Years*. "For all practical purposes the election was over."[79]

Chapter Two
Dark Secrets

I WAS AT MY KITCHEN TABLE WHEN I FIRST LEARNED THAT OUR democracy might have been stolen from under us.

It was the morning of April 15, 1991, I sat down in my apartment on the Upper West Side to read the *New York Times*. A few weeks earlier, I had just gotten back from Prague, where I had chronicled the early days of post–Cold War Czechoslovakia for the *Los Angeles Times*. Now that I was between projects and on the lookout for something new, I was suddenly transfixed by a *Times* op-ed piece, "The Election Story of the Decade," by Gary Sick, a former Iran specialist on the National Security Council.

The article coincided with a *Frontline* documentary broadcast on PBS that was to air the next day on the same subject, "The Election Held Hostage," by reporters Robert Parry and Robert Ross. Together, the op-ed and the documentary put forth narratives that shattered the widely accepted origin story of how the Reagan-Bush era and modern conservatism came to power. To almost everyone in America the election of 1980 had seemed perfectly normal. It was ordinary, routine. But as Sick laid it all out, nothing could have been further from the truth.

At the time, we were more than a decade into the Reagan-Bush era. After eight years of Ronald Reagan's sunny optimism, George H. W. Bush was now in the third year of his presidency and was extraordinarily well positioned to run for a second term. In 1989, the first year of Bush's presidency, the Berlin Wall had come down, bringing a symbolic end to the Cold War. The Soviet Union was on life support and would code out in a matter of months. The ideological battles with communism were over. Neocons heralded the death of history. Liberal Western democracy reigned triumphant.

Then, in late 1990 and early 1991, Bush's high-tech war machine stunned the world during the Gulf War in Iraq. American forces quickly accomplished their objective by driving Iraqi troops out of Kuwait, and emerged victorious and relatively unscathed. Bush's numbers surged accordingly, to a stratospheric approval rating of 89 percent after the war. Even with a recession and rising unemployment, in April 1991 he boasted an approval rating of more than 80 percent.[1] So daunting was Bush's hold on the country that the giants in the Democratic Party at the time—Sen. Bill Bradley (D-NJ), Sen. Sam Nunn (D-Ga), and others—put their presidential ambitions on hold because they thought no one had a chance of beating Bush. (Ultimately, that left the door open for a little-known governor of Arkansas named Bill Clinton.)

The *Times*' op-ed piece, though, punctured the conventional wisdom of inevitability surrounding Bush's second term.

Sick had been Jimmy Carter's Iran specialist during the hostage crisis and had worked on the National Security Council for both Republican (Ford and Reagan) and Democratic administrations. A career intelligence analyst who had served twenty-four years in naval intelligence, Sick had been first appointed to the National Security Council by Republican president Gerald Ford. "He wasn't a Carter appointee," Carter press secretary Jody Powell told me in a 1991 interview.[2] "He's not a political guy, and he wasn't some silly son of a bitch who goes off half-cocked."

While some of the op-ed's allegations had been made previously, Sick's work was based on meticulously assembled facts, and he brought a new and authoritative voice to the charges. His insider status during the hostage crisis and his sober, rational manner gave a certain gravity and credibility to the October Surprise charges for the first time.

"Frankly, to have this story come from him and to have it put together by him suggests a lot more than just a rumor flitting around the edges," State Department spokesman Hodding Carter told me in 1991.[3] "It suggests that at least one very serious, knowledgeable person has decided there's more to it than smoke."

As Gary Sick and *Frontline* both reported, the key to the October Surprise lay in the interaction between Reagan-Bush campaign manager William J. Casey, who had died in 1987, and a pair of arms-dealing Iranian brothers, Cyrus and Jamshid Hashemi. Sick had met the Hashemis when he was in the Carter administration during the hostage crisis. Back then, Cyrus had presented himself as an Iranian national and sophisticated international businessman who claimed to have a doctorate in economics from Oxford University[4] and ran a small independent merchant bank, which was said to be backed by his wife's family. Over the years, Cyrus had offices in Geneva, London, Paris, and New York. Along with his two brothers, Jamshid and Reza, Cyrus saw the Iranian Revolution as a potential opening to significant business opportunities.

Though secular himself, Cyrus had managed to remain close to anti-Shah clerics and had influential contacts in the government, including powerful clerics and members of Khomeini's immediate family.[5] Moments after the hostages were seized on November 4, Cyrus went into action and got an introduction to the Carter State Department as someone who was in daily contact with "high levels of the Iranian government." For several months, Cyrus had been involved in a frequent back-and-forth with the Carter administration, attempting to act as an intermediary for them to help free the hostages.[6] In the end, though, not much had materialized from Cyrus's offer.

And that seemed to be that.

But in 1990, ten years after the hostage crisis, Sick reestablished contact with Cyrus Hashemi's brother Jamshid. Cyrus had died back in 1986, but talking with Jamshid now, Sick was stunned by what he heard. Jamshid told Sick that in late February or early March of 1980, just after one of the meetings between the Hashemis and Carter officials regarding the hostages, Jamshid was in his room at the Mayflower Hotel in Washington when an unexpected visitor knocked on the door. It was Bill Casey, newly appointed campaign manager for Ronald Reagan.

"Mr. Casey quickly made it clear that he wanted to prevent Jimmy Carter from gaining any political advantage from the hostage crisis," Sick wrote. "The Hashemis agreed to cooperate with Mr. Casey without the knowledge of the Carter Administration."[7]

In other words, the Hashemis had initially offered to help the Carter White House, but in reality, they were double agents working for the Reagan campaign instead. More specifically, Jamshid told Sick that he and Cyrus had helped arrange two critical meetings in Madrid between high-level Iranians and William Casey. One meeting was said to have taken place in late July 1980. Jamshid said the second meeting took place a few weeks later to firm up an agreement "with the Reagan campaign about the timing of any hostage release."[8]

There was more, of course. Sick reported on a series of meetings in Paris in October 1980 between officials from Iran and representatives from the Reagan-Bush campaign. As many as fifteen sources with direct or indirect knowledge of those meetings gave Sick varying accounts of what happened at the Paris meetings, but by and large, the sources agreed on three things: (1) that William Casey was a key player in the meetings; (2) that the hostages would not be released until after the November 4 presidential election; and (3) that Israel would facilitate the transfer of arms and spare parts to Iran.[9]

Sick added that at least five of the sources said that George H. W. Bush was present for at least one meeting in Paris. Given Bush's reelection prospects, this was the most explosive charge of all.

The response to Sick's op-ed and the *Frontline* story was immediate. Despite the whispers about the October Surprise for the last decade, the mainstream media had largely relegated it to the realm of conspiracy theorists. On occasion, highly regarded journalists—Flora

Lewis at the *New York Times*, Alfonso Chardy at the *Miami Herald*—had waded into these dark waters, but they were ignored. Almost no one pursued the story. In 1991, for the first time, and more than ten years after the fact, national newspapers, magazines, and TV news operations finally began seriously investigating the October Surprise.

Of course, back then, there was no mass use of the internet. Email, text messages, and social media were either nonexistent or not widely used. Even Fox News was five years away from launching. Instead, there was what is now known as "legacy media." That meant the *New York Times*, the *Washington Post*, the *Wall Street Journal*, among other papers and nightly newscasts from the three major networks, ABC, NBC, and CBS. These were the organs that shaped the national conversation. The media world had not yet morphed into an atomized ecosystem filled with countless impenetrable silos.

Nevertheless, insofar as it was possible in that predigital era, the October Surprise went viral. PBS's *Frontline* aired the first of two hour-long investigative documentaries on the subject. ABC's *Nightline*, which had been born out of the Iranian hostage crisis ten years earlier, chimed in with a half hour devoted exclusively to the subject and continued to pursue the story throughout the summer, assigning a team of producers and reporters to investigate the October Surprise. More than a hundred newspapers across the country picked up the story. Major organs in the European press did so as well. *Esquire* and *Newsweek*, then still a powerful weekly, and others launched investigations. The *Chicago Tribune*, *USA Today*, and syndicated columnists Jack Germond and Jules Witcover joined in. The *Seattle Times* ran a letter to the editor stating that the investigations were necessary "to defend something all voters and parties should value: Democracy."[10]

Even President Carter spoke out. When the hostage crisis had unfolded in 1980, Carter had been told of clandestine dealings between Reagan campaign officials and the Iranians. After Sick came forward, Carter concluded that it seemed "inconceivable" to him "that this could be done by Bill Casey or anyone else. It's almost nauseating to think that this could be true—that any responsible American citizen could possibly have delayed the release of American hostages for one day, for any purpose."[11]

"But the evidence, I believe, is so large," Carter said, "the number of people and reports and so forth—that I think it has aroused a genuine question." Carter said enough evidence had been accumulated to warrant an investigation by Congress or a "blue ribbon panel."

He subsequently met with Speaker of the House Thomas S. Foley and urged him to launch a full-scale congressional investigation. On August 6, 1991, eleven years after the alleged conspiracy, House and Senate panels convened a formal inquiry into the charges.[12]

Bush's White House struck back ferociously. His press secretary, Marlin Fitzwater, called the *Times*' op-ed piece "trash," and derided Gary Sick as "the Kitty Kelley of foreign policy," a reference to the bestselling author of dishy celebrity biographies.[13]

A few weeks later, on May 3, 1991, President George H. W. Bush denied all charges that he was in Paris in 1980. "I can only say categorically that the allegations about me are grossly untrue, factually incorrect, bald-faced lies," he said.[14]

And, for many people, it was hard to believe such heinous allegations about the genteel president and his allies. After all, for more than a decade, Republican administrations had been trumpeting the threat posed by Islamic fundamentalism. With his black turban and silver beard, Ayatollah Khomeini had become its foreboding talisman, providing Republicans with a terrifying, new, and necessary villain throughout the 1980s.

So the idea that the Republicans had been secretly conspiring with Iran—those were Khomeini's supporters, marching in the streets of Tehran, chanting "Death to America!"—defied the imagination. It seemed too counterintuitive. To most Americans, the hostage crisis was the story of how the Carter era of humiliation, weakness, and disgrace had come to an end and was replaced by Reagan's new morning in America.

But now that version of history was being called into question.

WHEN I BEGAN INVESTIGATING THE OCTOBER SURPRISE, I'D already been in journalism twenty years. I had started out in college, writing for the *Harvard Crimson*, the university's daily, and long a training ground for the men and women who ended up writing for, running, and, often enough, owning the *New York Times*, the *Washington Post*, CNN, NPR, and other establishment organs. It provided a uniquely privileged perch from which to chronicle the sixties, an era marked by the Vietnam War, civil rights and antiwar protests, and the assassinations of Martin Luther King Jr. and Bobby Kennedy. The university went on strike. An office that had once been Henry Kissinger's workplace was bombed. There were riots in Harvard Square. Banks were set afire.

And when it came to the most divisive issue of the era, Harvard offered two diametrically opposed paths. On the one hand, Harvard's nearby Center for International Affairs employed one of the architects of the Vietnam War, Henry Kissinger, later Nixon's secretary of state. And on the other, there was former *Crimson* editor Daniel Ellsberg, who was responsible for the Pentagon Papers getting into the hands of *New York Times* reporter Neil Sheehan, another *Crimson* alum.

It wasn't hard for me to figure out which side I was on.

In 1969, when I was "comping" for the *Crimson*, Seymour Hersh exposed the slaughter of hundreds of unarmed men, women, and children by American soldiers in the small Vietnamese hamlet of My Lai.[15] Women were gang-raped, hacked up, mutilated, herded into a ditch, and shot. Infants were murdered. By the dozens. For the millions who had been told America was fighting a heroic battle against communism, the My Lai Massacre was a gory refutation of our noblest ideals and showed that even true-blue American soldiers had committed Nazi-like atrocities.

The Pentagon Papers, the My Lai Massacre—these were stories of lasting significance. They showed that all was not as it seemed, that the history we had been taught was full of lies. They showed me how the system worked—or, rather, *didn't*. This was the journalism that showed why freedom of the press was so sacred that it was codified in the First Amendment to the Constitution.

And not long after I graduated, there were Bob Woodward and Carl Bernstein's revelations about Richard Nixon's sprawling dirty-tricks operations known as Watergate. Nothing could have done more to infuse journalism with a powerful sense of mission. Suddenly, pavement-pounding ink-stained wretches were transformed into heroic truth seekers dedicated to preserving democracy. The highest ideals of a free press had been realized, and, thanks to Hollywood, a hefty dose of glamour had been added to the equation.

For anyone who had missed out on Watergate, the October Surprise seemed to offer another shot. It had Islamic terrorism, kidnapped hostages, a hostile foreign power, spies, arms dealers, covert operations, arrows pointing blame all the way to the top, and vital questions about treason poisoning our democratic processes. This was treachery on an epic scale—and many thought it went all the way to the White House.

As if all this weren't enough, my initial interest, natural as it was, was spurred by the memory of another Iran story, one I had missed—a regret that had been with me ever since. After graduation, I'd spent some time kicking around the innovative media scene of the alternative press in Boston, which gave me and many others the freedom to take a more expansive approach to journalism than most mainstream journals allowed. That eventually led me to three memorable years as co-owner and co-editor of *The Paris Metro*, an English-language fortnightly city magazine in the French capital.

The original *Metro* folded in late 1978, but a few weeks later I got a call from Sergio Gaudenti, one of the magazine's ace photographers, who had an idea for my next adventure. Over the preceding few months, anti-Shah demonstrations had gripped Iran. Ayatollah Ruhollah Khomeini, a Shi'ite cleric in his late seventies who had been exiled from Iran for his anti-Shah activities, had arrived in Paris just a few weeks earlier. In Iran, more than one thousand protesters had been killed in demonstrations,[16] many of them demanding that Khomeini be allowed to return.[17] The Shah was hanging on to his throne by a thread. On November 6, 1978, he had imposed military rule.

In response, Khomeini warned that he would call for a civil war in Iran if "the present method of political struggle doesn't work."[18] Suddenly, this Shi'ite cleric who was barely known in the West was hailed all over the world as a crusader in exile who was the political and spiritual leader of the Iranian people. From afar he called for strikes and demonstrations, and millions of Iranians responded. The Shah's government began to crumble. Americans fled Tehran, with the Shah following them soon after. In Paris, Khomeini responded, "*Allahu akbar* [God is great]. It is not a final victory but a preface to our victory. Our first step is to reconstruct the country, which has been destroyed by the Shah and the foreigners."[19]

And then Sergio Gaudenti called me out of the blue to say that he knew some Iranian guys in the suburbs—Islamic fundamentalists—who were going back to Iran to start a revolution. He said they were for real. And we could be on the plane with them as they made history.

With the *Metro* just folded, I was trying to figure out my next move, but I had no special knowledge of Iran. The Shah was gone, but what about SAVAK, his brutal secret police force?

"Are you out of your mind, Sergio?" I said. "Think about it. Do you know how powerful SAVAK is? And you really think there's going to be an Islamic revolution?"

On February 1, Khomeini loyalists took over Tehran's Mehrabad International Airport. The Ayatollah landed there in a chartered Air France 747 jumbo jet, on a plane full of Western journalists, that I could have been on. As I later learned, they had been invited—*we* had been invited—to provide protective cover lest the CIA or unseen Western forces try to shoot down the plane.

Since the 1953 coup d'état, Iranians had come to see—often with good reason—the CIA as imbued with mystical powers that allowed it to perform extraordinary feats on the world stage. But, they reasoned, even the CIA wouldn't shoot down an Air France airliner if it had a few dozen Western journalists on board. It was a decision that I've regretted ever since.

When Sick's op-ed landed in 1991, I had been working mostly for magazines like *New York*, *Esquire*, and *Vanity Fair.* Serious investigative reporting typically was the province of daily newspapers, which could follow up on a story day after day after day. But this was the heyday of the print era, and magazines still paid enough that I could spend several months on one long investigative article. My goal was to write an extended narrative that would be, I hoped, the first comprehensive account about the October Surprise.

Both Sick's piece and the *Frontline* documentary made it clear that this was no simple task. Gary noted that many of the sources "are low-level intelligence operatives and arms dealers who are no boy scouts. A number of them have been arrested or have served prison time for gunrunning, fraud, counterfeiting or drugs."[20]

As a result, he concluded, "There is no 'smoking gun' and I cannot prove exactly what happened at each stage. In the absence of hard documentary evidence, the possibility of an elaborate disinformation campaign cannot be excluded."[21]

Frontline's documentary had similar disclaimers. Again, that was no surprise. Any serious investigator would have to wade through a world polluted by disinformation, precisely because the most knowledgeable sources—spies, arms dealers, and the like—were professional liars of one kind or another. Not to belabor the obvious, but spies do not leave calling cards. As a result, proving beyond a shadow of a doubt that the October Surprise took place might be impossible.

But, using Gary Sick's op-ed and the *Frontline* documentary as road maps, I knew I could put together a compelling narrative that would make a powerful circumstantial case and advance the investigation. My job, essentially, would be to take the skeleton of a story that was not yet fully fleshed out and put some meat on its bones, to take the stories from as many sources as possible and lay them on top of one another like the anatomical transparencies in a medical textbook. At the center of the stories was Bill Casey, a brilliant spymaster who oversaw a clandestine network of covert operatives including dodgy arms dealers, rogue Israeli agents, corrupt bankers, and the like. With secret meetings involving Casey, mysterious deaths, and exotic locales in London, Paris, Madrid, Tehran, and Tel Aviv, how could there not be a great spy thriller?

In any case, I was hooked. I went to my editor at *Esquire* to make my pitch. Before long, I got a green light.

Over the next four months, I conducted more than 150 interviews with national security officials, White House aides, arms dealers, military officers, and intelligence operatives from the United States, Iran, and Israel. I interviewed former CIA heads William Colby and Stansfield Turner, former national security adviser Zbigniew Brzezinski, former attorney general Elliot Richardson, officials on Jimmy Carter's National Security Council, White House press secretary Jody Powell, a renegade Israeli spy, arms dealers, CIA agents, lawyers, congressmen and their aides, and friends of Bill Casey. I reviewed thousands of pages of official documents, court records, and congressional hearings.

I searched for dispositive evidence as well—that is, data that might refute the October Surprise thesis, interviewing some forty Republicans—staffers in Congress, the CIA, the State Department, the White House, the Reagan-Bush campaign, and elsewhere. For all the excitement about the October Surprise, there was plenty of resistance—and not just from the Republicans.

By the standards of that relatively innocent era, the October Surprise allegations were far beyond the pale, and many mainstream journalists also regarded these stories as the spectral tales of crazed publicity hounds.

One of the most outspoken critics of the October Surprise scenario was Bob Woodward. The celebrated *Washington Post* reporter had written about Bill Casey and the CIA in his best-selling book *Veil: The Secret Wars of the CIA, 1981–1987*, but found the new allegations too hard to swallow.

"The whole thing sounds counterintuitive," Woodward told me in 1991.[22] "I know Casey hated communists, terrorists, and leftists, but when it came to the question of his fellow citizens, I found him quite reverential on the subject. He thought of himself as a patriot. That doesn't rule it out, but it's counterintuitive. I really don't see a smoking gun or even much smoke in the room. Maybe a little haze."

Woodward was far from alone. Writing in the *Washington Post* in April 1991, Mark Hosenball dismissed the allegations as the product of "fashionable publications," the "chattering classes in New York, Washington and Hollywood . . . and a small brigade of conspiracy theorists and journalistic gadflies."[23] Ultimately, he concluded that "the only witnesses who might have persuasive evidence of such a plot" were Bill Casey and Cyrus Hashemi, and they were no longer around.

Except there was another witness, Jamshid Hashemi, Cyrus's brother. Jamshid had spoken to Gary Sick for his op-ed in the *Times* and, later, a richly detailed interview to ABC's *Nightline* in June 1991. Jamshid was the one and only on-the-record source who claimed to be present at the meetings in Madrid between his brother Cyrus and Bill Casey where the October Surprise deals were allegedly made. This made the Madrid meetings and Jamshid's firsthand account critical to the accusations; Madrid was where the terms of the agreement between the Republicans and Iran were originally articulated, where the line had been crossed and the Republican operatives had moved into the world of treason.

In the story he told to Sick and to *Nightline*, Jamshid Hashemi had arrived in Madrid a few days before the meetings and greeted the Iranian delegation when it arrived at the Madrid airport.[24] He and Cyrus were there as hosts, introducing Casey to another pair of brothers from Iran, Ayatollah Mehdi Karroubi and his brother Hassan, both of whom wore clerical robes.[25]

Though not particularly well known at the time, the forty-three-year-old Mehdi Karroubi was a highly placed member of the Majlis, the Iranian parliament, and a longtime student of Ayatollah Khomeini. A lawyer and theologian who had handled investments for prominent businessmen, he'd been imprisoned several times by the Shah's government and had emerged as a relatively moderate and pragmatic voice in the Revolution. According to Gary Sick's *October Surprise*, Hassan was less prominent than his brother but served as a link between Khomeini's inner circle and the shadowy world of intelligence operatives and arms dealers. Also present were two Americans who accompanied Casey but who were identified only by their aliases. They remained relatively silent throughout the day.

According to Jamshid, the meetings were conducted in Farsi and English, with the two Hashemis alternating as translators. Karroubi started by attacking the policies of the United States in general and Jimmy Carter in particular. Casey responded by saying the Republicans traditionally had better relations with Iran than the Democrats did—a banal statement, but one that was utterly pregnant with meaning. If you help us, we'll help you, Casey seemed to be saying—and that could have far-reaching ramifications.[26]

The discourse of this first session was so vague, according to Jamshid, that when it ended after nearly three hours, Mehdi Karroubi said he still was unclear as to why he was there. He asked the Hashemis what had been the purpose of the meeting. What did Casey want?

The following day, Karroubi asked Casey directly about the hostages and the release of Iran's frozen assets. The United States had also been holding large amounts of weapons bought and paid for by

Iran under the Shah, and Karroubi wanted to know if there was some way to get them. This was a matter of real urgency because Iraqi troops were threatening to attack Iran. Since the Republicans were not in power, Karroubi acknowledged that such a transfer would be difficult. But it might be possible, he said, if the weapons were transferred through a third country.

Here, Casey knew precisely what to say, how to phrase it—but also what not to say. He was perfectly at home in the world of covert actions, where he used unofficial channels to execute unofficial policy, often without the knowledge of duly elected officials. He responded to Karroubi with questions of his own, asking if Iran was ready to deal with Republicans and hand over the hostages. Could Karroubi act on Khomeini's behalf? Would the hostages be well treated?

Then there was the matter of timing. Moderate Iranian officials were anxious to release the hostages right away—presumably so the arms embargo and sanctions could end, and Iran could reestablish normal trade relations with the West. But Casey knew that the immediate release of the hostages would aid Jimmy Carter's electoral chances. So he finally cut to the heart of the matter and broached the idea of *delaying* the release of the hostages, asking if they could be freed to Reagan *after* the election. If that happened, Casey added, the Republicans would arrange for the release of Iran's frozen assets and the military equipment that had been held up.

As Jamshid told ABC *Nightline*, for the first time, Karroubi thought progress was being made. "I think," he replied to the Iranians in the room, "we're now opening a new era and we are now dealing with someone who knows how to do business."[27]

Translation: Iran was ready to make a deal with Bill Casey.

One of my first interviews was with Sick, who had become an adjunct professor of Middle Eastern politics at Columbia

University, at a bistro called Goodbye Columbus on Manhattan's Upper West Side. To all appearances, it was the kind of run-of-the-mill Yuppie joint that was ubiquitous in those days, but Sick had been meeting gunrunners and shadowy intelligence operatives there for the previous two years.

My impression was of an earnest, scholarly man with a stiff military bearing, whose assumptions about the limits of political warfare had been shaken to the core by surreal conspiracies he had never imagined. Few people had been more intimately involved in the crisis than Sick. On November 4, when the hostages were taken, he was still at home in bed when he got a call from Zbigniew Brzezinski, and quickly made his way to the State Department.[28]

In fact, Sick had initially been quite skeptical about the October Surprise. In 1985, he had published *All Fall Down: America's Tragic Encounter with Iran*, a book that examined the hostage crisis in detail and made no mention of any possible October Surprise deal. At that early date, Gary was aware of the allegations, but with so many aspects of the story still cloaked in mystery, he dismissed the October Surprise as "little more than a coincidence in timing."[29]

But in the late eighties, Sick told me, his assumptions began to change when "seemingly inexplicable fragments of information began to appear. My experience was not unlike that of a medieval scholar discovering traces of a hidden text beneath the script on an old parchment."

At first, he was reluctant to pursue this curious line of inquiry because it contradicted much of what he had already published. But as he uncovered more details, his original, more benign explanation of what happened during the hostage crisis no longer seemed satisfactory. As he put it, that initial account had proven "to be not only inadequate, but grossly incorrect."[30]

"You take events you know very well and strip off a layer and suddenly there is a whole different world," Sick told me. "I was in the White House then, but now I'm forced to go back and rethink every stage. Things happened for different reasons than you thought. There is another world. A whole different reality."[31]

In a movie or a novel, Sick noted, such challenges and twists of reality can be enormously entertaining. But real life is a different matter. What if hundreds of millions of people believe in "a reality" that is actually a lie? What if that false reality was *intentionally* created as part of a political agenda that resulted in seizing state power and changed the course of history? And if the unseen forces behind all this could change the past and get away with it, if they could convince all of America to believe in a false history that concealed acts of treason and enormous political crimes, didn't that mean they could shape the future?

Sick's initial reluctance to believe in the October Surprise suggested how it often seemed to be both opaque and transparent, both blatantly obvious and brilliantly well concealed. In 1981, nearly forty-two million people had seen Reagan take the oath of office just moments before the hostages were released. Because he had been on the podium for all five minutes of his presidency, Reagan could not possibly have conferred with Iran. "You'd have to be the village idiot to believe Iran released them at that time without talking to the Republicans," one congressional staffer told me. "And before then, Reagan had no authority to negotiate."[32]

It wasn't until later that I learned that what was really taking place—something unseen but in plain sight—was best articulated by the man who was most responsible for it. "The hardest thing to prove," Bill Casey later said, "is something that is self-evident."[33]

And, as I soon learned, Casey really knew what he was talking about.

Part of the mystique of the October Surprise was that everyone who really knew Bill Casey said it was exactly the kind of thing he'd do. The premise behind the October Surprise was completely in character with the great spymaster, but figuring out what he did and how he did it was another matter entirely.

Even his Republican colleagues—make that *especially* his colleagues—thought the October Surprise was just like Casey. John Sears, who was Ronald Reagan's campaign manager until he was fired and replaced by Casey, told me that he genuinely didn't know if the October Surprise took place and was somewhat skeptical, given the high risk of getting caught. Still, he said, he took the story seriously precisely because "it would have been so much like Casey."

"That's the one thing that makes sense. It's so much a part of his background, of who he was, of his love for his days spying against the Nazis. I knew him for over twenty years, and he had that kind of mind, that kind of mentality. So, it's believable."[34]

Scott Thompson, a Casey aide who later became a professor at the Fletcher School of Law and Diplomacy at Tufts University and associate director of the US Information Agency, went even further. "I have no way of knowing everything, but Casey would have had people doing very compartmentalized tasks so that no one knew everything that was really going on," he said. "He always had three or four people doing things for him in a very compartmentalized way so that no one knew the ultimate objective."[35]

Thompson, who died in 2017, had served as an aide to Casey in the 1980 Reagan-Bush campaign, and met with him at least once every week or two during the campaign. "He was unattractive, hard driving, brilliant, disorganized, disheveled, always marching to his own drummer, incapable of being chained down to one program, and played everything close to his vest," Thompson told me. "He understood something that very few people get. If you introduce yourself and say who you are, people will talk, and you can get them to do what you want. Casey liked to call people and push them around as if to compensate for his ugliness. He thought nothing of calling *anyone* late at night. His mind worked vertically and horizontally at the same time, and he would jump levels to pursue his objective."

In the end, everything pointed to one man. "So they finally figured it out," Thompson said.[36] "What the fuck did they think was going on?"

Chapter Three Mumbles

As a final act, the last weeks of Bill Casey's life could not have been more fitting. Throughout November and December 1986, Casey, then in his fifth year as director of the Central Intelligence Agency (DCI), had been hauled in to testify before Congress along with his Reagan administration colleagues one after another.

As he saw it, this was the ultimate indignity. It wasn't just that Congress was an institution for which Casey had complete and utter contempt—though that was certainly part of the equation. More to the point, Congress was holding Casey accountable—or trying to. Casey had ducked, dodged, sidestepped, and otherwise evaded accountability his entire life. In many ways, Casey was a physically awkward, clumsy man, but when it came to breaking rules, circumventing regulations, and leapfrogging hierarchies, no one was more adroit.

And no one had ever really held him accountable—until now.

The occasion was the congressional investigation of the Iran-Contra scandal, the conspiracy through which Reagan administration officials ran off-the-books operations involving illegal arms sales to Iran, and then funneled the profits to right-wing Contra rebels in Nicaragua who were fighting the country's socialist government.

Both facets of the operation—the arms sales to Iran and the funding of the Contras—had been *specifically* outlawed by Congress. But nothing was more like Bill Casey than doing an end run around Congress. Off-the-books operations were right out of his playbook. In World War II, Casey had pulled out all the stops to save Western Europe from the Nazis. Now, in the Reagan administration, he was doing everything he could to save Central America from going communist, and he wasn't going to let Congress get in the way. The only problem was everything had spilled out into the open, and now he was being called to answer for his role in it.

The Iran-Contra hearings were the first such nationally televised spectacle to command the nation's attention since Watergate in 1973, but this time around the Republicans fared far better in terms of creating a counternarrative that won the hearts of the American people. Throughout most of the hearings, Lt. Col. Oliver North, a Reagan staffer on the National Security Council, held center stage and seized the opportunity to transform himself from a thrice-convicted felon (whose charges were later vacated) into a widely feted celebrity on the right-wing media circuit, a brave and patriotic soldier with a chest full of medals supporting Latin American "freedom fighters," following what he thought were the legal orders of his superiors.[1]

The real story, however, was that Congress had finally trained its gunsights on the highest-ranking official at the heart of Iran-Contra—William J. Casey. As Iran-Contra unspooled for the public, it was becoming clearer by the day that this operation could be traced back to Casey's door. Did anyone really believe that the buck stopped with Oliver North? He knew all too well what happens when Congress and the bureaucrats start meddling with covert ops and he made a point of leaving no fingerprints. In Iran-Contra, Casey had overseen the illegal sale of arms to Iran as if he already had plenty of experience in such covert operations. And Congress knew it.

So, in November 1986, Casey shuttled back and forth between the House Intelligence Committee and the Senate Intelligence Committee. Even members of his own party, Republicans, were calling for his resignation. Being forced to explain himself to lawmakers, or anyone really, was Bill Casey's version of hell.

When he actually came before Congress in November 1986, however, at least some of the rules played to his advantage. For one thing, Casey was testifying in top-secret closed-door sessions—so he would not have to endure the full-bore glare of the media. Moreover, he was not required to testify under oath. The rationale for this was that it was in the interests of "free exchange."[2]

But in the end, Congress got nothing from Casey. The Senate Select Committee on Intelligence characterized his testimony as misleading and incomplete.[3] When he had finished testifying, and his mumbling had been deciphered, his inquisitors had managed to elicit from this "free exchange" such explosive bombshells as these:

"I'm not sure."

"I don't know all the details."

"It's hard to be precise on that."

And, later, the stunningly candid: "I don't have it at my fingertips."[4]

But it wasn't quite over yet. On Monday, December 8, Casey went before the House Defense Appropriations Subcommittee, which wanted to know if profits from Iranian arms sales were being diverted to Afghanistan. On December 10 and 11, he was grilled before the House's Foreign Affairs and Intelligence Committees, respectively.[5] "The guy had lost his stuff," said CIA officer Alan Fiers, according to *Casey*. "He stumbled and fumbled. At times, it seemed he couldn't talk. He had to be carried."

Even then, Casey still had to prepare for testifying before the Senate the following week.

Finally, on the morning of December 16, Casey was in his seventh-floor office at Langley, well into a busy day. Visitors were backed up in his waiting room—among them Jeane Kirkpatrick, the former ambassador to the United Nations. He also had scheduled some last-minute prep work to do before for his Senate testimony the next day. [6]

At 10:05, however, CIA physician Arvel Tharp made a quick stop by the DCI's office to check up on Casey. The seventy-four-year-old CIA director had just stopped taking his blood pressure medication after complaining about its unpleasant side effects, and Tharp wanted to make sure Casey was okay.[7]

But just moments after Tharp took his blood pressure, Casey started flailing about spasmodically. He opened his mouth to speak, but no words came out. Tharp called for help. Two minutes later, an emergency medical team arrived and took Casey to Georgetown University Hospital, where he was admitted with "a minor cerebral seizure"[8] under the alias "Lacey."[9] He was diagnosed as having a lymphoma of the brain.

Four days later, a malignant tumor was removed from the left side of Casey's brain. Initially, hospital officials said the growth appeared "treatable," and Casey would likely be able to resume normal activities after the surgery.[10] He did regain consciousness and the ability to talk. But he never fully recovered, and he never finished his testimony before Congress. And on January 29, 1987, William Casey resigned as DCI.

Sometime over the next few weeks, Watergate reporter Bob Woodward says he snuck into Casey's hospital room for what turned out to be the highly controversial deathbed interview of Casey reported in Woodward's bestseller *Veil*. It ended with one last question about whether Casey knew that funds from arms sales to Iran had been diverted to the Contras in Nicaragua.

"You knew?" Woodward asked. "Didn't you?"

Casey was frail, but his head jerked up suddenly. He stared and then nodded yes.

Why? Woodward asked.

"I believed," Casey said twice.[11] Then, he fell asleep.

And that was it.

At the time, of course, no one realized that Iran-Contra was the tail that wagged the dog of a much, much bigger scandal that had started six and a half years earlier and would come to be called the October Surprise. Consider the similarities: Both scandals involved arms-for-hostages deals with Iran, a hostile foreign power that was under embargo. Both scandals involved secret agreements in which Israel played a key role in facilitating arms shipments to Iran. And both scandals were done through elaborate off-the-books mechanisms that were designed to ensure secrecy.

In fact, the more you looked at it, the more you began to realize they were the same story—the October Surprise was the origin story of Iran-Contra. The biggest difference between the two scandals was that when the October Surprise took place, Casey was not even in the government. But Congress had not figured that out. And if Casey wasn't going to fess up, they probably never would. Aside from nodding his assent—as if to tell Woodward, yes, I knew—Casey said nothing. His secrets had died with him.

YOU WOULDN'T KNOW BY HIS APPEARANCE, BUT WILLIAM Joseph Casey was one of the greatest spymasters in American history. He just didn't look the part. Gruff and perpetually disheveled, his demeanor suggested a profoundly distracted, bumbling Mr. Magoo more than James Bond. He was tall, but somewhat stooped and ungainly. As Tim Weiner put it in *Legacy of Ashes: The History of the CIA*, Casey looked like "an unmade bed."[12] Or, as his deputy, Robert Gates, later director of the CIA himself, said, when Casey walked he resembled "a committee of bones and muscles all trying to amble more or less in the right direction."[13]

He muttered unintelligibly. In fact, the joke went, of all the intelligence operatives in the United States, Casey was the only one who *didn't* need a scrambler on his phone. Behind his back, they called him "Mumbles" because no one could understand him.

One on one, in the room, Casey could be unstoppably persuasive. He was always in motion, going in a million directions at once. Highly animated and always excited, his unkempt appearance made him seem simultaneously omniscient and inscrutable.[14] He asked questions no one else dared ask. And in response, he got not just answers, but action.

He got things done.

Yet for all the power and mystique and intrigue and secrets around him, when it came to Georgetown society, Casey was the guy you *had* to invite but you hoped wouldn't come. His table manners were mortifying. He was a noisy eater. When he became excitable, he was known to chew on his necktie.[15] Those who entertained him were warned not to serve him soup.[16] During her husband's presidency, the ever-fastidious Nancy Reagan lived in fear that Casey might show up at a state dinner "spilling food down his cummerbund."[17]

Mumbling was just one of Casey's many exasperating traits, but at times it was less an impediment than a potent passive-aggressive weapon, whether he was reluctantly testifying before Congress or was serving President Reagan as director of Central Intelligence. Indeed, several of Casey's associates thought he was intentionally incomprehensible—*especially* when it mattered.

"My problem with Bill was that I didn't understand him at meetings," Reagan told William F. Buckley, who, in turn, related it to Casey biographer, Joseph Persico.[18] "Now, you can ask a person to repeat himself once. You can ask him twice. But you can't ask him a third time. You start to sound rude. So, I'd just nod my head, but I didn't know what he was actually saying."

All of which gave rise to the specter of Casey proposing daring, off-the-books operations, while Reagan smiled genially and vacantly nodded his assent—without hearing a single word.

CASEY HAD LEARNED HIS CRAFT—INTELLIGENCE, THE ART OF deception—in World War II as head of Secret Intelligence for Europe in the Office of Strategic Services (OSS), the precursor to the CIA, where he played a key role in preparing the way for the Allied invasion of Normandy and the Allies' subsequent penetration into Nazi Germany. He called it "the greatest experience of my life,"[19] and revered the man responsible for putting him there, William J. "Wild Bill" Donovan, one of the great legends in American intelligence.

A highly successful antitrust lawyer, Donovan had pressed the case with President Franklin D. Roosevelt that the United States needed its own intelligence service as World War II approached.[20] In July 1941, he was named head of what was soon to become the OSS.[21] Its purpose was to make sure that American forces were not entering blindly into the battles being fought in North Africa and the Pacific, not to mention its forthcoming invasion of Europe.

Donovan assembled a team of young men and women, many of whom came from wealthy, socially prominent families, that would define American intelligence over the next two generations. There was Alfred DuPont of the eponymous chemical company; Lester Armour of the meat packing fortune;[22] diplomat David Bruce and his brother-in-law Paul Mellon of the eponymous banking dynasty; Cornelius Vanderbilt Whitney (shipping, railroads, cotton); and no fewer than five Roosevelts (Archibald Jr., Cornelius II, Frances, Kermit II, and Quentin II).[23] Four members of Donovan's team—Allen Dulles, Richard Helms, William Colby, and Bill Casey—went on to become directors of Central Intelligence.

Thanks to the surfeit of blue bloods in its ranks, it was sometimes said that OSS really stood for "oh-so-social." As a columnist for the *Washington Times-Herald* put it, "If you should by chance wander in the labyrinth of the OSS, you'd behold ex-polo players, millionaires, Russian princes, society gambol boys, and dilettante detectives."[24] Indeed, *Long Island's Gentlemen Spies*, a publication by the Nassau County Historical Society, noted that of thirty-one so-called intelligence agents whose presence graced the local beaches and golf courses,[25] all but two went to Ivy League colleges.

One of the non-Ivies, of course, was Casey, a Fordham graduate of Irish stock whose father was a Tammany Hall bureaucrat. (The other non–Ivy Leaguer, George Tenet, went to Georgetown University.) Casey referred to his old monied colleagues as the "white-shoe boys."[26]

After getting his law degree at St. John's, Casey worked at the Research Institute of America and devised plans to help put the US economy on a wartime footing, work that won favor with the man who would forever change his life, Wild Bill Donovan. Casey learned a lot from Donovan, but he particularly admired Donovan's success in overcoming the obstacles posed by intransigent bureaucracies. "It is no exaggeration to say that Donovan created the OSS against the fiercest kind of opposition from everybody," Casey said, "the Army, Navy, and State Departments, the Joint Chiefs of Staff, regular Army brass, the whole Pentagon bureaucracy, and, perhaps most devastatingly, the White House staff."[27]

Casey watched how Donovan operated and learned at the foot of a master. "You didn't wait six months for a feasibility study to prove that an idea could work," he said, according to Persico.[28] "You gambled that it might work. You didn't tie up an organization with red tape designed mostly to cover somebody's ass. You took the initiative and the responsibility. You went around end, you went over somebody's head if you had to. But you acted. That's what drove the regular military and the State Department chair-warmers crazy about the OSS."

Lesson learned, Casey, a mere lieutenant when he joined the OSS, immediately decommissioned himself and got rehired as a civilian. What better way for a low-ranking officer to start barking orders at three-star generals?

Casey adored Donovan, and in his highly distinctive way—clumsy and physically awkward—sought to be his own kind of swashbuckling buccaneer. Rules meant nothing to him. They were made to be broken. He was the anti-bureaucrat. Hierarchies, organizational charts, and chains of command were there to be ignored.[29] That was the way Wild Bill Donovan did it—and Casey did, too.[30]

Donovan also inculcated in Casey a sense of what intelligence was, of how intelligence really works. "By the time Pearl Harbor came, Donovan had gathered hundreds of the finest scholars in America and had them processing geographic, scientific, politics, and military information in the Library of Congress," Casey said in a 1981 speech at Brown University.[31] He went on:

> Two years later, Donovan had scoured our campuses and mobilized thousands of the finest scholars in America. He had assembled what had to be the most diverse aggregation ever assembled of tycoons and scientists, bankers and foreign correspondents, psychologists and football stars, circus managers and circus freaks, safe crackers, lock pickers and pickpockets, playwrights and journalists, novelists and professors of literature, advertising, and broadcasting talent. . . .
>
> What did he do with this array of talent? He used it to create intelligence networks behind enemy lines, to support the resistance forces that oppression always creates, to bring disaffected enemy officers over to our side, to dream up scenarios to manipulate the mind of the enemy in deceptions and psychological warfare programs.

All these machinations were not entirely new to Casey. Before the war, as a consultant for the Board of Economic Warfare, he carved out a sophisticated strategy: "pinpointing Hitler's economic jugular and investigating how it could be squeezed by blockade, preemptive buying and other economic warfare."[32] From there, it was not a giant step to identify specific targets that would most effectively impede the movement of Hitler's reinforcements. That was why Donovan had hired him.

According to Persico's biography, before Casey joined the fray, US forces had not even fully mapped out what would happen once Allied soldiers landed on the beaches of Normandy. "The Army hadn't always wanted our help," Casey said. "But they saw what we could do in Southern France. And they were taking a beating in the Ardennes—terrible casualties. And why? A colossal intelligence failure. So now the brass was more receptive to us."[33]

By December 1944, six months after D-Day, Donovan gave Casey blanket authority to head up the seemingly impossible task of penetrating Germany so Allied forces were not merely running blindly into Nazi territory.[34] "The man had a natural bent for what the Germans call *fingerspitzengefühl*, a feel for the clandestine," said Richard Helms, Casey's roommate in London and later the head of the CIA himself.[35]

In France, Casey got scores of Maquisards in the French Resistance to sever telephone and telegraph lines, thereby disrupting the Wehrmacht's communications.[36] He recruited operatives from neutral countries who could zip in and out of Germany with ease and trained them to infiltrate the Third Reich and collect data for the Allied assaults.[37]

Realizing that the talent pool was tiny when he was looking for American spies who might pass for Nazis, Casey flouted Geneva Conventions rules and began enlisting German prisoners of war as spies for the Allies. He parachuted agents into Berlin to find remnants of the anti-Nazi movement. Once they had infiltrated Germany, Casey had them radio back intel about Wehrmacht troop movements through important rail centers such as Hanover, Mainz, and Munich.[38]

This was his finest hour.

CASEY EMERGED FROM THE WAR ARMED WITH A MANICHAEAN ideology that served him for the rest of his life and the seeds of an extraordinary network with which to achieve its ends. When the war ended, Casey resolved that the battle was only half over, that there was another global totalitarian power as dangerous as Nazi Germany: the Soviet Union.[39]

In Tim Weiner's *Legacy of Ashes*, Bob Gates, who served as Casey's deputy for six years and later took Casey's job as DCI, explained the enduring power of Casey's wartime experience. "His view of how you fight a war against a totalitarian power had clearly been shaped in World War Two," said Gates. "Where there were no holds barred. Where everything went."[40]

Covert ops were in his blood.

His modest background aside, Casey had squeezed his way into the elite world of old money by being smart and fast and getting things done. But once the war ended, he also needed money, and became a venture capitalist. He backed an inventor who created a sophisticated new radar device for the Army Corps of Engineers. He invested in a handgun that could be converted into a rifle. He backed a man who was developing a new computerized tax return system.

Not all of his projects succeeded, but enough did that by 1948 he lived in a grand eight-acre Victorian estate, Mayknoll, in Roslyn, Long Island, not unlike the "white-shoe boys" in the OSS. His relationship to them is best described in Persico's biography *Casey*.

Of Casey's colleagues in the OSS, bestselling author Walter Lord noted, "Bill *appeared* to be on an intimate basis with all those people. But it looked to me, putting perhaps a harsh light on it, that they were using him. The establishment types were only too happy to have this bright, hardworking guy around. He was with them. But he wasn't *of* them."[41]

He was useful. And in civilian life, as a tax attorney, he continued to be useful. Not long after the war, Casey came up with the idea of the tax shelter. It was a means for his high-powered friends to avoid taxes, not by violating the law, but by creating new ways to act outside the scope of the regulations themselves.[42]

When it came to politics, Casey put his money on Nixon early, and his support never waned. Their relationship began in the late forties when they were drawn together by their mutual hatred of Communism, and Nixon, then a congressman on the House Committee on Un-American Activities, insistently pursued Alger Hiss as an accused Soviet spy, and so helped inspire Joe McCarthy's anti-communist witch hunts.

Meanwhile, Casey's law partner, Len Hall, who became chairman of the Republican National Committee in 1953, provided him with entrée to the reigning GOP powerbrokers of the times. As a director on the board of the right-wing Regnery Publishing, Casey had become close to William F. Buckley, the standard bearer of the modern conservative movement and founder of *National Review*, which was on the verge of collapse until Casey, ever the tax expert, came to the magazine's aid with imaginative fiscal solutions to its financial woes.[43]

The two men were Catholic, anti-communist, and conservative, and got along famously. Buckley soon came to anchor his sailboat occasionally at the dock at Casey's Mayknoll estate on occasion. Before long, Casey and Buckley joined forces in 1960 with a young PR man named William Safire to fight the liberal Rockefeller wing of the Republican Party on behalf of Richard Nixon. Safire, of course, went on to become a powerful GOP operative and, later, an op-ed columnist who touted Casey's fortunes in the pages of the *New York Times*.[44]

NOT TO BE OVERLOOKED IN CASEY'S NETWORK WAS A MAN WHO was not one of the "white-shoe boys" either but who may have been Casey's best friend of all—John Shaheen.[45] Shaheen had served in the Office of Strategic Services along with Casey during World War II, beginning a lifelong friendship.[46] Shaheen also hosted reunions for OSS alums that Casey never missed. Both men maintained active ties in the intelligence community.

After Nixon lost to John F. Kennedy in 1960, Casey and Shaheen remained Nixon men, with Shaheen enlisting Nixon as his attorney.[47] When Nixon was elected in 1968, Shaheen, a major contributor to the presidential campaign, was rewarded with an appointment as special ambassador to Colombia. As for Casey, Nixon eventually made him chairman of the Securities and Exchange Commission before moving Casey into the State Department in 1973, and later gave him the chairmanship of the Export-Import Bank of the United States.

After the Nixon administration, Casey had a lucrative practice at Rogers & Wells, a string of successful reference books such as *The*

Tax Shelter in Real Estate and *The Accounting Desk Book*, and highly profitable investments including one in a tiny media company he represented called Capital Cities that ended up taking over ABC. In all, by 1980, he had put together a fortune of an estimated $10 million (nearly $40 million in 2024 dollars).[48]

Both men remained active in Republican circles. In 1979, as the field of presidential aspirants took shape, Casey made $1,000 contributions—the maximum allowed at the time—to three Republican candidates, John B. Connally Jr., George H. W. Bush, and Ronald Reagan.[49] Of the three, Connally was the longest shot. The former Democratic governor of Texas, he had switched to the Republican Party in 1973 and was now running for president, but going nowhere fast. Still, Connally might prove useful to Casey in the future.

George Bush, however, was a different case. For many years, he and Casey had moved easily in high-level foreign policy circles, but their relationship, initially at least, had never been entirely comfortable. Where Casey made millions on his own as a stock speculator, Bush had plenty of family help, and grew prosperous in the oil business before his political rise in Houston. He was the offspring of Connecticut gentry—his father had been an investment banker who served in the United States Senate. Like him, Bush had attended Yale, and was tapped for Skull and Bones.

Casey and Bush also had political differences. Casey was part of the new rising right-wing movement within the Republican Party, the historic antagonist of Bush and his ancestors. Throughout the Cold War, Casey saw every stirring in every corner of the world through an unchanging ideological prism. He believed not in containment of Communism but in rollback, as it had been called in the late forties and early fifties. Bush, by contrast, was a consummate pragmatist, capable of rapidly adopting new positions if expediency or advancement seemed to demand it. Over time, though, Casey began to see Bush as a man of great personal discipline who understood accommodation as a way to achieve goals.[50]

Finally, there was Ronald Reagan. Casey had begun meeting with Reagan privately in early 1979 and soon became firmly convinced that Reagan not only had serious presidential prospects, but also that the Reagan team needed a guy like him. "The guys who have the brains can't get elected and the guys who get elected don't always have the brains," Casey told Republican congressman Henry Hyde (R-IL), according to Persico.[51]

By the fall of 1979, Casey had taken charge of lining up donations to Reagan fundraising dinners and sent out scores of solicitations to the makers and shakers in New York extolling Reagan as "the only one who has shown consistent dedication to the philosophy the country now needs and the ability to turn a government around as he did in California."[52] Casey would supply the brains—not to mention power and money.

Reagan, of course, was very much a creature of the West Coast, but anyone who was serious about becoming president had to be wired into the powers that be on Capitol Hill and Wall Street. In September, Casey put together an intimate evening for Reagan at the Hotel Pierre with two dozen of the richest and most powerful Republicans in New York. Next, he organized an enormous fundraiser on November 9 that raised more than $800,000 for Reagan from the top powerbrokers of the Eastern Establishment.[53] He also put together an event for November 13 at the New York Hilton at which Reagan was to declare his candidacy. He met with Reagan foreign policy adviser Richard Allen, campaign manager John Sears, and other top advisers to get a peek under the hood of the Reagan operation. Casey quickly concluded it was a mess.

But on November 4, 1979, with the hostage takeover in Iran, the calculus suddenly changed. Casey's experience in the OSS and the network that grew out of it became invaluable. Many in his network had been involved with Operation Ajax and were responsible for putting the Shah into power. And now Carter had lost it all in an embarrassing and public fashion. Twenty-six years earlier, as they saw it, the CIA had done exactly what the CIA was supposed to do. That had come to an end—temporarily, at least—in the wake of the Church Committee and Stansfield Turner's reign at Langley. The spies and ex-spies were horrified.

Once Casey took over as Reagan's campaign manager in March 1980, he went to work on the hostage crisis. Acutely aware that its resolution might well determine the outcome of the election, he knew that the fall of the Shah represented not just the end of one era but also the beginning of a new one. Jimmy Carter had lost Iran, but, Casey realized, the web of interdependent relationships that had tied together the United States, Israel, and Iran together for decades wouldn't disappear overnight. And the most immediate way to nurture it was by sending weapons to Iran. But that was the very last thing Carter wanted to do.

Casey, however, had no such scruples. Unlike Carter, he was merely a private citizen, so arming Iran would mean making illegal, clandestine arms shipments to a hostile foreign power under sanctions from the United States and its allies. How could anyone possibly pull off such an elaborate and treacherous operation?

According to his associate Robert Sensi, even though Casey did not join the CIA until he became its director in 1981, he made a point of cultivating a wide range of contacts in the intelligence world in the thirty-six years after his heyday in the OSS. Sensi, who became a Casey operative in the late seventies and played a significant role in the events of 1980, said that even during his time as a corporate lawyer at Rogers & Wells, Casey developed a close relationship with Robert B. Anderson, who served as secretary of the treasury in the Eisenhower administration, and in later years acted as "shadow director" of the CIA, as Sensi put it. "He was like a sounding board for the actual director of the CIA," Sensi told me in a 2024 interview.[54] "And he would say these are the covert operations we're working on now. . . . And he would voice an opinion one way or another. And this man had a lot of experience. He guided Eisenhower, and everything flowed from that."

Casey also still maintained active relationships with highly placed intelligence officials in Israel, France, the Palestinian Liberation Organization, and other sensitive outposts. He had established close relationships with corrupt banks willing to finance illegal arms deals with renegade arms dealers, intelligence operatives, and arms procurements officers all over the world.

Most critically, Casey's secret network also had a sophisticated operational infrastructure. He had cutouts—that is, go-betweens—who could facilitate clandestine communications with his network. He had high-profile emissaries who could lobby the powers that be in the Middle East. He could line up cargo ships that would sail under false flags, cargo planes disguised as commercial passenger jets, and crews that were very, very discreet. And, of course, there were the old hands who had been purged from the CIA's Directorate of Operations, unreconstructed Cold Warriors who were hankering for the days when they had carte blanche to execute coup d'états, assassinations, and the like with impunity.[55]

When the time came, they would all spring into action.

In March 1980, just after Casey became Reagan's campaign manager, the *Washington Post* noted that during World War II, when Casey became head of secret intelligence for the European theater, Wild Bill Donovan, the head of the OSS, saluted his handling of a crucial intelligence-gathering mission during the Battle of the Bulge. "You took up one of the heaviest loads which any of us had to carry at a time when the going was roughest," Donovan had written Casey, "and you delivered brilliantly, forcefully and in good time."[56]

Other than that, however, no one paid much attention to Casey's expertise in intelligence. As a result, his greatest asset during the 1980 presidential campaign was largely secret.

Chapter Four
The Secrets Men Die For

By modern political standards, it's somewhat hard to fathom that someone like Elliot Richardson, the former attorney general under Richard Nixon, ever existed. He was a Republican. He was a politician. And he was a hero—a moral hero at that.

He was also one of the first people I turned to in 1991 when I started reporting the October Surprise. With his anvil jaw and Hollywood good looks, Richardson was straight out of central casting as a scion of the Eastern Establishment, and he had the résumé to go with it. A Boston Brahmin who could trace his family roots back to the Puritans, Richardson graduated from Harvard and enlisted in the Army, then led a platoon landing on the beaches of Normandy on D-Day. After the war, he went to Harvard Law School where he became editor and president of the *Harvard Law Review*. He clerked for Supreme Court Justice Felix Frankfurter. And he served in no fewer than four cabinet posts—as secretary of health, education, and welfare; secretary of defense; attorney general; and secretary of commerce—for Presidents Nixon and Ford.

But Richardson made his most enduring mark on history when he served as Richard Nixon's attorney general during the Watergate scandal at a time when the walls were closing in on the president. In a last-ditch effort to stave off impeachment, Nixon ordered

Richardson to fire special prosecutor Archibald Cox, who was leading the Watergate investigation. But Richardson refused. Instead, he resigned as attorney general on principle in what became known as the Saturday Night Massacre. Thanks to Richardson, the investigation continued, and, ultimately, Nixon was forced to resign.* If any politician came out of Watergate a hero, it was Elliot Richardson.

All of which meant that in the squalid and murky world of the October Surprise, Richardson had suddenly appeared as Mr. Clean, a man of unimpeachable integrity. Next to spies and arms dealers, he was gold. Given his standing, his reputation, and his appearance, I had initially expected him to be somewhat stuffy, but whenever we spoke he was always refreshingly straightforward. He didn't know all the answers to the October Surprise, but he knew something horrible had happened, and he thought it vital that the country learn the truth.

In a series of interviews with me and, separately, with Bob Parry, Richardson offered a candid assessment of the scandal. "Whether the October Surprise happened, I don't know," Richardson told me.[1] "Some of the bits and pieces assembled suggest that maybe it did. Like everyone else in Washington, I have the attitude that one shouldn't put anything past Bill Casey. If it happened, it was despicable. Compared to the October Surprise, Watergate was an innocent child's frolic."

When I called him, Richardson had gone back into private practice with the white-shoe firm Milbank, Tweed, Hadley & McCloy. That made him an intriguing source for several reasons, one of which was that he had been Cyrus Hashemi's lawyer in the early eighties

---

* After Richardson resigned, Nixon ordered Deputy Attorney General William Ruckelshaus, the next in line, to fire Cox. But Ruckelshaus refused, and also resigned. Finally, the third-most-senior official at the Justice Department, Solicitor General Robert Bork, carried out Cox's dismissal as Nixon asked. But by then so much damage had been done to President Nixon that for all practical purposes, he was finished. The impeachment process against Nixon began just ten days after Richardson's resignation, on October 30, 1973.

when Hashemi was indicted for dealing illegal arms to Iran. Cyrus had died in July 1986, reportedly from leukemia, which meant when Parry and I interviewed Richardson on separate occasions in the early nineties, he was freer to discuss his former client. He painted a portrait of Cyrus as a high-roller who secretly lived a double life.

Cyrus, along with one of his older brothers, Jamshid, had been active in prerevolutionary politics in Iran. Once the Shah fell, they saw potential opportunities opening as various factions jockeyed for power in Iran. At the time, Cyrus had been living in high style with a Rolls-Royce in London and a chauffeured limousine in New York.[2] Meanwhile Jamshid was a civil engineer educated in England with his own construction business, but he too had been active in the anti-Shah movement in the seventies.[3] After the Revolution, Jamshid received an appointment from the new government to run the national radio network. That, in turn, put Jamshid in touch with other powerful Iranians, including the influential cleric Mehdi Karroubi, a onetime student of Ayatollah Khomeini's who later became Speaker of the Parliament, and his brother, Hassan.

Of the two, Cyrus was the mover and shaker. Elegantly turned out by a Bond Street tailor, Cyrus presented himself to clients as a sophisticated, well-traveled Iranian businessman who ran First Gulf Bank & Trust, a small merchant bank. With homes in London, Paris, and Wilton, Connecticut, he traveled the world on the supersonic Concorde. "He was very personable, unassuming, softspoken, intelligent, and gracious in manner, consistent with having an advanced degree from Oxford and moving comfortably in international banking circles," Richardson told Parry.[4]

"Everything about him was entirely consistent with his being a moderate, responsible, internationally oriented Iranian, who would have been embarrassed by fundamentalism, embarrassed by the seizure of the hostages, and would have seen it as in the long-term interest of his own country to reestablish relations with us and who would have been motivated by these and humanitarian concerns as well."[5]

But Richardson later realized that he had misjudged Cyrus Hashemi and learned things about him "that would have astonished me at the time."[6] Among other things, Richardson said, Cyrus died owing London casinos more than three million pounds sterling.[7] He left his family destitute. His wife's family fortune, which he said had funded his bank, did not exist.

"Hashemi was capable of playing more than one role simultaneously and seeming quite convincing to his audience, whatever it was," Richardson said. "What I know now is certainly not wholly inconsistent with the possibility that he could have been playing a double or triple game."[8]

And a dangerous one.

Indeed, it was Cyrus's sudden death in 1986 that was most troubling to Richardson.[9] During the Reagan administration, Cyrus had become an arms dealer who was a potential rival to Saudi billionaire Adnan Khashoggi in the illicit arms trade with Iran. According to the *Los Angeles Times*, Cyrus, forty-seven years old at the time, was acting as a confidential customs informant in a $2.5 billion sting operation that led to the arrests of an Israeli general and two of Khashoggi's associates.[10]

Then, on July 19, 1986, Cyrus was diagnosed with a rare and virulent form of leukemia. Two days later, he was dead.

Afterward, though, his lawyers and other observers raised questions about the diagnosis and whether injections or sprays that create similar symptoms caused his death. The *Los Angeles Times* cited an unnamed source saying Cyrus might have been "'bumped off' by government agents to protect the then-secret Iran initiative."[11]

That source was not alone. William Wachtel, who was Cyrus's lawyer at the time of his death, said that he was "ninety-eight percent certain" that Cyrus had been murdered.[12] Jamshid Hashemi and Richardson also both believed that Cyrus had been murdered, but the case was never solved. "No one I know believed that he died of natural causes," Richardson told Parry.[13] "There were plenty of people who wanted him dead."

As it turned out, firsthand information on the mysterious Cyrus Hashemi was not all Richardson had to offer. At the time I interviewed him in 1991, Richardson was representing a software company called Inslaw, whose programs had allegedly been pirated in a byzantine case of international espionage and cybertheft that involved Israeli intelligence. In that case, he had deposed a rogue Israeli operative and freelance arms dealer named Ari Ben-Menashe who happened to know a lot about the October Surprise.

An Iranian-born Jew of Iraqi parentage, Ben-Menashe had begun working for Israeli Military Intelligence in 1977[14] at the age of twenty-five. He spoke Farsi, Arabic, Hebrew, and English, and had acquired a richly detailed storehouse of knowledge about the Middle East by the time I met him in 1991. Knowledgeable as he was, he was also so deeply unreliable that even supporters of the October Surprise thesis—people like Gary Sick, who had spent considerable time with Ben-Menashe—were highly critical of him.

"Ari plays games that are so convoluted I can't follow them," said Sick. "I can't honestly say what his agendas are—and I use the plural intentionally. Money, vindication, Israeli American relations could all play a role.

"Does he ever lie? Yes. In many ways, he's reprehensible. But whether he is nice or always tells the truth is not important. The real question is what happened—and he knows a lot.

"Do we reject everything he says even when it is backed up by independent evidence?"[15]

Similarly, when I asked Richardson how credible Ben-Menashe was, the former attorney general reminded me that the people who are really the most knowledgeable about crime are themselves criminals, and that's why prosecutors often do everything they can to get the foot soldiers in a mob family to turn state's evidence and testify against the boss. At the time, mobster John Gotti, the boss of the Gambino crime family, was being prosecuted by the feds who were trying to "flip" a key witness against him—underboss Salvatore

"Sammy the Bull" Gravano, a sociopathic killer who had murdered at least nineteen people.[16] Was Gravano reliable? Of course not. But he *was* knowledgeable and his testimony, once corroborated, was enough to convict Gotti. That, Richardson suggested, was how I should handle Ben-Menashe: Hear him out. Then, corroborate or refute.

And that was what I did.

First, I tracked him down by phone at his temporary home in Australia, where he was writing a book on his life in Israeli intelligence. Since much of Ben-Menashe's story was spread out over five continents, and required penetrating the international intelligence world, separating fact from fiction required enormous patience and resources. In more than ten hours of taped interviews with me, he spoke with the fervor of a man whose life was in danger, regaling me with revelations about the October Surprise that were stunning: He told me that in 1980, he had been part of the Israeli team that provided security for the key meetings at which the October Surprise deal was hatched. As a result, he claimed, he had been present at meetings in Paris between Iran and the Republicans, which, he alleged, George H. W. Bush had also attended. He was telling me—on the record—that the incumbent president had participated in a treasonous conspiracy. That was the kind of explosive allegation on which the next presidential election could turn.

Ben-Menashe spun a riveting narrative about how the seizure of American hostages by Iran had boxed the Israelis into an awkward position where the most obvious solution to their dilemma was an arms-for-hostages deal. Much of what he said was impossible to corroborate or refute, and he delighted in playing reporters off each other, and tantalizing us by hinting at great secrets to be revealed later. Ben-Menashe could be irresistible, *and* he was unreliable.

The ball started rolling, he told me, in February 1980, when Robert "Bud" McFarlane—then an aide to Sen. John Tower—and Earl Brian, a businessman who had been secretary of health in Reagan's California cabinet, met highly placed Iranian officials in Tehran. This

February meeting was one of the first meetings about the October Surprise, he said, one that paved the way for later meetings in Madrid, and, eventually, the crucial October rendezvous in Paris.[17]

In a sworn affidavit submitted by Richardson on behalf of Inslaw, Ben-Menashe had said that both McFarlane and Brian had a "special relationship" with Israeli intelligence.[18] When I asked what he meant by that term, Ben-Menashe told me that McFarlane had been recruited as an intelligence asset by Rafi Eitan, a legendary Israeli agent who was the model for a leading character in John le Carré's *Little Drummer Girl*. Then, he reminded me that in the trial of Jonathan Pollard, an American convicted of spying for Israel in 1987 and sentenced to life in prison, there were persistent allegations about another, unnamed American who secretly worked for the Israelis. "McFarlane was the famous Mr. X in the Pollard case," Ben-Menashe told me.[19]

In other words, Robert "Bud" McFarlane, a former national security adviser to Ronald Reagan, had been an Israeli spy—or so said Ari Ben-Menashe.

Now things were getting interesting. (When I called McFarlane and Brian, both men declined comment.)

Ben-Menashe had first surfaced in the American press in 1990 when he was acquitted by a New York jury in federal court for trying to sell three Lockheed C-130 Hercules cargo aircraft to Iran in violation of the Arms Export Control Act. Ben-Menashe argued that the sale was part of a US government–approved deal with Iran to obtain the release of American hostages. Eventually, he was acquitted after arguing that the sale of the cargo planes were part of a US-sanctioned arms-for-hostages deal.[20] But before his acquittal, Israel denied having anything to do with Ben-Menashe's arms sales, and let him twist in the wind for nearly a year in New York City's Metropolitan Correctional Center. In return, Ben-Menashe struck back by leaking various tightly held Israeli secrets about arms deals to Iran—including the October Surprise.

For an investigative reporter like me, there was nothing worse than having a vital and knowledgeable source who was a liar. And that was especially true if he was a really important source and very easy to discredit, a source so toxic that merely quoting him by name could destroy your career.

There were many possible interpretations of what Ben-Menashe was doing. According to former CIA officer Victor Marchetti, Ben-Menashe's leaks to reporters like me were just part of a disinformation scam he was running for Israel, and he was merely posing as a renegade who knew the greatest secrets in the world. "He's still working for the Israelis and is putting out shit," Marchetti told me in 1991.[21] "He's a liar."

As I later reported in *Esquire*, when Ben-Menashe took a lie-detector test for ABC News, he failed miserably. "There was no ambiguity," Chris Isham, then a senior producer for ABC's investigative unit, told me at the time.[22] "He goes way off the chart on all relevant questions. My theory is that a lot of what he says is true, but that Ari exaggerates his own role and muddies the water."

That assessment made sense to me. After all, spies lie. That's what they do for a living.

But to me it also seemed possible that Ben-Menashe was in a pissing match with Israeli intelligence because they abandoned him, and he had gone rogue. The bottom line was that I didn't know the answer, but in either case, I didn't want to be collateral damage.

Yet I also knew that some of Ben-Menashe's most startling allegations had checked out. In 1986, he had told reporters about Iran's involvement in what came to be known as the Iran-Contra scandal, well *before* the story broke. Specifically, Ben-Menashe had gone to *Time* journalist Raji Samghabadi with explosive unreported details about the biggest story of the Reagan era. "It was the story of Iran-Contra," Samghabadi told me.[23] "I tried to get it printed, but it relied on a number of unidentified sources. I had the view that for accusations so earth-shaking and so provocative, you needed more than unnamed sources."

For six months, *Time* tried to corroborate Ben-Menashe's allegations and failed. But the ensuing congressional investigation into Iran-Contra backed him up. Samghabadi's story, and others like it, proved that Ben-Menashe did indeed have access to highly sensitive, classified information. To test Ben-Menashe further, I set up a three-way conference call with Avraham Bar-Am, a former Israeli brigadier general who was initially quite skeptical about Ben-Menashe's claims. But after grilling him extensively, with me listening in, Bar-Am told me, "He knows what he is talking about. Half of what he says is correct. The other half . . . who knows?"[24]

Elliot Richardson gave me a similar response when I asked if he genuinely believed Ben-Menashe or if he had submitted Ari's affidavit merely as a legal gambit. "I take him seriously as being who he says he is, and he does know quite a lot," he replied. "I can't always tell if the son of a bitch is telling the truth. My guess is that some of it is. One thing that is true of people like him is that they live in a world of such constant deception that they are used to moving without a misstep between truth and fabrication."[25]

When it came to Ben-Menashe's claims about the October Surprise, Richard Babayan, an Iranian who began working for the CIA in the '70s, also backed up some of Ari's claims about the Paris meetings and told me that William Casey was there for key meetings with the Iranians in October 1980. "I was meeting in Paris with Iranian expatriates, and I became aware of Casey meeting with Islamic individuals," said Babayan, in a phone call from jail where he was serving time for securities fraud.[26] "There were meetings, and I was able to debrief some of the people on the Iranian side who were present. I later met with Casey in June 1981, and he confirmed that he was at the meetings."

With all this in mind, I saw three possible ways to deal with Ben-Menashe. One option was to not use him at all because even mentioning his name would set off a firestorm of criticism. That was the safest option, but it meant abandoning his story entirely.

Option number two would be to talk to Ben-Menashe on background and not cite him by name. That might shield me from criticism, but if I were to use any material from Ben-Menashe I felt readers had a right to know where it came from. After all, he was not asking for his identity to be shielded.

Finally, the last option was to cite him as a knowledgeable but flawed source and let the chips fall where they may. At *Esquire*, I chose that route because I thought readers should know where my information was coming from and make up their own minds. Rule number one for investigative reporting is *not* to bury dispositive evidence. If you do, it's likely to come back and bite you in the ass.

Clearly, there were plenty of reasons to suspect Ben-Menashe was inflating his own importance, and even more clearly, everything he said needed to be double-checked. But just as clearly, he knew a lot about Israel's role in illegal arms deals that predated Iran-Contra. In fact, as he told the story, there was a direct line from the October Surprise to Iran-Contra in that both scandals involved illicit arms sales to Iran via Israel with oversight by William Casey, first as campaign manager for the Reagan-Bush campaign and later as CIA director. To understand the October Surprise, there was no choice but to enter that world, and Ben-Menashe was the only way in I knew.

BEN-MENASHE WAS JUST ONE OF MANY DUBIOUS FIGURES TO emerge following Gary Sick's op-ed. For most of them, their association with the October Surprise was rooted in Iran's need for weapons. After the hostage crisis and the US arms embargo began, freelance arms dealers and operatives from all over the world—many with loose or direct connections to Israel or the CIA—opened secret lines of communication with Tehran in the hopes of profiting off the situation. For most reporters, the problem was not so much getting in touch with these operatives as it was deciphering their unsavory pasts.

The very first person I investigated when I started working on the October Surprise was Richard Brenneke, a Portland, Oregon, businessman, arms dealer, and wannabe spook affiliated with the CIA. He had been in vogue as a so-called super source after spilling his guts about the October Surprise and clandestine arms deals to reporters all over the country. In the course of his work, he learned just enough to tantalize reporters with a few juicy secrets that checked out. A low-level intelligence operative, Brenneke claimed to have been under contract to Mossad, the FBI, French and Italian intelligence, and the CIA. At times, he might have worked on phony arms deals as a smokescreen, thereby diverting attention from the real weapons trade. Unfortunately, for reporters who spent time with him, he laced his goodies with lies and fabrications, invariably inflating his importance.

It didn't take long before it became clear that Brenneke did not have the CIA ties he had claimed and had not even been in Paris at the time of the October meetings.[27] A Senate investigation later concluded that he had spent considerable time trying to become an intelligence operative and, when that failed, an arms dealer. Some of the evidence he presented about the October Surprise was suggestive and true, but it soon became clear that the story of his "'secret' life as a spy" and secret arms deals with Iran had come from business associates who in turn had learned about them from Iranians.

And it wasn't just Brenneke. Suddenly, my Rolodex was filled with renegade Israeli operatives, South African arms dealers, arms procurement officials, Israeli generals, and the like. Before the October Surprise, I had never even spoken to an arms dealer; now there were operatives from five continents offering their stories to me—each one more disreputable than the next. Who *were* these guys? They raised the specter of an endless series of wild-goose chases. Figuring out who was authentic and serious, whether they were telling the truth, and why they came forward was not always easy.

Gradually, I put together a posse of sorts to help guide me through this shadowy world, people I could come back to repeatedly and were willing to share information and compare notes. There were congressional aides, sources in the intelligence world, and independent researchers. Foreign journalists like Pazit Ravina of *Davar*, in Israel, and Martin Kilian from *Der Spiegel* were particularly helpful in that they came at the scandal from completely fresh angles and had very different sources.

In 1989, Kilian, then Washington correspondent for *Der Spiegel*, had been one of the first serious reporters on the October Surprise. Among the people he interviewed was Austrian-born Oswald LeWinter, a self-proclaimed CIA agent and noted American poet who had a fabulously eccentric résumé. A literary figure of some repute, LeWinter had taught at Penn State, Columbia University, and Marist College, and published poetry in various literary journals. His work had been hailed by Saul Bellow, Robert Lowell, and William Carlos Williams, and they had likened him to Rimbaud, Goethe, and Rilke, respectively.[28]

LeWinter invited himself over to *Der Spiegel*'s Washington bureau, explained that he preferred to be known as "Razine," and proceeded to regale Kilian with wild October Surprise tales.[29] Kilian figured out just one key facet of LeWinter's spiel. "He was lying through his teeth," Kilian told me.[30] LeWinter admitted as much himself later when he swore under oath before congressional investigators that his October Surprise allegations were complete fabrications.[31]

Similarly, Heinrich Rupp, who claimed to have been a pilot for the CIA, had said he piloted two flights to Madrid in the summer of 1980 to facilitate "secret contacts between Casey and the Iranians."[32] There was also Gunther Russbacher, an inmate of the Missouri State Prison, who said he piloted Bush, Bill Casey, and their entourage to Paris on a BAC-111, a narrow-body British jet, in October.[33]

And yet, even if one discounted LeWinter, Rupp, and Russbacher—and I certainly did—there were several other sources who made the same charge against Bush: that the current sitting president who was up for reelection had participated in a treasonous covert operation eleven years earlier. These were echoes of the same claim Gary Sick had made in his *Times* op-ed piece when he had written, "At least five of the sources who say they were in Paris in connection with these meetings insist that George Bush was present for at least one meeting. Three of the sources say that they saw him there."[34]

Back in the seventies, when Bob Woodward and Carl Bernstein were covering Watergate for the *Washington Post*, one of the unwritten rules they followed was that they would not publish allegations about criminal wrongdoing unless they had at least two independent sources.[35] Yet, even with five sources, Sick felt it necessary to add that he had not made up his mind about whether the allegations were true. That was how murky this world was.

A bigger question was why so many arms dealers and renegade intelligence operatives suddenly were coming out of the woodwork and divulging secrets? Why was all this happening now, in 1991, just as a new presidential election season was getting underway?

No one had definitive answers, but it soon became clear that some of them were disseminating disinformation. Oswald LeWinter later said as much, under oath, before Congress.

LeWinter attributed his deceit to a variety of amorphous, self-serving reasons.[36] But he wasn't the only one, and there was more to it than that. Who, if anyone, was paying for it? To what ends? And which other "super sources" were also spreading disinformation?

I thought some of it might have come from Israeli intelligence or American operatives who would start by spoon-feeding a legitimate hot scoop or two to an unsuspecting reporter. Then, having won his trust, the operative would feed the reporter disinformation that would explode in his face and bring down his career. This way, they could destroy the reputation of anyone trying to unravel the October Surprise.

Figuring it out wasn't easy. There were multiple layers of deception, involving both sources and documentation. "In the world of fabrication, you don't just drop something and let someone pick it up," Milt Bearden, a thirty-year CIA veteran, explained to me.[37] "Your first goal is to make sure it doesn't find its way back to you, so you do several things. You may start out with a document that is a forgery, that is a photocopy of a photocopy of a photocopy, which makes it hard to track down. You go through cutouts so that the person who puts it out doesn't know where it came from. And you build in subtle, nuanced errors so you can say, 'We would never misspell that.' It's a chess game, not checkers."

Martin Kilian at *Der Spiegel* had a few ideas about what was really going on. "My suspicion is that it's part of an operation by the Israelis going after Bush for being too friendly towards the Palestinians," he told me.[38] Bush had been the first US president to call for the establishment of an independent Palestinian state, and the Palestinians hailed him as the only president to stand up to Israel.[39]

Normally, our instincts tell us either to trust or distrust a source, but to investigate the October Surprise one had no choice but to enter a clandestine world peopled with knowledgeable yet deeply flawed sources. As Gary Sick told me when I first started investigating in 1991, "If you want to deal with the October Surprise, those are the people you have to deal with. It's a very special world with its own rules."[40]

Indeed, if Bill Casey were planning a covert operation, he might look for operatives who were skilled in arms dealing, but above all else, in his world, being a skilled liar was a highly desirable, even necessary, trait. If such contractors—pilots, arms dealers, and the like—found themselves in a compromising position, you would want people who could lie easily about what they had done.

Moreover, freelance operatives, driven as they are by mercenary motives, would have little incentive to remain loyal, so it also made sense to hire people who were expendable. Convicts, spies, arms dealers. The taller their tales, the more exotic their imagined adventures, the wackier they appeared, the better. People—like Ben-Menashe or Brenneke—who could be easily discredited. At a certain point, what they divulged would be irrelevant because their stories could be totally undermined. And it would be equally easy to discredit any reporter who cited them as well.

Needless to say, that last part concerned me a great deal.

Despite the disparate backgrounds of many of these sources, a common theme running through many of their stories—most notably Ben-Menashe's—was that Israel had played a key role in the October Surprise. A decade after these events supposedly took place, perhaps the only thing about the October Surprise more counterintuitive than Republicans wanting to arm Iran, was the idea that Israel would help the Islamic fundamentalists they decried as their mortal enemy.

After all, in the wake of Iran's Islamic Revolution, Ayatollah Khomeini demonized Israel as the "Little Satan"—the Big Satan, of course, was the United States—while Israel returned the favor by labeling Iran an existential threat. "Israel was of one mind," former prime minister Shimon Peres told me in a 1992 interview.[41] "We could not accommodate Khomeini in any way."

Officially.

But unofficially, all the rhetoric from both sides masked a secret: the Israeli-Iranian partnership that had lasted for decades prior to the Islamic Revolution could still be mutually beneficial for both countries, at least in the short term. While the Shah was still in power, Israel had enjoyed a rewarding relationship with Iran that included military, economic, and intelligence sharing. Right up until the Shah was overthrown, Israel had pumped in as much as 1.2 million barrels of oil a day from Iran through the Trans-Israel pipeline, a joint project built by Israel and Iran when it was under the Shah to transport Iranian crude oil from the Israeli Port of Eilat across Israel to the Mediterranean and Europe.[42] The military in both Israel and Iran relied heavily on American hardware, which meant that Israel had plenty of spare parts for F-14 Tomcat fighter jets and other weapons that Iran needed.

And then there was Iraq. Iranian posturing aside, Israel was far more concerned with Iraqi dictator Saddam Hussein acting as an aggressor in the region. At the time, Israeli foreign policy was known as "the doctrine of the periphery," a policy which called for Israel to forge strategic alliances with non-Arab Muslim states in the Middle East—most notably, Iran—to counteract Arab opposition. Or, as the Israelis often framed it: "The enemy of my enemy is my friend."

Israel also *needed* an Iran that was strong enough to fight off Saddam Hussein. As I saw it, the value of Ben-Menashe, and some of the other sources, was that they provided entry to a mysterious sub-rosa world that rarely saw the light of day, a world in which, with a wink and a nod, Israel facilitated covert arms shipments of weapons to Iran.

By prying that world open, by corroborating as many of those arms deals as possible, a new paradigm gradually started to emerge that repeatedly echoed the contours of the Iran-Contra scandal. In Iran-Contra, Bill Casey had overseen illicit and clandestine arms shipments to Iran starting in 1984. With the October Surprise, the arms shipments to Iran, also overseen by Casey, had started four years earlier. Otherwise, they were identical.

At the same time, I was haunted by the risk posed by so many unreliable sources. The possibility of fraud tainting any serious attempts to investigate the October Surprise called to mind the Hitler diaries hoax of 1983, when half a dozen major newspapers and magazines including the *Sunday Times* of London, *Stern* in Germany, Paris *Match*, and *Newsweek* in the United States paid $3.7 million for a trove of Nazi memorabilia including sixty volumes of journals, poems, and diaries said to have been written by Adolf Hitler.[43] The diaries had been authenticated by no less an authority than Hugh Trevor-Roper, the esteemed British historian and Oxford professor who had authored *The Last Days of Hitler*.

But they were fake.[44]

After the hoax was exposed, Brian MacArthur, who covered the story for the *Sunday Times*, explained that the journalists involved "were so gullible" because "the discovery of the Hitler diaries offered so tempting a scoop that we all wanted to believe they were genuine. . . . The few of us who were in on the secret fed on the adrenalin: we were going to write the most stunning scoop of our careers."

When the story blew up in their faces, however, Trevor-Roper's lofty reputation was forever tarnished, as were those of the journalists involved, many of whom lost their jobs. With the October Surprise, however, the dangers were even greater than mere reputational harm.

CYRUS HASHEMI WAS NOT THE ONLY FIGURE INVOLVED IN THE October Surprise who had died mysteriously. That was the thing about the October Surprise. Everywhere you looked there was another rabbit hole. Another conspiracy. Another deep dive into the weeds. And no one went deeper than Danny Casolaro. Most recently, Casolaro's story has been told in a four-part docuseries, *American Conspiracy: The Octopus Murders*, on Netflix.

At first, all I knew was that he was another freelance reporter investigating the October Surprise. I was told he saw it as part of a larger global conspiracy that tied together several scandals and alleged scandals—the Iran-Contra affair, the Inslaw case that Richardson was involved with, among them.[45] He called the overlapping intrigues "The Octopus." And because Elliot Richardson was representing Inslaw, he and Danny had been working the same network of sources.

A forty-four-year-old freelance writer who worked at and then acquired small computer and data-processing trade journals, Casolaro had published one novel—*The Ice King*—with a small publisher, and had mixed success in journalism, publishing in supermarket tabloids such as the *National Star*, *National Enquirer*, *Washington Crime News*, and various tech trade publications. He also presented himself as a veteran investigative reporter who had dug up major stories—published or not, it's unclear—about Fidel Castro's intelligence network, how the Chinese were smuggling opium into the United States, and the like.[46]

In early August 1991, Casolaro had gone to Martinsburg, West Virginia, to interview an unnamed source for a book proposal on The Octopus. *Wired* magazine said Casolaro had ventured into "the Bermuda Triangle of spooks, guns, drugs and organized crime."[47] Before leaving for Martinsburg, Danny told his brother, Dr. Anthony Casolaro, about threatening calls he had received and said if something were to happen to him there, it would not be an accident.[48]

At about the same time, Casolaro's housekeeper said she answered several frightening phone calls including one that promised to slash Danny up and "throw [his body] to the sharks."

Just a few days later, on August 10, Casolaro was found dead in the bathtub of the Sheraton hotel in Martinsburg, his wrists slashed ten to twelve times. His death was ruled a suicide, and no evidence was found showing that Casolaro had been murdered. But it had been widely reported that the cuts were deep enough to sever his tendons, which would have made it impossible to slash *both* wrists.

As soon as I heard about it, I got on the phone and touched base with half a dozen people who might know more about it—among them, Martin Kilian, Elliot Richardson, and Bill Hamilton, the president of Inslaw, the computer company that had been targeted in The Octopus, which Danny had been investigating.

With Richardson, I was struck with how such a stalwart pillar of the establishment took even the darkest allegations quite seriously. "Casolaro had been working on this for a year, so he cannot have been ingenuously expecting the material," Richardson told me. "He told four people he had already received hard evidence and was going to Martinsburg, West Virginia, to get more. There is reason to believe that he did not die by his own hand."[49]

Later, Richardson wrote about it in a *New York Times* op-ed: "I believe [Casolaro] was murdered, but even if that is no more than a possibility, it is a possibility with such sinister implications as to demand a serious effort to discover the truth."[50]

Richardson's sentiments were shared by Inslaw president Bill Hamilton, as well as Danny's friends and family. "The people we had talked to were warning us that he would be killed, a week before he died," Hamilton told the *Washington Post*.[51]

"It's not like we're all in mass denial," Ann Klenk, a television producer and Danny's former girlfriend, also told the *Post*. "It's the fact that we knew him for so long. And you'd think there would be something, some crack in that exterior."[52]

She found suicide by razor to be a most unlikely possibility. "He would have jumped off the Empire State Building, with firecrackers," she added.

And that, in essence, was the October Surprise—even the deaths didn't add up in a way that made sense. The Danny Casolaro story—his fate, the real story behind his death—had absolutely nothing to do with whether the October Surprise happened. And yet no single component of the October Surprise was as evocative of its culture of conspiracy. I never met Casolaro or talked to him, but I had heard his name bruited about as a freelance journalist who was on the trail of the October Surprise. And now I was hearing various names tossed around of people who might have killed Danny, and tales of renegade spooks gone wild working out of an obscure Indian Reservation in California.

The press, all over the world, went crazy for the story. The Danny Casolaro story allowed the press to see itself—that is, it allowed *us* to see *ourselves*—as similar to Danny, an intrepid, martyred reporter who heroically gave his life in his search for truth. CNN began investigating. In England, Australia, and Canada, the media couldn't get enough of it. *Newsweek* jumped in. "As U.S. Battles Computer Company, Writer Takes Vision of Evil to Grave," read the headline in the *New York Times*.[53] In London, the *Independent* said that he had died from "the Oliver Stone Syndrome, the belief that all malefaction is ultimately connected, that a network of crime and corruption underlies American life."[54]

Casolaro's death added a sensational new layer of paranoia to the October Surprise—and made it that much easier to dismiss later on. And that was the thing about investigating it. In the public imagination, the October Surprise had metastasized into a morass of new mysteries and conspiracies faster than anyone could process them. Some of them were only vaguely related to the October Surprise and more often than not the evidence was merely circumstantial.

In late July 1991, just before Casolaro's death, Anson Ng, a stringer for the *Financial Times*, was found shot to death in his Guatemala City apartment.[55] Ng had been investigating arms sales to Guatemala brokered by the Bank of Credit and Commerce International (BCCI), a massively corrupt and secretive Pakistani bank. BCCI had fueled arms deals and money laundering at the center of various covert operations around the globe, and counted Cyrus Hashemi, as well as many other arms dealers, as major customers.[56] With more than four hundred branches in seventy-three countries all over the world, BCCI earned the nickname the Bank of Crooks and Criminals International as it laundered money for and financed arms deals for dictators, gangsters, and terrorists including Saddam Hussein, Manuel Noriega,[57] the Medellín Cartel, and Abu Nidal.[58]

According to Sen. Alan Cranston (D-CA), the Ng assassination appeared to be the work of professional hitmen. He added that journalists in Guatemala suspect that Ng's murder was related to his probe into arms trafficking allegedly carried out by BCCI.[59] (FBI wiretaps of Cyrus Hashemi recorded a call alerting Hashemi that "money from BCCI [is] to come in tomorrow from London on Concorde."[60] But the full story of the bank's ties to October Surprise arms shipments remain murky thanks to the CIA's decision to withhold "sensitive operational information" from congressional investigators.[61])

Nor were Casolaro or Ng alone. In November 1988, Amiram Nir, the chief counterterrorism adviser to Israeli prime ministers Shimon

Peres and Yitzhak Shamir, met his demise in a small plane crash in Mexico that gave rise to countless conspiracy theories. Nir had not become counterterrorism adviser[62] until 1984, and in many ways the illicit arms sales to Iran that he oversaw appeared to be nothing more than a continuation of those that began with the October Surprise.

According to the *Times of Israel*, there were "unsubstantiated allegations that he was silenced because he was about to spill details of his role in Iran-Contra that might prove hugely embarrassing to [then vice president] George H. W. Bush."*[63] Many years later, Amiram's son, Nimrod Nir, investigated his father's death and concluded that he had been assassinated by American agents who didn't want the truth to come out.

All of which added up to a number of unsolved crimes that were enormously intriguing but, in the end, were nothing more than a sideshow.[64] Any evidence that their deaths were directly tied to the October Surprise was largely circumstantial. On the other hand, they *were* dead. And the mystery behind those deaths made paranoia a perfectly natural response. After all, the specter had been raised, repeatedly, that somewhere in this morass were secrets that men died for.

And killed for, as well.

AFTER FOUR MONTHS OF WORK FOR *ESQUIRE*, AND MORE THAN 150 interviews, I concluded that many pieces of the puzzle were still open to question, but that a persuasive case could still be made that the October Surprise did take place. My ten-thousand-word article came out in the October issue in early September 1991. I was anxious to see how much pushback I would get. Initially, it got a respectful write up

* Later, in 1992, in a story entitled "In the Loop," Murray Waas and I reported on Bush's briefing from Nir in *The New Yorker*. So there was no question in my mind that Bush, contrary to his protestations, was very much in the know about secret and illegal arms deals to Iran, and Nir had firsthand knowledge of it.

in a handful of newspapers, and a mention on ABC's *Nightline*, which had an investigative unit that was still going after the story.

While all this news was breaking, more action was going on in Congress. In August, Speaker of the House Tom Foley (D-WA) and Senate Majority Leader George Mitchell (D-ME) had announced an investigation of the October Surprise to be conducted by the Senate Foreign Relations Subcommittee on Near Eastern and South Asian Affairs and, in the House of Representatives, a special task force headed by Rep. Lee Hamilton (D-IN). The first phase of the investigation was to take place behind closed doors and involve sworn testimony and subpoenaed documents, Foley told the *Los Angeles Times*.[65]

Shortly after my article came out in *Esquire*, I got a call from *Newsweek*'s Jonathan Alter, who said the magazine wanted to talk with me about playing a key role in investigating the October Surprise for them. Working at *Newsweek* was appealing because, with the exception of ABC's *Nightline* and PBS's *Frontline*, serious investigative reporting on the October Surprise had largely been absent from the Capitol Hill press corps.

Newsweek, which today is under different ownership but back then was owned by the Washington Post Company, the paper that broke Watergate, was now offering me a venue to bring the issue into the mainstream national conversation. At *Esquire*, I had been a solo practitioner who turned in his story and was essentially given a free hand to write whatever was on my mind. *Newsweek*, by contrast, had veteran correspondents all over the world and could finance costly international jaunts at the drop of a hat. Monthlies like *Esquire* could not chase breaking stories, simply because they published so infrequently. At *Newsweek*, we'd be able to pursue the story as it unfolded week after week, and shape the national conversation.

Or so I thought.

Chapter Five
Pretty Poison

On October 10, 1991, I nervously paced back and forth at the Qantas gate at LAX, waiting to meet a man who was widely considered to be a complete fraud. The plan was for me to meet Ari Ben-Menashe, who was coming in from Australia, and then fly with him from Los Angeles to Houston where we would meet up with a member of the *Newsweek* team. The multiple plane rides all felt a bit too cloak-and-dagger for my taste, but Ari had legitimate reasons to be concerned. During a previous entry to the United States, he had been busted by US Customs agents, who arrested him for illegal arms dealing, and spent nearly a year in jail. In the end, he was acquitted after the jury bought his story that the Israeli government had authorized the arms sales, but he didn't want to go through that again alone.[1]

But as I weaved my way through the airport, Ben-Menashe's spotty past wasn't the only thing on my mind. I'd only been at *Newsweek* for about five weeks, but I was already concerned about how things were playing out there.

Even back then, there was something about *Newsweek* that harkened back to an earlier era. For decades, it had cultivated a swashbuckling ethos that resembled a latter-day version of the great newspaper movies of the forties like *His Girl Friday.* Reporters had traveled the world dressed like ambassadors—bespoke suits, Chesterfield coats with black velvet collars. They expected to be treated as equals of the diplomatic corps. They spent freely from bottomless expense accounts. There was sex, money, and three-martini lunches.

That era was over, and pundits had already begun to predict the demise of the newsweekly. But there were still big expense accounts, international travel, and the romance of being a foreign correspondent. *Newsweek* was still near its peak circulation of 3,400,000. And on the top floors, the editors were known as the Wallendas—a reference to the aerial circus act, the Flying Wallendas—for their daring feats of journalistic derring-do, ripping up the book and crashing massive cover stories at the last minute about the latest catastrophe gripping the world.

Jonathan Alter had helped set up my meeting with *Newsweek* executive editor Maynard Parker, and just after Labor Day in 1991, I made my way to Parker's office in the Newsweek Building at 444 Madison Avenue. Then fifty-one, Maynard had begun his career as a reporter for *Life* magazine and soon became a foreign correspondent in its Hong Kong bureau. In 1967, he went to *Newsweek* in Hong Kong, and went on to lead *Newsweek*'s coverage of the Vietnam War. As the editor in New York, Maynard savored the use of military phrases like "scramble the jets" while he played a larger-than-life field general moving reporters around the globe to cover a breaking story. "What would daunt most people would thrill him," Evan Thomas, assistant managing editor at *Newsweek*, told the *New York Times*. "The later, the harder, the better. He was never happier than when we were either at war or on the brink of war."[2]

It was a short meeting. To make sure Maynard and I were on the same page, I made a point of discussing my *Esquire* piece with him. He hired me on the spot.

I began work the first week of September. At a noon meeting on the fourteenth floor, I was introduced to the rest of the October Surprise team. There were two other reporters—Pentagon correspondent John Barry and Tony Clifton, a *Newsweek* foreign correspondent from Australia who had considerable experience covering wars in the

Middle East. Tom Morganthau was to be the writer for the project. In addition, there were editors, research assistants, and various correspondents all over the world to assist as needed.

John Barry was put in charge. Working out of Washington, he split the project into manageable sections that Clifton and I could investigate. Since I was the only one who had interviewed Ben-Menashe, I was deemed the Ben-Menashe expert and was put in charge of debriefing him by phone while he remained in Australia. I called him regularly, and gradually a more fully fleshed-out picture began to emerge of who Ari was and what he had done. Part of the idea too was to lure him to America where an in-person interview could take place.

Ari was the son of Iraqi Jews and had grown up in Tehran. Armed with a familiarity of Arabic, Farsi, and Israeli cultures, Ben-Menashe told me how he carved out a place for himself in Israeli intelligence administering a secret Israeli arms channel to Iran that he called the Joint Committee. He said it consisted of a network of freelance Israeli operatives working in an unofficial capacity with US operatives. He told me he worked with Yehoshua Saguy, the director of military intelligence, and his chief of staff, Moshe Hevrony. He explained how fraudulent export licenses were obtained, what military bases were used for arms shipments, and the relative roles of Mossad and Israeli Military Intelligence.[3] I spent hours on the phone with him in taped conversations and tried to figure out what could be corroborated or refuted.

Meanwhile, John Barry queried the magazine's correspondents all over the world. To expedite the project, in a pre-email world, *Newsweek* put together a jerry-rigged variant of the Unix operating system that was woefully primitive by today's standards, but state-of-the-art technology at the time. As a result, we were able to file our memos in a computer queue that would be shared automatically with the whole team. At least in theory.

At Barry's request, I had prepared a list of a dozen or so documents that I thought would be a propitious starting point, including court records, arms deals, and the like. I also sent Barry a list of more than two dozen potential Republican sources, many of whom had been involved in the Reagan and Bush presidential campaigns of 1980 and had had fallings-out. When I first called them for *Esquire*, I was astounded at how openly some had discussed Casey's role. I was certain it was worthwhile to ping-pong back and forth with Casey's aides to reconstruct what happened. In the past, I'd often had good luck with low-profile sources like Scott Thompson or Susan Clough, people who were not household names but were in the room and knew what was going on. Now, among his other duties, John Barry said he would follow up with Thompson and the like, so that part was out of my hands.

I didn't get ahold of it until several weeks later, but on September 25, Paris correspondent Christopher Dickey had filed a report with *Newsweek* editors, after interviewing former Iranian president Abolhassan Bani-Sadr; Alexandre de Marenches, the former head of Service de Documentation Extérieure et de Contre-Espionnage (SDECE), the French counterpart of the CIA; and others. According to Dickey's file, the picture Bani-Sadr painted "takes as a given that there was some contact between members of the Republican campaign and aides to Khomeini—probably Casey and Karroubi."[4] Dickey, who had covered Central America for both the *Washington Post* and *Newsweek*, added that it all reminded him of "the way Republican operators were muddying the waters in Central America at the same time, telling all kinds of conspiracy-minded loonies (including the leaders of the Salvadoran death squads) that the Carter administration was on the way out and they were the representatives of the government-to-be who really counted."

The Bani-Sadr interview was promising but unsurprising, given that the banished Iranian president had given similar interviews to the *New York Times*[5] and the *Miami Herald*.[6] But Bani-Sadr could easily open the door to other Iranian sources. In addition, I was hoping Dickey would turn his attention to the October Surprise meetings that allegedly took place in Paris.

As for Ben-Menashe, it would be an understatement to say that I was wary about checking him out; nevertheless, I went to work. On October 1, I sent Barry a memo noting that two sets of "official" Israeli records on Ben-Menashe were available for inspection. When he had first been arrested for arms dealing in 1989, the Israelis had insisted that Ben-Menashe had no ties to Israeli intelligence whatsoever, and they sent around a bunch of documents that showed him to be merely a low-level translator. But Bob Parry had dug up documents that contradicted the official Israeli story in the form of "letters of reference" that noted Ben-Menashe served in "key positions" with the External Relations Department of the Israeli Defense Forces while undertaking "complex and sensitive assignments."[7]

In addition, Ben-Menashe had presented his passport during his trial as evidence indicating he had made trips to Peru, Chile, Guatemala, and other destinations that simply did not jibe with Israel's description of him as a low-level translator. Yes, he had mastered all the major languages in the Middle East—but none of those languages were relevant to his Latin American travels. After reviewing both sets, I suspected that the first set represented an attempt to discredit Ben-Menashe as "a minor translator" because he had gone rogue.

During the months of my reporting for *Esquire* and the first few weeks of my time at *Newsweek*, my relationship with Ben-Menashe had been confined to phone interviews with him in Australia. But in mid-September, he flew to New York City, and I met with him briefly, the first time in person.

My partner in checking out Ben-Menashe was Tony Clifton, and on the morning of Monday, September 23, 1991, Clifton and I had walked into a nondescript Midtown hotel to meet the man causing confusion and controversy across three continents. At forty years old, Ben-Menashe wore a maroon Lacoste polo shirt and faded blue jeans. He was unshaven, stood about five ten, and chain-smoked Marlboros. On a table were the business cards of congressional investigators to whom, presumably, he was divulging all his secrets. At his feet was an open suitcase with the documents he displayed temptingly, but guardedly. There were hundreds of business cards and scraps of paper that had the names of arms dealers, transport companies, and the like and notations about TOW missiles and spare parts for various fighter jets. There were gunrunners, aircraft brokers, shipping companies, arms procurement officials all over the world. According to Ben-Menashe, they had the phone numbers and addresses of the various proprietaries that serviced the Joint Committee.

Theoretically, these papers should tell us whether Ben-Menashe was completely full of shit or not. With all those names and phone numbers, there would be hundreds of leads.

I wanted them.

"Not now," Ben-Menashe said in a whisper. He leaned forward conspiratorially as he spoke. The documents were currency to him, and before I knew it, our meeting was over, leaving me empty-handed.

When I had discussed Ben-Menashe with Clifton after we left, he pointed out that Ben-Menashe's claim that the amount of weapons funneled to Iran—more than $80 billion worth—was so astronomical that he could not possibly believe it. No one did. (Seymour Hersh in the *New York Times* later cited a CIA official saying the figure was about $2 billion per year.)[8]

Still, Clifton did not dismiss Ben-Menashe entirely. "My own assessment of Ben-Menashe is that he has been involved in the Israeli-Iranian arms traffic," Clifton wrote in a memo that week. "But I don't believe his claims that he was a central figure on the Israeli committee which did the Israeli side of the deals."

Clifton concluded that Ben-Menashe was "a quite valuable and very flawed source whose every 'fact' will need to be double checked if we intend to use it."

I agreed. "I am well aware that Ari could turn out to be working for the Israelis, feeding disinformation, a fabulous fantasist or just an asshole like Brenneke," I wrote in a memo. But, I added, it was important to hear out his story and to corroborate or refute it.

Meanwhile, Ben-Menashe had gone back to Sydney. But, about a week later, he called me from Australia with a proposition. He was ready to talk and deliver people, places, and a paper trail of evidence that could be independently verified. He insisted on a number of unusual security precautions: He stipulated that *Newsweek* pay round-trip airfare from Sydney to an American city that he would name only at the last minute. There were to be no leaks about our meeting, what we were discussing, or where it would take place. Finally, he demanded that I fly from New York to LAX to be there with him in case he was harassed by US Customs officials. Maynard quickly gave me a green light, and I arranged to meet Ben-Menashe in Los Angeles on October 10.

The man who knew too much, the spy who came in from the cold, the man without a country—Ben-Menashe savored every cliché that the literature of espionage had to offer. All the drama made me somewhat skeptical. But, he had promised, once we got down to business, to unravel a key element of the October Surprise scenario—the massive arms network that the CIA and Israelis set up in 1981.

At the same time, *Newsweek* Jerusalem correspondent Ted Stanger was also investigating Israel's role in the operation. On October 3, he filed a memo saying, "[T]hat Israeli agents may have facilitated contacts between Casey and the Iranians is no surprise to me. I was working in Israel at the time, and it was clear the [Menachem] Begin government opted for Reagan as early as June 1980, despite Camp David, or because of it."

Stanger was right about that. Menachem Begin had won the Nobel Peace Prize jointly with Egyptian president Anwar Sadat for signing the Camp David Accords between Egypt and Israel in 1978, which led directly to the Egypt-Israel Peace Treaty the following year. This peace treaty—still intact and operational forty-six years later—was Jimmy Carter's greatest foreign policy achievement, but it came at a steep price: returning the Sinai peninsula to Egypt. For Israel, the cost was dear, and Begin had never forgiven Carter.

Stanger also pointed out Israel's need to discredit the October Surprise: "We cannot expect the GOI (government of Israel) to let down its hair even a bit on this issue. . . . [A]lthough Bush may be disliked at the political level, the Israeli Defense and espionage establishment are more concerned about linking themselves in any way with a dirty piece of work like delaying release of the US hostages in 1980. Some GOI officials would love to teach Bush a lesson, but the lesson for future presidents and CIA directors would be a negative one: don't trust the Israelis."

General as Stanger's assessment was, his words reaffirmed my own instincts around using Ben-Menashe as a source. Yes, he was problematic, but because he was giving reporters like me the information we needed to uncover Israel's role in the October Surprise, the Israelis, it seemed, were out to destroy his credibility—and ours.

Then, in the second week in October, just as I prepared to leave New York to meet Ben-Menashe, Tony Clifton dropped a bombshell: He said *Newsweek*'s London bureau had accounted for all of William Casey's time in late July 1980 during the crucial window when the October Surprise meetings were taking place in Madrid. Casey, they said, was in London, not Madrid.

I was stunned. This was absolutely critical. If Casey wasn't in Madrid, the single most important piece of evidence was gone. If there was a smoking gun for the entire October Surprise narrative, Casey's presence in Madrid was it. If Casey had met with the Iranians there to delay the hostage release, he had committed an act of treason. If not, there was really no story. Clifton, however, said he didn't know the specifics about the new information.

When I asked John Barry about it, he declined to give me details. As a freelancer parachuting into *Newsweek* from the outside, I was intruding on Barry's turf. One *Newsweek* veteran told me that Barry was wary of an outsider being brought in. Others said this was simply the way Barry worked, that he was notorious for keeping things to himself and filing at the last minute.

But the way the entire *Newsweek* investigation was unfolding didn't sit right with me. Clifton had been a colleague of Barry's for many years and thought the reasons behind *Newsweek*'s lackluster efforts lay elsewhere. To him, the unseen hand here had more to do with *Newsweek*'s infamous connection to the Hitler diaries hoax in 1983. Maynard Parker had been held responsible, and his reputation went into freefall. Now, eight years later, he had miraculously recovered, and, under his aegis, *Newsweek* had been catching up to *Time*.

"On the one hand, Maynard wants to beat *Time* on the October Surprise project," Clifton told me. "On the other, he cannot afford another Hitler's diary."

AFTER BEN-MENASHE ARRIVED AT LAX, WE CAUGHT THE next flight to Houston. Once we arrived, Tony Clifton joined us, and we sat down together in a room at the Westin Oaks hotel, near the posh River Oaks section of Houston.

At the time, President Bush had just nominated Clarence Thomas to the Supreme Court, and Anita Hill, an attorney who had worked under him when he was in the US Department of Education, had accused him of sexual harassment. As Clifton and I sat down with Ben-Menashe, the entire nation was glued to Anita Hill's testimony before the Senate.

Tony and I, however, were participants in another spectacle that was far less public. For four consecutive days in a suite at the Westin, Ben-Menashe regaled us with astonishing tales of intrigue in sessions lasting eight, ten, twelve hours at a shot. As he unspooled his story, he explained how he used his language skills and Iranian connections to carve out a unique place for himself in the external relations department of Israeli Military Intelligence. Chief among them, he said, was his friendship with Ahmed Kashani, the son of Ayatollah Abol-Qassem Kashani, a powerful Shi'ite cleric in prerevolutionary Iran. Ahmed had become a friend of Ben-Menashe's at Tehran University in the late 1970s.

To an Israeli intelligence operative in Iran during these prerevolutionary times, Kashani was an interesting contact. He came from a famous Iranian family, and the Kashani name still retained influence. According to Ben-Menashe, he often used the first name Mehdi to blur his identity. Ari described Ahmed to me as "good-looking," and a bit of "a womanizer," and said he had loads of funny stories about long weekends they had spent in Marbella together.

It was through Kashani that Ben-Menashe first became aware of the powerful Shi'ite movement that was coming together to overthrow the Shah, information he dutifully shared with Israeli intelligence.[9] As a result, Israeli intelligence knew by early 1978 that the Shah's days were numbered, at a time when US intelligence was in the dark. Indeed, just a few weeks earlier President Carter had dubbed Iran "an island of stability in one of the more troubled areas of the world."[10]

According to Ari, after the Revolution, Kashani became a key Iranian operative who was close to Khomeini. In January 1980, just weeks after the embassy takeover, Kashani reached out to Ben-Menashe saying Iran urgently needed weapons and spare parts for their military. Israel was the obvious place to go, as both countries had been armed by the United States and had similar military hardware.[11]

Highly verbal and engaging, Ben-Menashe was at his most persuasive in providing a rare and revealing prism—distorted and self-serving though it was—into how Israel's secret relationship with Iran was serving its strategic needs now that the Shah had gone, and how Iran's anti-Arab sentiment at the time also governed its political calculus.

"To defend Iran against Saddam Hussein," Ari said,[12] "Iran will actually deal with Satan. Politically, it's acceptable for Iran to buy arms from Israel. Iran never saw Israel as such a great evil. Americans don't have a clue. Remember, the Iranians are so anti-Arab that they were always willing to deal with Israel because of its anti-Arab stance."

And now that the Shah was gone, Israel was vulnerable to Iraq. "The initial motive was to arm the Iranians against the Iraqis," Ben-Menashe told me. "It didn't start out as a malicious thing. They only decided to delay the release of the hostages later."

Ben-Menashe made it clear that he had not personally attended the infamous Madrid meetings with Bill Casey and Karroubi, but that he had gotten all his information from Kashani. As a result of Kashani's trips to Israel, Ben-Menashe said, Israel sent approximately three hundred F-4 Phantom jet tires to Iran in March or April 1980,[13] in violation of the Carter administration's embargo. When Carter found out that Israel had violated the Iranian arms embargo, he demanded that Prime Minister Begin observe it rigorously, and Begin reluctantly ordered the IDF to stop selling anything to Iran—even shoelaces.[14]

But the Israeli prime minister wasn't happy. Prior to this, no arms had gone from Israel to Iran since the Shah's exile. This was a small transaction, but it broke the logjam.

For all this to happen, there had to be back-channel communications between Iranian intelligence and Israel, and with Casey and his associates as well. If Ben-Menashe was telling the truth—a big if—this was how one back channel grew out of the friendship between him and Kashani. My plan was to corroborate or refute what Ben-Menashe was saying, and, if it checked out, to keep fleshing out the network—on both sides of the Atlantic—that could have produced these kinds of arms deals.

I would also need to tie the arms sales to Casey and the Reagan-Bush campaign. If Ben-Menashe turned over the documents scattered about the room, presumably we would be able to check it out. While he might have been lying about certain things, it was clear Ben-Menashe had real ties to the arms trade. After all, that was why he had been arrested in an undercover operation by US Customs.[15]

Interestingly, Ben-Menashe also fleshed out *Newsweek*'s Ted Stanger's reporting about Israel's preference for Reagan over Carter. Still smarting from its humiliation at having been forced to give back the Sinai peninsula, Ben-Menashe said, Israel was only too happy to do what it could to make sure Carter was not reelected. Menachem Begin made that pointedly clear to Ben-Menashe.[16] "He would have done anything to get rid of Carter," said Ben-Menashe. "That's why there were orders in Israeli intelligence for us to cooperate with the Republicans."

As Ben-Menashe explained, Israel's top officials viewed President Jimmy Carter with such dismissive contempt that they began dealing with American intelligence operatives who were loyal to the Republicans. And so began the chain of events leading to the October Surprise and a multi-billion-dollar arms pipeline.

AT THE END OF OUR MARATHON SESSION WITH BEN-MENASHE, even Clifton, a skeptic, said he was impressed by the performance. When it was over, Tony flew back to New York alone, while I shared a later plane with Ben-Menashe. There were plenty of direct flights available from William P. Hobby Airport in Houston to New York, but, at the last minute, Ben-Menashe switched to one that had a stopover in Chicago. When I asked why, he looked at me like an impatient Sherlock Holmes talking to a dull-witted Watson. "They can't check every flight," he whispered. The message was clear: this was standard tradecraft for shaking someone off your tail. I hadn't seen any spooks hiding behind the potted palms, and I winced a bit at his theatrics.

In general, when interviewing a subject, I normally played the mild-mannered reporter, gently prodding the source in the direction I wanted to explore. I was rarely adversarial, even when I knew I was being lied to. But Ari's extravagant chronicles of espionage, arms deals, and covert ops, the epic dimensions of his tales, their historic significance, his grandiosity, his narcissism, and the slow and deliberate way he gradually teased out the story, as if dropping breadcrumbs on the path to the Holy Grail—were such that I had to speak out.

"Ferrchrissake, Ari," I finally said. "Who the fuck are you? What are you doing? What's your agenda? What are you trying to do? Why are you leaking it out bit by bit?"

Ari was silent for a moment and smiled. "We have a saying in Hebrew," he said. "'When you pull the Devil's dick, you pull it very, very slowly.'"

My first thought was that the Devil in question was Israeli intelligence. Ari had betrayed them and become a renegade, so they were after him. They had sicced US Customs on him in 1989 when he was arrested for arms dealing, and now, as he traveled the globe spilling secrets, they were doing their best to discredit him.

But that was the problem with Ari Ben-Menashe: even his metaphors went in multiple directions.

When we got to New York, Ari checked into the Algonquin Hotel. I knew its restaurant/bar as the home of the Algonquin Round Table, where the likes of Dorothy Parker would trade barbs and witticisms with playwrights, screenwriters, actors, and humorists such as George S. Kaufman, Alexander Woollcott, Franklin P. Adams, and the like. To Ben-Menashe, however, it was just another old haunt from his gunrunning days. He checked in, unpacked, and we took the papers to a nearby photocopy center. There were hundreds, perhaps thousands of pages: invoices, requests for prices, and telexes for TOW missiles, automatic weapons, and C-130 cargo planes; the names of hundreds of people who allegedly helped funnel arms to Iran; and the numbers of bank accounts in Zurich, Geneva, and Panama that handled money for the arms deals and bribing Iranian officials. There were names of contacts in Iran's Ministry of Defense and companies that leased airplanes for cargo transport, intermediaries who were involved in money laundering, and Israeli "proprietaries" that were allegedly involved in various aspects of the arms trade.

On October 18, I filed a memo in the *Newsweek* computer's October Surprise queue: "I have photocopied all the documents

Ben-Menashe brought with him from Australia. . . . BM claims the hundreds of names and phone numbers in them represent the Israeli network in the U.S."

I added that the key problem with Ben-Menashe had always been that there was no way to corroborate what he said, but at last we could review the paper trail that could either confirm or refute key elements of his story.

Over the next few days, I set out to make sense of Ben-Menashe's documents and compiled a list of alleged spies and arms dealers. To my surprise, no one at *Newsweek* responded to my memo about the documents. Not a peep.

The October Surprise team had been working together for nearly a month and it would be an understatement to say that it had not gelled. We'd had only one actual meeting and very limited phone contact. When I raised questions about the lack of progress, one old hand explained, "*Newsweek*'s never been good at investigative reporting, and there's no reason to think that's changed now."

Like *Time*, *Newsweek* was a practitioner of the team game—group journalism, corporate journalism. Both magazines had far-flung correspondents all over the world who moved on from one topic to another each week. They went wide, not deep, and if you wanted to make headway on this kind of story, you had to keep coming back to it again and again. Come closing time, files poured into New York from *Newsweek*'s foreign correspondents all over the world—in this case, London, Paris, Lisbon, Jerusalem, and more. But once their files arrived at 444 Madison, they were promptly chewed up and run through the corporate meat grinder.

I had wrongly presumed that if we managed to dig up one scoop after another on a breaking story, the magazine would eagerly snatch it up. But, as I learned, when reporters managed to uncover explosive material, they had no control over what got in the magazine and what ended up on the cutting-room floor. Instead, each reporter was reduced to being a disposable and easily replaceable component of the group project. Local bureaus—in New York, Washington, Paris,

Hong Kong, or wherever—never saw anything through from start to finish. The process was broken up into units of journalistic production that were put together as if on an assembly line. Correspondents reported verifiable facts that might or might not make it into the final product. Fact-checkers verified what they reported. The writer wrote it up. Copy editors copyedited. And the editor finalized everything.

"Ultimately the editors in New York decided what went in the magazine," said Jonathan Alter, a *Newsweek* columnist at the time.[17] "You could argue about it, but you had to know when to stop. After all, there's always next week."

So the job of the reporter—*my* job—was not so much to uncover startling revelations as it was to put together a huge file for "New York," most of which—perhaps *all* of which—might go unused. As it turned out, that was precisely what happened.

LATE IN THE AFTERNOON OF FRIDAY, OCTOBER 25, A FEW DAYS after I returned with Ben-Menashe's documents, Assistant Managing Editor Evan Thomas called me into the office of Alexis Gelber, then editor of the Nation section at *Newsweek*. Thomas was based in Washington and was a key player in shaping *Newsweek*'s political coverage. I didn't know him well, but we had both started out in journalism in college, on the *Harvard Crimson*, as had Alexis Gelber.

I took a seat. The mood was glum, but I didn't know why. Between Alexis, Evan, and a few other *Crimson* alumni, this, in effect, was my old boys' club. But somehow, I had a very bad feeling.

Alexis went first. "We are going to cast doubt on Ben-Menashe as a source," she said.

Then Evan explained. Seymour Hersh's new book, *The Samson Option*, had just been published in England, and in London, the Fleet Street tabloids were having a field day. *The Samson Option* exposed British media mogul Robert Maxwell as an Israeli agent who used his

Mirror Group Newspapers to disseminate Israeli propaganda and to facilitate the illegal and clandestine sale of Israeli arms to Iran. For the last few months, the impending publication of *The Samson Option* had been of special interest to me; Hersh's key source for his explosive charges against Maxwell was none other than Ben-Menashe, who claimed to have worked with Maxwell on the arms deals.

Maxwell was the billionaire newspaper baron whose daughter, Ghislaine Maxwell, later won notoriety as the companion and sex-trafficking partner of sex criminal Jeffrey Epstein. In the 1970s and 1980s, he had won fame himself as a self-invented Citizen Kane of sorts, albeit an Anglicized one, a precursor to and rival of Rupert Murdoch who owned newspaper, broadcast, and publishing properties in New York, London, Israel, and all over Europe. Known as the corpulent "bouncing Czech," Maxwell was a man whose Falstaffian bonhomie dwarfed his enormous crimes and daring exploits. But was it possible, as Hersh had reported, that he was also an Israeli intelligence asset? The British media was in an uproar.

"Maxwell Man in Arms Storm," blared the *Daily Mail*, publishing Ben-Menashe's charges that Nicholas Davies, foreign editor at the *Daily Mirror* in London, had been an Israeli operative who had partnered with Ben-Menashe in selling arms to Iran for Israel. The allegations were outrageous, but Ben-Menashe had documents—among them, telexes with Davies's name on it to the defense minister of Iran confirming an order for four thousand TOW missiles, orders for arms from Yugoslavia, and more. Furthermore, Davies's ex-wife, actress Janet Fielding of the *Doctor Who* series, backed up Ben-Menashe's allegations. Members of Parliament were calling for an investigation.

With this book's publication, Ben-Menashe's notoriety spread all over the world, and a wave of suits and countersuits regarding Hersh and Maxwell's properties ensued. Ultimately, Hersh was vindicated when the Mirror Group agreed to pay him "substantial damages" and apologized for its "attempts to impugn" his integrity, but that resolution would be a long time coming.[19] In the immediate aftermath, because Ben-Menashe was a key source for Hersh's book, *Newsweek* had decided to run an article on Ben-Menashe himself. The *Newsweek* editors found Hersh's accusations against Maxwell so breathtakingly wacky that they were shaking their heads in laughter. The story on him was closing in less than twenty-four hours, Gelber told me, and would be delivered to subscribers on Monday.

I was baffled. Doubt Ben-Menashe? Of course. Ari was a reporter's ultimate nightmare: a valuable source of great secrets who was also completely unreliable. He'd failed a lie detector test. You'd be nuts to *trust* him. But all of that was old news.

What had they come up with that I didn't know about?

"Casey couldn't have been in Madrid," said Thomas. "We've been able to check on Casey's presence every two hours." He paused. "Ben-Menashe is really fucked up."

I recalled that a couple of weeks earlier Clifton had told me that *Newsweek*'s London bureau had proven Casey wasn't at the Madrid meetings. I'd asked John Barry about it, but he wouldn't go into details. Now Thomas was answering that mystery. The most damning piece of evidence, he said, was that Ben-Menashe had apparently lied about a critical piece of the October Surprise puzzle—the attendance of Bill Casey at the secret meetings in Madrid in July 1980.

If there was one thing we all agreed on, it was that Casey's presence in Madrid was the most important piece of the October Surprise conspiracy. Proving or disproving his attendance at the meetings in Madrid was at the heart of whether the October Surprise happened. Evan was saying Ben-Menashe lied about Casey's presence in Madrid, something that was evidently bolstered by what the London bureau had found, and taken together, it meant Ben-Menashe was completely full of shit.

There was a crucial flaw in *Newsweek*'s rationale, though: Ben-Menashe wasn't the primary source that put Casey in Madrid. Jamshid Hashemi was the main source on those meetings; Jamshid was the only one who had been in Madrid and actually gave a first-hand account, which he had done with Martin Kilian at *Der Spiegel*, Gary Sick, ABC's *Nightline*, and Bob Parry for PBS's *Frontline*. In this case, Ben-Menashe had actually made it clear, for once, that he was *not* present in Madrid and had learned about Casey's attendance secondhand. There were plenty of reasons to challenge Ben-Menashe, but Casey's presence in Madrid wasn't one of them.

Still, Evan was telling me Casey had not been in Madrid, and if he was right, I had wasted an enormous amount of time on this project. What evidence did *Newsweek* have to support this conclusion? According to Thomas, the evidence came from *Newsweek* London correspondent Dan Pedersen. The information should have been filed in the shared October Surprise queue on my computer. But when I checked, Pedersen's files were not there. Evan Thomas went to my computer to look for himself. Still, no luck.

Finally, Evan left to find out what happened and returned with a hard copy of the memos filed by Pedersen and other *Newsweek* correspondents. According to Pedersen's memos, *Newsweek*'s conclusion that Casey was not in Madrid was based entirely on one interview with one person: Jonathan Chadwick, secretary of the Imperial War Museum in London. Chadwick had held the position in late July 1980 when William Casey had attended a reunion for World War II veterans of the OSS held at the Museum.

At the time of the 1980 reunion, Casey was one of the most prominent OSS alumni, having served as chairman of the Securities and Exchange Commission and head of the Export-Import Bank, and held other highly visible positions. As campaign manager for the Reagan-Bush operation in the midst of a heated presidential race, his presence surely would have been noted—as would his absence. No one disputed that Casey attended the conference. The real question was whether he was there for all five days without leaving. If so, he could not have been in Madrid. If so, there was no October Surprise.

But, what if Casey had used the conference as a cover, and slipped away to attend a couple of meetings in Madrid—just about a ninety-minute flight from London? That was the question.

Now *Newsweek*'s London correspondent was saying that he had uncovered attendance records of the reunion from Jonathan Chadwick proving definitively that Casey had been there for all five days. In sharing this information with me, *Newsweek*'s editors were acting as if they had scored some great coup because they had obtained these attendance records, as if *Newsweek* were the only entity in pursuit of this question: Was Casey in Madrid?

In fact, these attendance charts had been around for months. Gary Sick, *Nightline*, and *Frontline* had all seen them months earlier. Bob Parry had them. I had obtained copies myself. All of us—even the congressional task force that was just getting underway—zeroed in on them because, more than any other single piece of evidence we had back then, they could have been the smoking gun. If Casey was in Madrid that week, he was there to make a deal with Iran. If he had a solid airtight alibi in London, then . . . no smoking gun.

But by this point all of us—*Nightline*, *Frontline*, Gary Sick, and later the congressional investigators as well—had all reviewed these attendance charts and come to the exact *opposite* conclusion about Casey's attendance. To everyone except *Newsweek*, the records had showed there *was* a two-day window in which Casey could have gone to Madrid. Gary Sick, Ted Koppel and his producers at *Nightline*, Bob Parry and the team at *Frontline*, Martin Kilian at *Der Spiegel*, Christopher Hitchens at *The Nation*, and several other reporters had all come to the same conclusion—independently. And so had I.

It didn't seem possible that all of us were wrong and *Newsweek* was right. But if I was going to confront the higher-ups at *Newsweek*, there wasn't the slightest room for error. I went back to my office and worked late into the night, talking to Gary Sick. At his suggestion, I also talked to Martin Kilian at *Der Spiegel* and an ABC producer who had examined the same documents, making sure I had all my ducks in a row. Given the time difference, it was too late to call Jonathan Chadwick in London to see if I could get it straight from the horse's mouth. I'd save that for the next day.

On Saturday, October 26, I got up as if it were a weekday, and went straight to the office. Back then, if you worked at one of the big newsweeklies, Saturdays were the most pressure-packed days of all. In order to be on the newsstands or in subscribers' mailboxes on Monday, we had to have all of our stories finalized on Saturday. Workdays started in the late morning and often ended well after midnight when the magazine was put to bed.

I arrived just before 11:00 a.m. Tony Clifton came in at the same time, in a cheerful mood. "Well, I think this will just about drive a stake through Ben-Menashe's heart," he said.

Earlier, Clifton's memos had characterized Ben-Menashe as a knowledgeable but flawed source. For reasons I didn't understand, however, that notion, which had been prevalent among *Newsweek* correspondents in Jerusalem, Paris, and elsewhere, was no longer viable among the *Newsweek* editors in New York. As Tony put it in a memo, the intention of the article was to "identify Ben-Menashe and his importance as the only identifiable source for so much print, and then proceed to expose him as at best deeply unreliable, and at worst a pathological liar."

For weeks, a polite frisson had separated me from the rest of the staff. But now there was a sense I had been discredited, that I was a Ben-Menashe partisan. For all the warnings I'd filed about Ben-Menashe's reliability, John Barry told the others I was "practically Ben-Menashe's press agent," that I was a "true believer."

Rather than reply to Clifton, I went straight to my office, shut the door, and got on the phone to London where I reached Jonathan

Chadwick. I pressed him on his methodology and the exact meaning of his notetaking. I wanted to be prepared for the upcoming editorial meeting, when the October Surprise team would go over the story that was about to close.

At noon, we gathered in a small conference room on the fourteenth floor—John Barry, Tony Clifton, Alexis Gelber, writer Tom Morgenthau, researchers Gregory Cerio and Nancy Stadtman, and me. For the first five or six weeks of the investigation, I had exchanged very few words with John Barry, which was particularly disturbing given that he was in charge of pulling the whole project together. A few weeks earlier, I had asked Barry if he'd followed up with Scott Thompson, the former aide to Casey who had been such a promising source. "He's just a munchkin," Barry sniffed.

I was struck by his choice of words. Several years before Gary Sick's op-ed piece was published, Barbara Honegger, a former campaign staffer and policy analyst for Ronald Reagan, coauthored an article for *In These Times*, the political weekly, saying that just after October 22, 1980, an unidentified Reagan aide tried to ease fears that President Carter would bring the hostages home before the election. "We don't have to worry about an 'October Surprise,'" he reportedly said. "Dick cut a deal."[20] According to Honegger, "Dick" was a reference to Richard V. Allen, Reagan's top foreign policy adviser and a close associate of Bill Casey.

When Honegger spoke out about the October Surprise in one of the early rumblings about it, the Reagan White House derided her as a "low-level Munchkin" who had an exaggerated sense of her own importance.[21] To hear the echo of that word now, this time from the head of *Newsweek*'s investigation, was not a promising sign.

Then, John Barry, sporting his trademark bowtie, leaned back in his chair, and explained that there were two reasons that the October Surprise could not have taken place. First, he said, if there had been a secret deal between Iran and the Republicans, there would have been a payoff in the form of massive arms shipments, and, he claimed, there was absolutely no evidence that any such shipments had taken place.

This wasn't true, of course. Jerusalem correspondent Ted Stanger had sent in files backing up reports of an Israeli-Iranian arms pipeline as early 1981. So had I. Reports were coming in from correspondents all over the world. We had scores of new leads on the arms shipments.

Even more critical was the magazine's assertion that Casey had not been in Madrid in July 1980. Given Casey's highly visible presence running Reagan's presidential campaign, evidence would later surface that he could be accounted for in Washington as late as Saturday, July 26.[22] In addition, a *New York Times* story dated Wednesday, July 30, 1980, cited a Reagan spokesman as saying Casey was returning from a trip abroad that day.[23] That meant, in effect, that we needed to establish if Casey could have attended the meeting in Madrid for any two consecutive days between Sunday, July 27, and Tuesday, July 29, inclusive.

When Barry explained Casey's alibi, he referred to reports by *Newsweek* correspondent Dan Pedersen in London that said the attendance sheets proved that there was no two-day window during which Casey could have been in Madrid.

So now the attendance charts had become what Alfred Hitchcock called the MacGuffin, the arcane detail that no one cared about, but on which everything depended. I explained to Barry that I'd had the attendance charts for some time and, like other reporters, had concluded that there *was*, in fact, a two-day window during which Casey could have gone to Madrid. If this was his alibi, it didn't hold up, I said.

Barry leaned back in his chair. "We have our own reporters," he said.

Yes, I said. But I had not only obtained the documents, I had also interviewed Chadwick about them as well. In fact, I had just gotten off the phone with him—*that* morning. We'd had a lengthy discussion about his methodology in taking attendance and what his attendance charts revealed.

Chadwick's account was filled with hesitation, uncertainty, and, occasionally, contradictions—not surprising, perhaps, in view of how much time had passed. At times, he seemed to suggest Casey was in London during the critical period in question. At other times, he suggested the contrary. "I'll try to explain," he told me. "I couldn't be certain. . . . I might have forgotten or been distracted. . . . I would have intended if . . ."[24]

As for the charts themselves, they could not possibly have been more ordinary, consisting as they did of a horizontal grid with the names of the attendees listed in descending alphabetical order in the far left column. Immediately to the right of each name were twelve horizontal rectangles that designated three sessions and a lunch for each day of the three-day event.

If invitees were absent, Chadwick said, he put an *X* by their name in the appropriate box. If they were present, he put a check mark.

However, even a casual look at the chart showed that Chadwick's system was slightly more complicated than that. Some of the marks—both check marks and *X*s—were quite dark and were clearly made in ink. Others—again, both check marks and *X*s—were legible but quite faint and were made in pencil.

When I asked Chadwick what that meant, he said pencil marks indicated *expected* attendance, not actual. "It's an English custom," he told me, "as in 'I'll pencil you in for dinner.'"

He added that the pencil marks had *not* been made on the day in question. They were made in advance for planning purposes, so he would know approximately how many people were *likely* to attend the conference. Consequently, they indicated *expected* attendance and were not definitive about whether the person in question actually showed up.

Looking at the far left column, name number three was "William J. Casey." The grid to the right indicated what sessions he was present for on Monday, Tuesday, and Wednesday, July 28 through July 30. Of course, Casey was back in Washington by July 30, so only July 28 and 29 were relevant.

To make sure I was interpreting the chart correctly, I asked Chadwick to look at it, and take me through it day by day. On the grid marking day one of the conference, Monday, July 28, there were four ink check marks next to Casey's name, suggesting he had attended all three sessions and the lunch meeting that day. But there was also an anomaly in the form of a cursive handwritten notation, written in ink for the afternoon session that read, "came at 4 pm."

Chadwick said the handwriting was his. So what did that mean? "I suspect on seeing Casey arrive, I put checks all the way through the day," Chadwick told me. And, ink check marks notwithstanding, he told me he did not recall seeing Casey *before* then.

The bottom line: He could *not* attest to Casey's presence before 4:00 p.m. And with Madrid just around an hour and a half away, there was plenty of time for Casey to have attended a morning or lunch meeting with the Iranians that day and return to the conference in London by the afternoon.

On Tuesday, July 29, there were four faint check marks lightly penciled in next to Casey's name. That meant Casey was *expected* to attend. But had he?

Chadwick later gave contradictory accounts of his record keeping and wrote a letter to the editor of the *New York Times* insisting that attendance charts were "unequivocal and not ambiguous" evidence that Casey was in London and could not have been in Madrid.[25]

But he gave a very different story to me. Noting that he usually inked over pencil marks when they deviated from expected behavior, but that he sometimes varied his practice, Chadwick described his own record keeping as "inconsistent."

"I can't guarantee [what it means]," he added. "I might have forgotten or been distracted. When I did not ink over a [penciled] check mark, that leaves open the possibility that I overlooked someone's absence. That is a perfectly acceptable question to raise."[26]

Moreover, a year later, after congressional investigators examined the same issue, the House task force investigating the October Surprise came to the same conclusion that I had: "Credible sworn testimony supports the proposition that Casey was absent from the morning sessions on July 28 and refutes the check marks on Chadwick's chart to the contrary. Robert Dallek, an American professor who presented a paper on China between 11:30 a.m. and 1:00 p.m., gave credible testimony that Casey was not in attendance during Dallek's presentation. Dallek recalled that he was eager to 'strut my stuff' in front of Casey, that he looked around the conference room for Casey and Casey never appeared during Dallek's presentation."[27]

In other words, Casey probably didn't get there until 4:00 p.m., in which case he could easily have spent the morning meeting in Madrid with the Iranians, and then hopped on a ninety-minute flight to London for the afternoon session.

On Tuesday, July 29, Casey had given a talk to his assembled OSS veterans at 9:30 a.m. It lasted less than an hour. As for the rest of the day, however, the chart shows only light pencil marks for the entire day. Nothing was inked in that day.

When I asked Chadwick exactly what that meant, his response did nothing to bolster Casey's alibi. "He [Casey] could have left after the morning session," he told me.[28]

And that would have left plenty of time to get back to Madrid.

I told all of this to Barry, but he was unmoved. "Don't worry," he said. "It's well in hand."

I didn't know what to say. Until the October Surprise investigations started up, no one on the planet cared whether there were pencil or ink marks next to Casey's name on the attendance chart for the last week of July 1980. No one cared whether the marks were checks or *X*s. But now the stakes had become enormous. They might tell us whether the 1980 presidential election was sabotaged by an extraordinary act of treachery. They might determine the outcome of the next presidential election.

Frustrated as I was, I wasn't the only *Newsweek* journalist whose reporting was being discarded by Barry's decision to burn Ben-Menashe. When I asked Evan why I had not had access to the files of my other colleague on the investigation, he had looked into it and suddenly dozens of files appeared in my computer queue. After I went back to my office, I saw for the first time that Ted Stanger, *Newsweek*'s Jerusalem correspondent, had eviscerated Israel's cover story for Ben-Menashe. He pointed out in a memo that the military sources he interviewed would likely "be party to any attempt to minimize Ben-Menashe's role and responsibilities or to blacken his character."

It went without saying that Israeli officials, Israeli lobbyists, and Bush administration officials were on the warpath against Ben-Menashe, Stanger said. He was a *huge* security breach. In his internal memos at *Newsweek*, Stanger, who had never even met Ben-Menashe, had gone as far as anyone I read in deciphering the enigmatic Israeli. In one memo, he said that he could "not discount Ben-Menashe for one main reason: he was a member of the "Club." The Club, in Israel, includes anybody who has been cleared for security work, even minor. "It is hard to explain to outsiders," Stanger noted, "but members of the Club take in information with every breath. In addition, Ben-Menashe's job (which the Israeli Defense Forces admits to on the record) gave him access to considerable documents, memos, and more. I have spoken to two sources within the IDF today, who knew Ben-Menashe. Neither can explain how he managed to travel so extensively while working as a minor clerk translator in the Kiria in Tel Aviv."[29]

Stanger had investigated how Israel exported weapons through its arms procurement agency, known as SIBAT, "using field agents who know that they will be disavowed if caught." That made sense. In that regard, Ari's notoriety, his lies, his games, his untrustworthiness—in short, everything there was to hate about him—was a positive attribute from Israel's point of view. If he went rogue—and he had—think how easy it would be to discredit him. Furthermore, Stanger said, it was an "open secret" that the Israelis delivered "arms to Iran during the Iran-Iraq war, and by now the Israelis pretty much admit it." He added arms transfers to Iran were easily "ten to twenty times the figures of sales that had been disclosed."

In other words, there *was* an Israeli arms pipeline to Iran, and, Stanger concluded, Ben-Menashe was a participant in it: "My explanation is this: BM was probably one of the legions of theoretically free agents Israel sends into the field either to work for the Mossad or to work for SIBAT, and SIBAT offshoots, hawking everything from bazookas to jets. I also suspect that BM might be stretching what he knows of the truth a bit, but that's something we can work out."[30]

Stanger had pretty much nailed it. I'd spent six months cultivating Ben-Menashe as a source. I had roughly sixty of hours of taped interviews with him. Thousands of pages of transcripts. In addition, Ben-Menashe had given me thousands of pages of documents that I had just started checking out. They had the phone numbers of and information about small-time arms dealers, aircraft brokerages, pilots for hire, British and Israeli operatives, arms procurement officials from Iran to Latin America to Sri Lanka, proposals to sell C-130 cargo planes, and more. Dozens of leads, but, clearly, *Newsweek* was not going to follow up.

The magazine was going to bed in a matter of hours, so there wasn't much more I could do. My only recourse really was to go to Maynard Parker, the court of last resort. But when I went to Maynard's office and made my case, I got nothing more than a polite brush-off.

On my way back to my office, I went to a fact-checker who had been working on the story to see what he thought. After all, in the end, this was not a matter of opinion. It came down to facts.

"Do I have a case with this stuff?" I asked.

"I think you have a point," he said. "But my bosses have determined that they are not going to make it."

On Monday, October 28, the new issue of *Newsweek* appeared on the stands with a two-and-one-third-page story, "One Man, Many Tales," that discredited Ari Ben-Menashe, a man almost no one in America had heard of. Absolutely nothing was cited that corroborated any part of Ben-Menashe's stories. To read it, you would think Ben-Menashe had never been an Israeli intelligence official at all.

Instead, he was presented as "a former translator for the Israeli government who now lives in Australia" and had become "a leading evangelist for the cult of the October Surprise" by claiming to have been an Israeli agent.[31]

The magazine added: "'He was apparently a minor clerk in some military branch,' said David Kimche, a Mossad veteran and former director-general of Israel's Foreign Ministry, who says Ben-Menashe's claims are 'ridiculous.'"

You wouldn't know it by reading the *Newsweek* piece, but, far from being a neutral observer, Kimche was the deputy director of Mossad. In December 1980, he had three secret meetings with Robert "Bud" McFarlane, then the incoming State Department counsel, to arrange arms sales to Iran. In other words, *Newsweek* had conveniently omitted the fact that he was one of the key facilitators of the arms deals to Iran, that he was the fox in the proverbial henhouse. Instead, the magazine cited him as a knowledgeable, unbiased, and authoritative source denying that they ever took place.

Similarly, the magazine omitted any evidence that was dispositive to its central thesis. That meant Ben-Menashe's passport, official documents tying him to Israeli Military Intelligence, or, for that matter, anything reported by me, Ted Stanger, or Chris Dickey didn't prove that there had been contacts between the Republican campaign and Iran, arms shipments to Iran, or that the October Surprise happened.

Later, after the story hit the newsstands, I checked my voicemail to find a message from Seymour Hersh, who had returned to the *New York Times* and was looking into issues related to the October

Surprise. By this time, those of us who were on the story were being pummeled so much that we sometimes compared war stories. Hersh had just read *Newsweek*'s coverage on Ben-Menashe.

"Unger," the voicemail said. "Sy Hersh. I was agog at this story I just read. I presume you were agog. It was a motherfucker."

When I called back the next day, Sy offered me some friendly advice. "Drop it," he said. "Drop the story, Unger. Otherwise, they will crush you."

Then he repeated himself. "Believe me," he said, "they'll crush you."

Chapter Six
The Hand That Feeds You

Purely as a reader, my favorite rubric in *Newsweek* in those days was the Conventional Wisdom Watch, a short, edgy front-of-the-book chart, started by Jonathan Alter and Mickey Kaus, that artfully skewered the herd mentality of the Washington press corps. The chart used arrows going up and down to show the rising and falling fortunes of the personalities and issues of the day. The Conventional Wisdom Watch seemed to be saying that yes, we all know what happened last week, but its meaning and its political ramifications are all the products of transactional relationships between reporters and the politicians they are covering.

Implicit in the column was the notion that what journalists really owe readers is the truth, but what inevitably happens instead is that politicians feed the reporters an endless string of self-serving stories, and the reporters spread them around and keep coming back for more. And, of course, given that all parties concerned have their own conflicting agendas, multiple warring narratives emerge. The beauty of the Conventional Wisdom Watch was its shorthand way of explaining that we were seeing the world through the prism of these ever-changing relationships, and we should take everything with a grain of salt because there's a different spin every week. It implied that the news was performative, staged, and here's what we should look for as consumers of the latest spectacle.

But at *Newsweek*, I had not expected that a publication with such a finely hewn sense of irony would be simultaneously turning cartwheels to forge the conventional wisdom that the October Surprise was nothing more than a wild conspiracy theory. Indeed, if *Newsweek* had put the October Surprise on its Conventional Wisdom Watch back then, it should have been accompanied by a big thick arrow plunging directly downward to the bottom of the page.

The week after the Ben-Menashe article ran, the new issue of *Newsweek* hit the stands with the magazine's investigation of the October Surprise on the cover. Titled "The October Surprise: Making of a Myth," it concluded that "the key claims of the purported eyewitnesses do not hold up. What the evidence does show is the murky history of a conspiracy theory run wild."[1] By mutual agreement, the story did not have my byline on it.

What followed was a five-thousand-word piece that dismissed the scandal as "a mother lode for conspiracy junkies of all political persuasions." The most significant detail supporting *Newsweek*'s argument were Jonathan Chadwick's attendance records. *Newsweek*'s interpretation of those records had a certain finality to it: "There is, in short, no possibility that Casey could have held meetings with anyone on two successive days in Madrid," the magazine said.

That conclusion was a bald-faced lie, and the tell was right there in the form of a photo of the attendance sheet, published smack-dab in the middle of page twenty-two. One didn't need X-ray vision to differentiate between the faint, barely visible pencil marks and the much darker ink marks. But *Newsweek* declined even to note the distinction, much less explain its meaning, even though it was easily discernible to the naked eye. To do so would have destroyed the entire premise behind the piece.

Finally, as if this story and the Ben-Menashe hit job weren't enough, for its November 18 issue, *Newsweek* went at it again. That week, Gary Sick's new book, *October Surprise*, was published, and an article by John Barry concluded that it contained "no credible evidence" that such a conspiracy had taken place.[2]

Never before had I heard of a major news outlet devoting so much attention to saying something did *not* happen. Nor was *Newsweek* alone.

Critics of the October Surprise continued to have a field day. The *Wall Street Journal* attributed "the hoax," as they referred to it, to gullible reporters who had been taken in by dubious arms dealers, freelance operatives, fringe cults, and the like. The conservative *Washington Times* dismissed it as "the nutty story" about the Republican conspiracy to delay release of the embassy hostages.[3] Others blamed it on reporters who had unwittingly engaged in an international game of "telephone" gone wrong.

One of the most notable attacks came from *The New Republic*, where, in the November 18 issue, "The Conspiracy That Wasn't," by Steven Emerson and Jesse Furman, it called the October Surprise allegations "a total fabrication," and concluded that "William Casey and George Bush could not have been present at the meetings alleged by the sources."[4] Like *Newsweek*, *The New Republic* hauled out the old, unreliable sources—Richard Brenneke, Barbara Honegger, and the like—and, again like *Newsweek*, relied on a flawed interpretation of Chadwick's attendance sheets to exculpate Bill Casey. Not surprisingly, Emerson repeatedly concluded that anyone seriously investigating the October Surprise—Gary Sick, Bob Parry, or me, for example—was a gullible dupe.

That *The New Republic* was seemingly acting in concert with *Newsweek* only compounded the impact. Its modest circulation notwithstanding, *The New Republic* was highly influential in Washington policy circles and had become known as "the inflight magazine of Air Force One."[5] *Vanity Fair* called it "the smartest, most impudent . . . most entertaining and intellectually agile magazine in the country."[6]

Consequently, the phrase "Even the liberal *New Republic* says" became a new tool for discrediting the story.[7] The magazine's vaunted liberal past gave added credibility to Emerson's reporting because of the presumption that no "liberal" publication would criticize anything that served the interests of Democrats unless the evidence was overwhelming. Its articles had a ripple effect within the Beltway and far beyond.[8] Not everyone realized, however, that *New Republic* owner Marty Peretz had added a cadre of activist neoconservatives, including columnist Charles Krauthammer, Iran firebrand Michael Ledeen, and Emerson himself.

One of the more strident voices was Ledeen, who later won notoriety for what he called the Ledeen Doctrine: "Every ten years or so, the United States needs to pick up some small crappy little country and throw it against the wall, just to show the world we mean business."[9] In the mideighties, articles in the *Wall Street Journal*, *The Nation*, and elsewhere had linked Ledeen to two major international disinformation operations. One of them targeted Billy Carter, President Jimmy Carter's hard-drinking younger brother, for having ties with Libyan dictator Muammar Qaddafi in what became known as the Billygate scandal. The second one, known as the Bulgarian Connection, falsely tied the attempted 1981 assassination of Pope John Paul II to Russia's KGB. In the *Journal*, investigative reporter Jonathan Kwitny wrote that Ledeen had been paid handsomely to write stories in *The New Republic* disseminating false information that would aid right-wing forces.[10]

It was not until many years later that I learned that Ledeen also happened to be a close associate of Bill Casey's and had attended meetings of the Reagan campaign's October Surprise Group.

Meanwhile, Emerson began to fashion October Surprise–bashing into an ongoing cottage industry. He threatened to sue Parry.[11] He urged Congress to confiscate the earnings from Sick's book *October Surprise* to help defray the cost of the task force investigation.[12] He saw fit to attack Parry and me in *The New Republic*, the *Wall Street Journal*, *The American Spectator*, the *Los Angeles Times*, *American Journalism Review* as well as on National Public Radio, ABC News,

CNN, and more. (Emerson declined to return multiple phone calls and emails.)

And why were they doing this? As far as *Newsweek* was concerned, Evan Thomas, the magazine's assistant managing editor, told me he had been impressed by the work of his colleague Mark Hosenball, a national security correspondent and investigative reporter, who had done several stories in the *Washington Post*, *The New Republic*, and elsewhere attacking the credibility of Richard Brenneke, the fallen "super source" behind the October Surprise.[13] Bob Woodward didn't believe in it.[14] Michael Isikoff, then an investigative reporter at the *Washington Post*, dismissed it as a hoax.[15] All of which suggested an echo chamber effect in which they were simply repeating similar views.

As *Newsweek* knew all too well, that's how the conventional wisdom is forged.

It wasn't just that the White House was pushing back with regard to the October Surprise. *That* was expected. But these were supposedly my colleagues and peers. I'd been hired by *Newsweek* based on the strength of my reporting on this story. I had also been an occasional contributor to *The New Republic*. Two of my friends had been its editor in chief. I'd gone to college with them. But now, just as America had finally tuned in to a national psychodrama that promised to outdo Watergate, *The New Republic* had joined the nation's entire investigative apparatus—journalistic, legislative, and otherwise—in abruptly shifting into reverse. The October Surprise began to be *unreported*. Everything that had been revealed was now being covered back up.

As a reporter, I'd had plenty of pushback before, of course—from politicians, businessmen, and the like. As an editor at *New York* magazine in the 1980s, I fondly remembered the day Roy Cohn, the ruthless fixer for Donald Trump and the Italian Mafia, called me trying to kill a story we were reporting about money laundering at Studio 54, the legendary New York disco. In the end, the magazine ignored him, we ran the story, and his clients went to jail. Standing up to a true master of the dark arts of politics was a badge of honor that was worn with pride.

But this wasn't just pushback. The entire story had been killed. In the end, a vitally important chapter in contemporary American history had been discredited at the time in which it was still politically relevant and actionable.

Nothing about the October Surprise lends itself to easy answers, but the roots of this unreporting at *Newsweek* and *The New Republic* and elsewhere came down to "access journalism," as it is known in the trade. Not everyone realizes it, but journalists essentially have two masters. On the one hand, we may get paid by *Newsweek*, CNN, the *New York Times*, or some other mainstream organ that is widely identified as being part of the liberal press. On the other hand, our sources, though not always visible, often play a greater role in determining what we actually write. After all, a steady flow of inside information—the more exclusive the better—from knowledgeable sources, well known or not, is vital to any reporter.

But access isn't free. Powerful public officials, well-placed staffers, and knowledgeable operatives are not going to dispense these goodies to me because they think I'm a terrific guy. The care and feeding of exclusive sources is an art in and of itself. It requires reporters to curry favor, to play the courtier. Occasionally, that means writing a so-called apple polisher to make the source look good. Or it may involve writing a story attacking their rival. And it always means *not* biting the hand that feeds us. All of which can be a steep price to pay if the sources are the very people you are investigating. With figures like Henry Kissinger or Bill Casey, the only reason such highly placed officials would deign to speak to journalists would be to have the reporter do their bidding. And that meant serving as a mouthpiece for their damage control operation, if and when the time came.

Moreover, once a reporter started down that road, there was no turning back. How could you betray a powerful internationally known figure like Kissinger or Casey if he was feeding you one story after another? If you wrote critically about him, you did so at your own peril. Access would end. Ultimately, a journalist had to decide to be either an insider or an outsider.

To me, real investigative reporting meant being the latter. I'd learned that early on from I. F. Stone, the great radical journalist and publisher of *I. F. Stone's Weekly*, and, briefly, a mentor of mine when I started out in the seventies. A heroic figure during the McCarthy era, Izzy, as he was known, has been the subject of three biographies and three documentaries and was legendary for his independence and integrity. In 1999, New York University's Journalism Department ranked *I. F. Stone's Weekly* near the top of its list of the best works of journalism in the United States in the entire twentieth century.[16]

When I lived in Washington in 1974, Izzy would often chastise me if I had not thoroughly devoured five newspapers by 8:00 a.m. Much of his work was unornamented, plain solid reporting based on endless hours poring over public records no one else bothered to read. It was all in the fine print. One night, I told him I was going to a party on Capitol Hill where I expected to meet several well-known senators.

"No, you're not," he barked. "You're not going. Once you start socializing with them, you'll never be tough when you write about them. If you dine with them or play tennis with senators and cabinet secretaries, you'll see them as friends or sources and you'll never write about them critically."

At the time, I was still in my early twenties, and I didn't fully understand what Izzy was getting at. I was going to a goddamn cocktail party. What was wrong with that? But that's how access journalism starts. You have drinks. You have mutual friends. Before you know it, you're invited into their social circle. Soon, you're flying across the ocean seated next to a cabinet secretary. They feed you stories. If it's Henry Kissinger, Casey, or someone of similar stature, a source like that can make a reporter's career. It's money in the bank.

But before long you're addicted to them, and, like it or not, you realize that the relationship between a reporter and a source is transactional. If the Henry Kissingers of the world were feeding you the latest inside dope, they want something in return, and if you want to keep the relationship going, you must dance to their tune.

Not that there was anything necessarily wrong with access per se. It was enormously valuable having unfettered access to knowledgeable officials at the National Security Council, the State Department, the White House, and more. But the transactional nature of such relationships often compromised reporters. You had to carry water for them and write their narrative. Only then would they keep feeding you. And sometimes that meant they were leaking you an exclusive that served their agenda—but wasn't true.

Over the years, I grew to see access journalism as one of the most irredeemable sins in my field. When I first came to *Newsweek*, it didn't occur to me that the magazine would fall prey to such practices. After all, its parent company, the *Washington Post*, had uncovered the biggest political scandal of the century.

But a lot had changed in the nearly two decades since Nixon's Plumbers had broken into the Watergate complex. *Newsweek*'s coverage of the Iran-Contra scandal had been noticeably weak. Celebrity journalism was ascendant. Rather than speak truth to power, many journalists had discovered that it was much more fun and lucrative to join in and hang out with the movie stars, politicians, titans of Wall Street, and other luminaries.

Consequently, I had questions about *Newsweek*'s ties to two key figures in the scandal, Henry Kissinger and Bill Casey. Katharine Graham, the owner of the *Post* and *Newsweek*, had become very friendly with Henry Kissinger and had signed him up to be a *Newsweek* contributor writing two or three times a year on major breaking international stories.

As a protégé of former vice president Nelson Rockefeller, Kissinger served as chairman of the international advisory committee of Rockefeller's Chase Manhattan Bank, which handled billions of dollars of the Shah's account as well as billions more from Iranian oil interests. In the Nixon era, when Kissinger served as secretary of state, he helped make sure that the Shah became the largest purchaser of American weaponry on the planet, assembling the largest navy in the Persian Gulf, the largest air force in Western Asia, and the fifth-largest army in the entire world.[17] And in 1980, he had been part of the so-called Rockefeller Group, which had been ferocious in its lobbying effort to admit the Shah to the United States, the very act that triggered the hostage crisis.

All of which was no secret, nor was the fact that Kissinger was a welcome and familiar figure both in Katharine Graham's social whirl and the pages of *Newsweek*, where he appeared frequently both as a subject and an author. Indeed, the week before I started at *Newsweek*, the magazine featured a major piece by Kissinger pontificating on the "New Russia."[18] In her memoir, *Personal History*, Graham asserted that she didn't believe her friendships with Kissinger, Casey, and other highly placed figures "interfered with our reporting at any of our publications."[19]

After several decades in journalism, however, I was well acquainted with the self-censorship that trickled down from editors and reporters who wanted to curry favor with the owner's friends. Maynard was thrilled to have Kissinger contribute to the magazine—which made any attempt to cover him critically difficult at best.

And, in 1985, when Katharine Graham was considering hiring John Barry as *Newsweek*'s Pentagon correspondent, she insisted he first make a special trip to Langley, Virginia, where he was vetted by the CIA director himself, none other than Bill Casey. At the time, CIA policy was that the Agency would give exclusive briefings to journalists on occasion—but *only* if they were American citizens. That was a problem because Barry was a Brit. However, thanks to Katharine Graham's special relationship with Bill Casey, John Barry became known as the "Casey exception." Barry was thrilled. "How many *Newsweek* hires have been checked out personally by the director of the CIA?" he later asked in a short personal essay about his time at *Newsweek*.[20]

When I talked to Barry about it in 2023, he immediately made it clear that he was still very much a naysayer about the October Surprise. "The sources were bullshit," he told me.[21] "They were fantasists. They were just making stuff up. It was very strange."

Barry insisted that after he was hired at *Newsweek* he rarely talked to Casey or, for that matter, relied on any CIA sources at all. Still, the fact that the man who wrote *Newsweek*'s investigative pieces dismissing the October Surprise owed his job to Bill Casey, the investigation's main target, seemed suspect at best.

It would have been easier to dismiss aspects of what happened to the October Surprise story at *Newsweek* if it didn't feel so eerily similar to how the magazine had treated Iran-Contra and the reporter it hired to cover the scandal—Bob Parry. In the years before the October Surprise came into view, Parry had learned the hard way what it was like to be at *Newsweek*, sitting on a truth that no one wanted to print.

In the mid-1980s, it had been thanks to Parry, then at the Associated Press, that Iran-Contra had initially spilled into the daylight. He'd written the first article tying National Security Council staffer Lt. Col. Oliver North, an adviser on Central American issues, to the secret funding of the Contras.[22] Then, six months later, with Brian Barger, Parry wrote an even more explosive story reporting that the US-backed Contras were engaged in cocaine trafficking to fund their operations.[23]

At the time, the nation was in the midst of a massive crack cocaine epidemic, First Lady Nancy Reagan had launched her "Just say No!" campaign, and President Reagan had accused the leftist government of Nicaragua of "exporting drugs to poison our youth."[24] Parry and Barger, however, showed that Reagan had it backward. In fact, it was the Contras—Reagan's proxies—who were using the profits from the drug trade to fuel their attempt to overthrow the Sandinista government.

Even after these scoops, however, Parry and Barger were pretty much lone voices in the wilderness. Few reporters followed up. At the time, the Democrats had a now-inconceivable eighty-five-seat majority, yet Rep. Lee Hamilton and the Democrats leading the House investigation into the early Iran-Contra reports took the denials of Oliver North over Parry and Barger's reporting.

And with that, Iran-Contra was apparently over before it started. As a result, at AP, Parry and Barger were hung out to dry. Barger was let go. Parry was marginalized. "I was basically told, more or less, 'Well, you know, take your medicine like a man,'" he recalled in a 1993 talk he gave.[25] "'You got it wrong; you know.' We were wrapping up our investigation—it was over." Parry had broken the biggest story of his life, the biggest political scandal of the entire Reagan era, and as a result, his career was in jeopardy.

Then, in October 1986, proof that Parry and Barger were right quite literally fell from the sky. Former marine Eugene Hasenfus was flying weapons to the Contras on behalf of the CIA when his plane was shot down.[26] His capture provided clear evidence of the ties between the Contras, the US government, and the White House. Parry and Barger were vindicated.

Like many news outlets, *Newsweek* was caught flat-footed on Iran-Contra, having largely bought into the Reagan administration's cover stories before Hasenfus was shot down. But in 1987, as the Iran-Contra scandal exploded in newspapers all over the country, *Newsweek* realized the error of its ways and brought Parry on board to investigate Iran-Contra.[27] But Parry was an uncomfortable fit at *Newsweek*. As an old-fashioned, hardscrabble, "just-the-facts, ma'am" shoe leather reporter, he was cut from a different cloth than the *Newsweek* editors who were regulars on the Georgetown party circuit, and who had cultivated cozy relationships with various officials in the Reagan and Bush administrations. At *Newsweek*, access to senior administration officials was coin of the realm.

"That's what *Newsweek* wanted—access to people who could give you the tick-tock of Ronald Reagan striding into the Oval Office and putting his feet on the desk," Parry later said. "There was this disconnect in which they relied on people who were deemed credible by the establishment. The attitude that [John] Barry and other editors had was if you had something from a really golden source, it didn't matter if it was true."

It was commonplace for *Newsweek* reporters to dine with highly placed officials who were key figures in such imbroglios. One such soiree took place at the height of the Iran-Contra hearings at the home of Assistant Managing Editor Evan Thomas and took the form of a privately catered dinner for National Security Adviser Brent Scowcroft and Dick Cheney—who was then the ranking Republican on the House committee investigating Iran-Contra and a relentless GOP attack dog. At the time, the Iran-Contra hearings were a nationally televised spectacle. Dinner table conversation naturally found its way to Adm. John Poindexter, the national security adviser under Reagan, who had testified about transferring weapons to Iran and diverting the funds to the Contras in Nicaragua.[28]

"I probably shouldn't say this," said Scowcroft to the other guests, including Parry. "But if I were advising Admiral Poindexter, I'd advise him to say that he hadn't diverted the funds."

Parry assessed the implications of that statement. "Are you saying you would advise Poindexter to perjure himself before Congress?" he asked.

A hushed silence came over the table. Later, Maynard told Parry that he thought "it was not good for the country to have this [the Iran-Contra scandal] brought out."[29]

Even as the Iran-Contra investigations made their way through the legal system, resulting in thirty-eight indictments and thirteen convictions for the most powerful figures in Reagan's national security apparatus, the powers at *Newsweek* were not about to announce that they had all been taken for a ride.

Finally, in June 1990, *Newsweek* and Parry parted ways in "one of those mutual partings where they don't want you and you work out a deal," as he put it.[30]

ALL OF WHICH RAISED THE QUESTION OF WHY *NEWSWEEK*, IF it was really so keen on investigating the October Surprise, had gotten rid of Parry and brought me in. Now, I realized that I was a readily disposable outsider who was easy to dismiss. When I asked around, I was told Maynard had tired of the steady drip of "small-bore" stories on illegal arms deals by Parry, and given *Newsweek*'s ongoing battle with *Time* magazine for newsstand supremacy, there was some logic to that argument. But when I read Parry's clips, I thought that his meticulously detailed, granular approach was precisely what was needed.

After all, Woodward and Bernstein didn't *begin* their Watergate investigation with stories implicating Nixon. They started out reporting on the burglars who broke into the Watergate complex. Only later did they gradually work their way up the hierarchy of the Nixon campaign until they finally got to the Oval Office. That's the way investigative reporting works.

But much of the reporting on the October Surprise had inverted the tried-and-true from the bottom-up paradigm of investigative reporting. "Follow the money" is a time-honored, though apocryphal, catchphrase* in Watergate lore, often attributed to Deep Throat, as advice he was giving to Woodward. In the case of the October

---

* In the film *All the President's Men*, screenwriter William Goldman attributed the phrase to Deep Throat, but the phrase was never used in Woodward and Bernstein's reporting. In the book, however, Woodward says to Sen. Sam Ervin (D-NC), "The key was the secret campaign cash, and it should all be traced."

Surprise, following the money meant uncovering one illegal arms deal after another to peel back one layer at a time. Instead we had tackled an accusation against President Bush that was so big, so outrageous that, in the opaque and mysterious world of the October Surprise, they had become relatively easy to dismiss.

As the old saying goes, if you are going after the king, you better go for his head. And if you are going after the president, you better have the goods. So far, we didn't have that evidence, but that didn't mean it wasn't out there.

BY THIS TIME, HOWEVER, FINDING NEWS OUTLETS THAT WOULD take on the October Surprise had become all but impossible. A war against the reporters on this story began. At PBS, Bob Parry suddenly went from being the George Polk Award–winning investigative reporter to being a marginalized conspiracy nut. In Hamburg, Rudolf Augstein, the founder and part owner of *Der Spiegel*, got a call from Henry Kissinger's office, complaining about the magazine's October Surprise coverage by Washington correspondent Martin Kilian. My three-month contract at *Newsweek* was over. I was unemployed.

Then, a few weeks after I had left *Newsweek*, an unidentified man was buzzed up to my Upper West Side apartment. When I answered the door, he gave me papers indicating that Robert "Bud" McFarlane, Ronald Reagan's national security adviser, was suing *Esquire*, the Hearst Corporation (its owner), and me for libel for $10 million. Each.

The figure was staggering, but the suit itself wasn't a total shock. A few weeks earlier, shortly after my marathon interview with Ben-Menashe in Houston, I'd gotten a call from my editor at *Esquire*, because the magazine had received a legal letter from McFarlane. McFarlane had been a significant figure in my article because, according to Ben-Menashe, he had played a key role in working with Israel to facilitate arms shipments to Iran. According to a sworn affidavit by Ben-Menashe, McFarlane had a "special relationship" with Israeli intelligence. When I asked Ben-Menashe exactly what he meant by that, he told me that McFarlane had been recruited by Rafi Eitan, a legendary Israeli agent.

In his letter to Terry McDonnell, *Esquire*'s editor, McFarlane decried my article as "the most mean-spirited, irresponsible and loathsome example of false journalism I have ever witnessed against a public official."[31] He further demanded that *Esquire* "cease and desist" from further distribution of the article and reserved the right to take legal action.

My reporting had been professionally fact-checked as usual, by *Esquire*, and vetted by Hearst Corporation libel lawyers who did not think it represented a problem. When I did my reporting, I had left at least three phone messages for McFarlane, who declined to comment. Ben-Menashe had sworn to McFarlane's "special relationship" with Israel under oath in a court document, and, therefore, was privileged.

Moreover, if McFarlane did sue, all his papers would be open to discovery. Finally, McFarlane was a convict. He had pleaded guilty to four misdemeanor counts of withholding information as part of the Iran-Contra cover-up and had attempted suicide by downing more than two dozen Valium tablets in 1987, because, he said, he had a deep sense "of having failed the country."[32] Besides, they had no evidence that anything I had reported was wrong. As a result, *Esquire* said, McFarlane had a very weak case.

Nevertheless, it seemed that we had unearthed something so toxic, so taboo, that the body politic had no choice but to deny its very existence. We had crossed a certain line and had to decide whether to go forward.

Chapter Seven
My White Whale

WHEN I THOUGHT ABOUT IT LATER, THE TIMING OF *NEWSWEEK*'S stories could not have been more bizarre.

Investigations, hearings, and lawsuits relating to the October Surprise were just getting underway. In the independent counsel's office, Lawrence Walsh was finishing the fifth year of his Iran-Contra probe, an investigation into a scandal that increasingly looked as if it were the tail end of the October Surprise. At the same time, the House of Representatives had assembled the House October Surprise Task Force (formally the Task Force of the Committee on Foreign Affairs to Investigate Certain Allegations Concerning the Holding of Americans as Hostages by Iran in 1980), led by Lee Hamilton (D-IN) to investigate the allegations.[1] Similarly, Senate Majority Leader George Mitchell (D-ME) had announced an investigation of the October Surprise to be conducted by the Senate Foreign Relations Subcommittee on Near Eastern and South Asian Affairs.

Also in the Senate, John Kerry (D-MA) and Hank Brown (R-CO) were leading an investigation of the BCCI (Bank of Credit and Commerce International), the massive international bank used by the CIA, Saudi intelligence, Cyrus Hashemi, and others to facilitate illegal arms deals.[2] And, at the time, Robert Gates, who had served as deputy director of Central Intelligence under Casey, was up for Senate confirmation to take the top job at Langley himself.

Few people seemed to realize it, but every single one of those cases led back to Bill Casey. Five years after his death, news about

Casey was more relevant than ever. In any case, to an investigative reporter, all these official inquiries meant that scores of congressional aides, Senate investigators, witnesses from the intelligence community, and other sources would be coming out of the woodwork. Ben-Menashe and his ilk would soon be called to testify—under oath. There would be the predictable partisan sparring, but that in turn meant more and more people were going to talk. And now that the gears of government were engaged, the hearings, the trials, and various proceedings provided narrative structures that would unfold over time, presumably, to reveal the truth about the October Surprise. With George H. W. Bush running for reelection in the upcoming presidential elections, the October Surprise was sure to be center stage. All this added up to a story that was growing and would keep evolving in the weeks and months ahead.

By this time, however, most of the media had already washed its hands of the story. The House task force finally got started in early February 1992,[3] followed, about two weeks later, by the Senate Foreign Relations Committee inquiry,[4] but, by and large, both investigations were conducted behind closed doors with no public testimony or television coverage. While they were taking place, the *New York Times*, the *Washington Post*, and other newspapers referred to the investigations only sporadically, and then largely in articles addressing procedural questions. Republicans and their allies in the press assailed the probes as "a ploy to smear Bush."[5]

Still, I was sure interest would return as the November elections approached. How could the media possibly ignore the fact that the incumbent president running for reelection was being accused of treason?

So, I stayed on it. Which is how, on a beautiful winter day in January 1992, I ended up in Mevaseret Zion, Israel, about six miles from Jerusalem, in the home of Moshe Hevrony, the former aide-de-camp to the director of Military Intelligence, Yehoshua Saguy.

The forty-five-year-old Hevrony had retired from Israeli Military Intelligence a few years earlier and was clad in a black sweat suit. Out his back window was a lovely view of the Azarim Valley. His wife and young children milled about as we talked. I was on assignment for the *Village Voice*, the counterculture weekly, to unravel Israel's role in the October Surprise.[6]

This was my first trip to Israel, and I was a neophyte when it came to Israeli intelligence. Israel, of course, had a justly deserved reputation for its legendary security forces—Mossad, which handles intelligence collection, covert ops, and counterterrorism; Shin Bet (officially, the Israel Security Agency), which covers internal security; and Aman, or Israeli Military Intelligence, which was where Ben-Menashe had worked and which handled intelligence for the vaunted Israel Defense Forces.

Ben-Menashe had reported directly to Hevrony, so I hoped he might clear up some of the mysteries surrounding the October Surprise. Given that I was trying to unearth Israel's most closely guarded greatest secrets, I did not expect it to be easy.

Hevrony had never talked to an American reporter before. At his insistence, an unnamed friend was present. At first, Hevrony asked that I not take notes—until, that is, he had carefully formulated what he wanted to say. For an Israeli intelligence officer—even one who is retired—to contradict his government is not a matter to be taken lightly. After more than two hours of hemming and hawing, Hevrony finally allowed me to put pen to paper.

"Ben-Menashe served directly under me," he said. "He worked for the Foreign Flow Desk in External Relations. He had access to very, very sensitive material."

And that was it.

Period.

Even after much prodding, he elaborated only minimally. "The matter is far too sensitive," Hevrony told the Israeli newspaper *Davar* in another interview.[7] "I know exactly what he knows, what kind of access he had to what kind of material that was not within his authority to know. I do not want to touch it."

Brief though his statement was, Hevrony had dispelled any lingering doubts I might have had about who Ben-Menashe was, but I still had other pressing questions. I wanted to know if Israel was knowingly engaged in a conspiracy that sabotaged an American presidential election. Had Israel secretly worked with Bill Casey and the Republicans?

In addition to Hevrony, I interviewed his former boss, Gen. Yehoshua Saguy, in the lobby of the Sheraton hotel in Tel Aviv. A burly, white-haired, fifty-nine-year-old man who had been forced to resign from military intelligence because of "his indifference and lack of concern" for the 1982 massacre of Palestinian refugees in Beirut, Saguy had subsequently been elected to the Knesset.[8] He confirmed that Ben-Menashe reported to Hevrony in the External Relations department of Israeli Military Intelligence but held the official Israeli line, insisting that Ari was just a translator who had no access to sensitive material.

That, I assumed, was all I would get from Saguy. But, as a long shot, I asked if he had had any contact with Bill Casey in 1980. If so, there was probably no way Saguy would let on, but I had nothing to lose.

To my astonishment, Saguy replied, "Yes, I had very good ties and contacts with Casey. I talked to him at least three or four times a year again starting in 1979, generally on the Middle East."[9] He added that he also had contacts with Robert "Bud" McFarlane, the Reagan aide who was suing me for libel. As it turned out, Saguy had met with him several times as well.

To state the obvious, Casey and McFarlane were not part of the reigning Carter administration at the time they were talking to Saguy. They were part of the Reagan-Bush campaign. Saguy told me that his talks with Casey did *not* include the hostage crisis, but that was difficult to believe, especially after another highly placed Israeli assured me it was at the *center* of Saguy's meetings with Casey. The Shah had just been toppled, the hostages seized, and the West was losing Iran. To both Casey and Saguy this was topic number one. Moreover, at the time, Israel was working feverishly to create a new foundation for trading arms and sharing intelligence with Iran, but was very much at odds with the Carter administration over the path forward.[10]

He also confirmed that Casey had met with Iranians in Europe that summer to negotiate the release of the hostages. All of which clarified how Casey communicated with Israeli intelligence and showed that if the Israelis decided to defy Carter's arms embargo, they had a direct line to the Republicans. That would be essential if Casey made a deal with Iran.

In terms of leads to pursue, I had an embarrassment of riches, but getting someone to publish it was another question. For one thing, McFarlane's lawsuit against me was just getting underway, making it treacherous for any news outlet to back me, especially since I was still being assailed from all quarters as a conspiracy nut. The Hearst Corporation, which owns *Esquire*, brought in a team from BakerHostetler, a giant international law firm, to defend *Esquire* and me from McFarlane's suit. Throughout the discovery process, we met regularly to discuss the voluminous notes on the story I had submitted to my lawyers so they could see what was relevant.

If and when I won the lawsuit, finding an outlet to pursue the investigation would still be almost impossible. The last thing *Esquire* wanted was another story on the October Surprise. The same for *Vanity Fair*. Phone calls to other publications went unreturned. I had already approached every publication willing to stick its neck out. It was a dangerous, costly, and labor-intensive project. The prospects of making a decent living pursuing the October Surprise were nonexistent. Continuing to pursue it was not a wise career move, and when I persisted, a friend described it as my white whale. I did not need to be reminded that things had ended badly for Captain Ahab.

Meanwhile, the congressional investigations were still moving along, and that made it hard for me to stop paying attention completely. In May 1992, a rich new vein of evidence to mine came to light thanks to the investigations.

Back in 1980, the FBI and US Customs had suspected Cyrus Hashemi of being an important financier for the Khomeini regime and that he was acting as a paymaster for Iranian agents in the United States. As a result, in September 1980, just as the final planning for the October Surprise would have been taking place, the FBI installed bugs and wiretaps in Hashemi's New York offices for the First Gulf Bank & Trust, and his home in Wilton, Connecticut. The wiretaps confirmed that Cyrus was extremely influential with senior officials in the new Islamist Iranian government, but when it came to finding evidence that Cyrus was a Khomeini operative, the FBI struck out.

The FBI's misstep, however, revealed that Hashemi was leading a double life. At the same time Hashemi was involved in the hostage negotiations with the Carter administration, he appeared to be making illegal arms deals with Iran in breach of Carter's arms embargo. Consequently, FBI surveillance of Hashemi continued from early September 1980 until February 1981, but this time with an eye toward prosecuting him for violating the embargo.

It had been more than a decade, but the contents of Hashemi's wiretaps had never been revealed. Finally, in May 1992, the FBI started to make these long-missing surveillance tapes of Hashemi available to the House October Surprise Task Force, including verbatim transcripts of classified conversations between Cyrus Hashemi, John Shaheen, Iranian operatives, and who knows who else. The tapes might be able to "establish whether Hashemi was a double agent who was secretly working for Reagan-Bush campaign manager William Casey, as his brother Jamshid Hashemi has alleged," I wrote in the *Washington Post*.[11]

They would likely provide scores of leads as to how Casey ran his operation—if, that is, they were released in full.

For the time being, however, all we had to work with were telexes and memos about the surveillance tapes that had been released by the FBI for public review. Unfortunately, those documents were of limited value because the few bits of conversation they included were almost incomprehensible. A typical exchange included Hashemi saying, "Right. . . . Fine. . . . Okay" in response to a person whose identity and dialog have been redacted.

"It is so heavily censored you can't tell who is talking to whom," Gary Sick told me at the time.[12]

Without a verbatim transcript of the conversations, no one was able to fully decipher them. "It is possible that the arms dealing discussed is part of the October Surprise," continued Sick. "But we don't know, except that this is contemporaneous material, and it should be full text and should include a wide range of individuals."

I was hoping that the FBI's wiretap transcripts would provide some of the answers, so I immediately filed a Freedom of Information Act request to get the full text of newly declassified documents. I assumed Bob Parry, who was also still working the story, would be after them as well. It could take weeks, months, or even longer before they materialized. When they came—or, rather, *if*—I could begin to unravel the mystery anew.

THEN, ON JULY 1, 1992, CONGRESSIONAL INVESTIGATORS threw cold water on the most explosive unanswered question of all regarding the October Surprise and announced that "all credible evidence" contradicted charges that George Bush went to Paris in October 1980 to delay the release of the American hostages.[13]

The *Washington Post* reported, "The head of the task force, Rep. Lee H. Hamilton (D-Ind.), said it had interviewed about 50 witnesses, listened to thousands of hours of FBI surveillance tapes and was sifting through tens of thousands of pages of documents provided by the CIA, the State Department and other agencies." Several people, including Ben-Menashe, testified that they had seen Bush in Paris on

October 19 or October 20, 1980, but their testimony was filled with so many contradictions the committee did not find it credible. Instead, the committee's conclusion regarding Bush was based on testimony from the Secret Service officers who were protecting the Bushes at the time.

In response to Hamilton's announcement, White House press secretary Marlin Fitzwater said, "We are glad that Congress, in a bipartisan report, concluded today what we know all along—that President Bush had no involvement with any alleged meetings in Paris."[14]

The announcement was surprising on multiple levels. A Democrat-led investigation was pushing to exonerate the chief Republican target of their investigation when he was still four months away from facing reelection. A go-along-to-get-along politician, task force chairman Lee Hamilton often bent over backward to accommodate his foes, but this was absurd.

To maintain the appearance of bipartisanship, his committee had absolved Bush of any wrongdoing and preempted his own investigation. And now that Bush had been exonerated, the Washington press corps meekly bought the House Joint Task Force's conclusion that George H. W. Bush had not been in Paris. That meant the October Surprise was dead as a campaign issue. No freelance reporter could possibly change that.

As it turned out, Bush's campaign foundered for other reasons. In the coming months, Bill Clinton and Al Gore focused on the recession, which had caused Bush's popularity to plummet. Using James Carville's celebrated battle cry—"It's the economy, stupid!"—the Democrats sailed to a comfortable victory in November.

ON NOVEMBER 19, 1992, ABOUT TWO WEEKS AFTER BILL Clinton was elected president, special counsel Reid Weingarten released the Senate Foreign Relations Committee's report, entitled *The*

October Surprise Allegations and the Circumstances Surrounding the Release of the American Hostages Held in Iran. Six weeks later, on January 3, 1993, as chairman of the House Intelligence Committee, Lee Hamilton published the *Joint Report of the Task Force to Investigate Certain Allegations Concerning the Holding of American Hostages in Iran in 1980.*

Both investigations had come to conclusions that were disheartening to anyone trying to prove the October Surprise. Allowing only that Casey "had been fishing in troubled waters," the Senate report concluded, "The great weight of the evidence is that there was no such deal."[15] Far worse, the House task force decided that almost nothing important happened, and determined "There is no credible evidence supporting any attempt or proposal to attempt, by the Reagan presidential campaign . . . to delay the release of the American hostages in Iran."

Sophia Casey, the spymaster's widow, hailed the House report and demanded an apology from people like Gary Sick, "who blackened Bill Casey's good name."[16]

Anyone who read these conclusions without taking in the entire 325 pages of the Senate report and the 999 pages of the House report might reasonably assume that the rest would be a waste of time. With its powers to subpoena witnesses and take testimony under oath, the House interviewed or deposed more than 230 witnesses,[17] the Senate more than 150. Both houses had access to documents and testimony regarding the October Surprise from a broad swath of federal agencies including the FBI, the Department of Justice, the Office of the Independent Counsel for Iran/Contra, the CIA, the State Department, and so forth.

The media were quick to jump on board. "House Inquiry Finds No Evidence of Deal on Hostages in 1980," headlined the *New York Times*.[18] "Bipartisan Probe Clears 1980 Reagan Campaign of Hostage Deal with Iran," read the Associated Press headline.[19]

The verdict was in stone: there was no October Surprise. One challenged the consensus at one's peril. Moreover, with the defeat of

George H. W. Bush, none of the key figures remained in office. And that meant it was unclear what publication, if any, would stick its neck out again. Anyone who pursued it now faced a much tougher challenge than Watergate. This was no longer just about uncovering political crimes. Making a case that would win over the general public meant overcoming an insurmountable wall of doubt.

But over the years I had learned that when it comes to congressional investigations such as these, bipartisan simply means that two adversarial parties have negotiated a mutually agreed-upon version of the truth. The final product—the official version of events—was usually the result of considerable political horse-trading, which is quite different from a fair, impartial, accurate, and complete investigation. In Congress, it is often the case that the most crucial parts of the investigation will be omitted or hidden precisely *because* they go to the heart of the very divisive allegations in question. For many such investigations, "bipartisan" is not the same thing as the truth—it's merely a draft of history that both sides can tolerate.

And so it came as no surprise to me, and certainly not to Bob Parry, that far from answering questions about the October Surprise once and for all, these reports merely posed new ones.

Chapter Eight
The Alibi Club

When it came to understanding the problems with the congressional investigations, it was hard to overlook the role of the man leading the charge in the House: Lee Hamilton, the chair of both the House Intelligence Committee and the House Foreign Affairs Committee, who happened to be a lapdog at a time when the Democrats needed a pit bull.

"Lee caved on the October Surprise, and he caved on Iran-Contra," said Spencer Oliver, who, as chief counsel of the House Foreign Affairs Committee, worked directly with Hamilton on both investigations.[1] "He had this reputation of being an above-the-fray, Abraham Lincoln kind of a guy who made great speeches. But he didn't have any guts."

"Lee Hamilton was a great failure in my mind," said Walter Pincus, a Pulitzer Prize–winning reporter who covered Iran-Contra for the *Washington Post*.[2] "He was the kind of guy who sent someone to the [Reagan] White House to ask for documents. That's not how you do it! You go to where the documents originate." Hamilton's methodology was akin to asking the fox about the terrible henhouse break-ins—and taking his word for it that absolutely nothing was amiss.

It had been Hamilton, of course, who'd taken Oliver North's word over the reporting of Bob Parry on Iran-Contra, almost single-handedly ending the Reagan administration's biggest scandal before it had begun. In August 1986, Hamilton called Oliver North for a briefing at the White House to address Parry's reporting about him. Talking to the committee, North assured them that Parry's allegations about the Contras were false.[3]

Afterward, a staff aide informed Parry that his allegations had not checked out. Hamilton had accepted North's word over Parry's reporting—without doing any independent investigation.

"Congressman Hamilton had the choice of accepting the word of honorable men or the word of your sources," he told Parry. "It wasn't a close call."[4]

In the end, it was Parry who got the last laugh when everything he wrote turned out to be true, and the "honorable" Oliver North was convicted. But this lapse in Hamilton's judgment and his general willingness to take Republicans at their word regarding possibly illegal activities during Iran-Contra should have disqualified him from leading an investigation that so closely mirrored that earlier scandal. After all, this was a man who appeared, at times, as though he didn't want to believe that Republicans were capable of the things that they clearly were guilty of. How could he effectively lead a search for truth as murky and nefarious as this?

Later, when the task force reports faced true scrutiny, its intrinsic flaws became all too apparent. But if it revealed any single development that was undeniable, it was that Republicans had learned a lot from Watergate—most notably how to cover up better.

Before a word had been written or interviews had been conducted, both October Surprise investigations were severely compromised by the appointment of personnel.[5]

The House task force in particular was highly partisan. The lead counsel for the investigation, Larry Barcella, had worked for Paul Laxalt, the chair of the 1980 Reagan-Bush election campaign, and had also played a key role in defending the corrupt BCCI in its indictment for money laundering, bribery, arms dealing, smuggling, and other crimes.[6] It was peculiar that Lee Hamilton had chosen a man who was so closely tied to Republican interests, not to mention the very same bank that funded so many illegal arms deals and covert operations.

The House task force was also embroiled in a pissing match from the start over the role of Spencer Oliver, the chief counsel of the House Foreign Affairs Committee that was overseeing the investigation. A seasoned Beltway insider, Oliver had long been active in Democratic Party politics, and had earned a footnote in history during the Watergate scandal after Nixon's Plumbers wiretapped two phones in the offices of the Democratic National Committee, one of which was Oliver's. In addition to being a veteran of Watergate, Spencer had been active during the Iran-Contra hearings, and early on had been one of the key House aides pushing for the October Surprise investigation.

Thanks to his rich experience with Republican transgressions, Oliver had acquired a rather jaundiced view of what was going on with the October Surprise. "When corruption reaches the highest precincts of government, the protection mechanisms for the people who inhabit those precincts are so powerful that they are almost impenetrable," he told Parry.[7] "The result is that the word has been conveyed that if you take on people with positions of power, you have to be prepared to pay the highest price in terms of your job, your career, and even your friends. The tools that are available to people of great power in the U.S. government are so frightening in their impact on an individual that it has the effect of making most people conclude that it is just not worth the candle to fight the battle."

Even before the investigation was officially underway, Spencer had flown off to Hong Kong to interview Dirk Stoffberg, a South African arms dealer who sold arms to Iran and who claimed to have met with William Casey in London in August 1980. As a result of his aggressive approach, Republicans were doing everything they could to keep him off the committee.[8] Ultimately, they succeeded.

The Senate investigation had even more severe restrictions. Investigators were prohibited from traveling abroad—thereby precluding the possibility of interviews with many prominent Iranian political figures, Iranian exiles in Europe, international arms dealers, and intelligence officials. They were denied access to Bill Casey's files until the last minute and even then, key files were missing. They had no independent subpoena authority and could compel attendance of witnesses only after being authorized to do so by a majority vote of the committee.[9] Worse, the entire budget for the Senate investigation was a pitiable $75,429.16.[10]

These constraints were just the start. Perhaps the biggest obstacle was how many key players—Casey chief among them—were dead. Yet even when interview targets were alive, the committees did not always pursue all the interviews that were available to them. Most notably both committees failed to interview President Bush, either under oath or otherwise.

Another problem the investigations faced was that in the eleven-plus years since the 1980 campaign, key bits of evidence had been destroyed—especially insofar as it concerned Casey and John Shaheen, both of whom, of course, were dead. According to the House task force report, after Casey's death, his files were sent to the CIA, and they included, among other documents, a file titled "Hostages," a standard diary, a "Monthly Minder 1980," and loose calendar pages for July 24, 1980, to December 18, 1980.[11]

After they were indexed by the CIA, the files were sent to Casey's house in McLean. But when House task force investigator Richard Pedersen examined the files on August 12, 1992, some of the materials were missing—among them, the "Hostages" file, the standard diary, the "Monthly Minder 1980," and the loose calendar pages from July 24, 1980, to December 18, 1980.[12] Later, most of the missing files were recovered, but, the Senate reported, loose calendar pages for

July 26–27, October 21, October 29, November 3–11, and November 13 were never found.[13]

Similarly, when the Senate sought John Shaheen's personal and business files, they found that Shaheen's Economist Pocket Diary for 1980, his passport, and certain financial ledger pages from 1980 were all missing, even though his pocket diaries for other years just before and after 1980 were available.[14] The task force concluded that the missing documents "might have assisted the investigation in obtaining further evidence on Casey's ties to Hashemi."[15]

I, on the other hand, surmised that the documents were missing precisely *because* they would have been so helpful to the investigation.

One of the first issues addressed by both the House and Senate investigations was the question of Casey's whereabouts during the Madrid meetings, and while the two legislative bodies addressed the matter differently, in the end, they both decided that the London conference didn't stand up to scrutiny as Casey's alibi.

Citing a number of inaccuracies in Chadwick's attendance chart, the House task force concluded that these diminished the chart's "reliability as an accurate record of the proceedings."[16] Similarly, the Senate Report on the October Surprise Allegations determined that the various irregularities in Chadwick's charts created so much confusion that the "only clear conclusion to be drawn was . . . that Casey walked into the [July 29] session (which had begun at 2:30) late, at 4:00 o'clock."[17]

Until now, all of the focus on Casey and those Madrid meetings had been on those attendance charts, and much like everyone else, save *Newsweek* and *The New Republic*, the committees had found those charts lacking. No other alibi for Casey had ever been presented except for the London meetings, which is why it was fascinating that as soon as the infamous attendance chart alibi was knocked down, another one popped up.

This second attempt to exculpate Casey came from a Republican operative named Darrell Trent, who had been an adviser to the Reagan-Bush campaign, and, according to the House task force, testified under oath that "Casey was his guest during the summer of 1980 at the Bohemian Grove, an all-male club retreat located on the Russian River."[18]

A rustic 2,700-acre camp in the California Redwoods, about seventy miles northwest of San Francisco, Bohemian Grove was founded by railroad barons who were members of the Bohemian Club of San Francisco in 1878 during the Gilded Age of California.[19] It became the site of secret meetings for a global elite that conducted an annual ritual in which they donned mostly red-hooded robes and worshipped a forty-foot stone owl.[20] In addition to Republican presidents Nixon, Reagan, and George H. W. Bush, its members and guests have included James Baker, Dick Cheney, Donald Rumsfeld, David Rockefeller, Henry Kissinger, and William Casey.*[21]

Again, as with the London alibi, there was documentary evidence that both Trent and Casey had been there, but the question was when. According to the task force report, the "records show that Casey incurred charges at the 1980 Bohemian Grove for a two-day period, although they do not reflect the actual dates on which the charges were incurred."[22] In addition, two attendees at Bohemian Grove testified that they either saw Casey there during the weekend of July 25–27 or that their "best recollection" was that Casey was present during that time.[23]

Also, like the London alibi, the question of whether Casey was attending the Bohemian Grove retreat was crucial. Once again, if the alibi held, there was no October Surprise.

But, as Parry first pointed out in the *Washington Post*, the documentary evidence suggested other possibilities. He wrote that

---

* In a tape made on May 13, 1971, while he was president, Richard Nixon offered his reflections on the club. "The Bohemian Grove that I attend from time to time. The Easterners and others that come there, but it is the most faggy goddamned thing you could ever imagine, with that San Francisco crowd that goes in there," he said.

at *Frontline* they had interviewed Matthew McGowan, a participant in the 1980 Bohemian Grove retreat, and he had "read to us a notation from his diary for Aug. 3, 1980, stating that 'we had Bill Casey, Governor Reagan's campaign manager, as our guest this last weekend.'"[24]

Consequently, *Frontline* concluded that Casey's alibi "almost certainly" didn't hold because he was at Bohemian Grove during that first weekend in August rather than the last weekend in July.[25]

But when the House task force examined the same material, they came to a radically different conclusion. "McGowan told the task force that the date on which a certain entry appears in his calendar does not necessarily correspond to the actual date of the event for which the entry was made," the task force noted, adding that McGowan "did not rule out the possibility that the reference to 'last weekend' in the calendar entry for August 3 actually pertains to the middle weekend of July 25–27."[26]

The Senate took a less categorical position on Casey's whereabouts that weekend and concluded that the evidence was "essentially in equipoise."[27] Ultimately, the Senate asserted that it was "extremely unlikely" that Casey made the trips to the Madrid meetings, but that his "missing 1980 passport would be highly relevant in making any final conclusions."[28]

The bottom line was that neither the House nor the Senate committees truly scrutinized this new wrinkle in Bill Casey's whereabouts at the end of July 1980. And much like the attendance chart alibi, this Bohemian Grove story had plenty of holes.

Not surprisingly, it was Parry who found even more holes in the task force's Bohemian Grove alibi and characterized it as nothing more than cherry-picked data that was contradicted by documents that had been conveniently overlooked or omitted.[29] First, Darrell Trent said he had left for Bohemian Grove on Thursday, July 24, but he didn't recall whether Casey came with him that weekend or arrived the following weekend. In other words, it might well have been the weekend of August 2 and 3, when Trent was also present. He just wasn't sure.[30]

Trent's presence at the Grove on July 24 was corroborated by three dated and signed bar receipts. When the task force investigated Casey's financial records from that time, they found an invoice for that same day showing that Casey was nearly 3,000 miles away at the Metropolitan Club in Washington.[31] They also discovered a photo of him accepting a check for $24.9 million from the Federal Election Commission that day in Washington.[32] That ruled out his travel with Darrell Trent on the same day in California.

An airtight alibi? I don't think so.

Nor was that the only documentation that refuted the task force's conclusion. Casey's calendar noted a meeting with a "Mrs. Tobin" on Saturday, July 26. Exactly who she was and whether she could remember the meeting was omitted from the House task force. But, as Parry wrote in *Trick or Treason*, when the task force interviewed Mary Jane Tobin, a New York–based right-to-life advocate, she confirmed meeting with Casey that day at his Long Island estate, though she could not remember the exact day. She recalled, Parry wrote, only that it was hot.[33] The temperature hit ninety-two in New York that day.

In the face of all this dispositive evidence, the House task force seemed to be grasping at straws that might exonerate Casey. Among them was a handwritten notation of Casey's Long Island phone number made by the Reagan campaign's foreign policy adviser Richard Allen on August 2, 1980. At his deposition, Allen said the notation meant that he had called Casey at his home in Long Island that day.[34] If Allen had spoken on the phone with Casey at Casey's Long Island home on August 2, that would have meant Casey could not have been at the Bohemian Grove on August 2 and 3.

But Allen also said he did not actually recall talking to Casey that day, nor was there any documentation that the phone call was actually made. And even if the call *was* made, there was no indication that

Casey answered the phone. Allen had simply written down the phone number—period. Writing down the phone number proved only that he had written down the phone number—nothing more.

Nevertheless, the House committee clung to that thin, thread-like reed as proof that Casey was at home in Long Island that August weekend.[35] As a result, they ultimately concluded "that the great weight of evidence places Casey at the Bohemian Grove on the weekend of July 25–27, 1980,"[36] and therefore he could not possibly have been in Madrid.

In other words, no October Surprise.

CASEY WASN'T THE ONLY ONE WHO NEEDED AN ALIBI.

For both committees, the most pressing question regarded Bush and his alleged presence in Paris on October 19 and 20, 1980, when the October Surprise deal was apparently finalized. Back on July 1, the committees had released their conclusion that Bush was not present on October 19, using the Secret Service records on Bush as evidence. But now with the full reports, it was possible to follow how they'd come to that conclusion. Though there were inconsistencies in it, Bush's alibi held up somewhat better under scrutiny than Casey's did.

With just a little over two weeks before the presidential election, the American presidential campaign was at a fever pitch. Bush was on the campaign trail nearly every day warning voters that Carter was going to pull an "October Surprise."[37] Throughout October, he campaigned all over the country. He traveled north and south and east and west, hitting cities, suburbs, and small towns—Eugene, Oregon; San Francisco; Baton Rouge, Louisiana.[38] The spotlight was on him day after day.

Would he have dared sneak away amid all this to participate in a treasonous covert operation? How could he have possibly pulled it off logistically? That was what the committees sought to answer.

Based on the interviews, depositions, and in some cases sworn affidavits that the committee conducted with members of Bush's Secret Service detail, the House committee decided that Bush could not have attended the October meetings in Paris. "Few of these agents had any current recollections of specific events during . . . October 18–22, 1980," the House task force reported, "all of the agents clearly recalled that Bush did not engage in any foreign travel during this period." This point about foreign travel seemed vital to the conclusion. While the agents interviewed or deposed recalled the hectic nature of the campaign, "each agreed, however, that anything out of ordinary, in addition to being reflected in the shift reports, would have clearly stuck out in their minds." And travel to Paris for Bush at this point certainly would have been out of the ordinary "both because of the incredible logistical burden it would have entailed for protection details to have travelled with him abroad and because any absence of the protected candidate would have been immediately noticed."[39]

Because twelve years had passed since the days in question and the hectic work pace of Secret Service agents, the committee did not find it odd that none of the agents in Bush's protective detail specifically recalled Bush's activities during October 18–22. However, there was one agent the House committee met with who recalled "that Bush went with his wife to Chevy Chase Country Club for about an hour and a half on Sunday October 19, 1980, to have lunch with Associate Supreme Court Justice Potter Stewart and his wife." The committee also found a Secret Service site survey that was prepared in anticipation of Bush's October 19 luncheon at the country club that also supported this version of events. Yet the agent's memory erred in at least one respect. Interviews with other agents about that day showed that Barbara Bush was *not* present at the country club.[40]

Despite this discrepancy, "in the opinion of the Task Force, these records and testimony conclusively prove candidate George Bush's whereabouts in October 1980. The Task Force has determined that Bush did not travel to Paris during the period of time in question as has been alleged by many October Surprise witnesses."[41]

Digging into Bush's alibi with all these newfound specifics, Parry began to investigate anew, discussing these details regarding the country club with Spencer Oliver, who figured it should be easy enough to check out. Even after being forced off the task force, Oliver continued to have a strong interest in the investigation and often compared notes with Parry, me, and other reporters. He wanted the truth to come out.

Since Bush supposedly was playing tennis at the Chevy Chase Country Club that day, Parry went to the country club and talked to the pro. No one remembered Bush being there that day playing tennis, but that didn't mean much. Twelve years had passed. People forget.

So that wasn't enough to knock down Bush's alibi. But the Secret Service records also noted the particulars of a lunch date Bush had that day. "Now they said Bush and his wife had lunch at the club that day with [Supreme Court Justice] Potter Stewart and his wife," recalled Oliver.[42]

By the time of the task force investigation, Potter Stewart had died, but his wife was very much alive. "So, we had a young woman from the General Accounting Office, Cecilia Porter, who was assigned to assist the investigation, and we had asked her to find Mrs. Potter Stewart," Oliver told me.

Cecilia Porter returned later that day. "I was advised not to go to see her," she told Oliver, "because they said she's senile and very, very frail. It would be very dangerous to her health to try to interview her. And she's not competent.'"[43]

But about a week later, Oliver was having dinner with a friend who knew Mrs. Stewart. "She's not old and senile!" he told Oliver.[44] "I was with her about a week ago and she was dancing through the night. Spencer, she's just as competent as you and I."

When Parry finally got on the phone, Mary Ann Stewart, then in her early seventies, was as "bright and chipper" as could be. "It was our custom to lunch together at the Bushes' home on Sunday mornings when we were all in town," she told Parry.[45] "But I don't know for sure if we did that weekend."

When Parry pressed further, she replied, "I don't remember anything about the Chevy Chase Country Club." Then, after a pause, she added a warning. "You should believe whatever the president tells you."[46]

So according to Mary Ann Stewart, it was possible she and her husband were never at the country club. Once again, this didn't prove anything conclusively about Bush's alibi, especially given how much time had elapsed, but it did raise the specter that the investigation into the matter had not been as exhaustive as claimed. A busted alibi did not prove that Bush was in Paris. It merely meant that Bush was unaccounted for during a period of time, long enough for it to be *possible*. "There was a twenty-two-hour gap in the middle of the campaign," Spencer Oliver told me. "How the hell can the vice-presidential nominee disappear for twenty-two hours in the middle of a campaign?"[47]

Still, I had spent enough time investigating the sources who claimed that Bush had been in Paris—Ari Ben-Menashe, arms dealer Richard Brenneke, various pilots who said they flew Bush and Casey to Paris—to know they would not hold up well in court.[48] In the end, the evidence for Bush's presence in Paris was not nearly as strong as it was for Casey's travels to Madrid. As a result, I remained agnostic about Bush's presence in Paris.

The task force was also focused on Casey's attendance at the Paris meetings. In its effort to exculpate Casey, the task force tried to determine his whereabouts on October 19 and 20, 1980, when the Paris meetings took place, and they had come up with an alibi. This one came from the spymaster's nephew, Larry Casey, who asserted that his parents had had dinner in Washington with Bill Casey that evening, so that he could not possibly have been in Paris.[49]

When Parry interviewed him for *Frontline*, Larry Casey said he "vividly" remembered having dinner with his parents and Casey that night at the Jockey Club in Washington. "It was very clear in my mind, even though it was eleven years ago," Larry Casey said.[50]

Never one to take alibis at face value, Parry dug up campaign sign-in sheets at Reagan-Bush campaign headquarters and Casey's American Express card receipts, discovering a very different story. As Parry reported at *Consortium News*, the sign-in sheets at the GOP campaign headquarters showed "Larry Casey's parents picking up Bill Casey for the dinner on Oct. 15, four days earlier [than Larry had asserted]. Larry Casey acknowledged his error, and indeed an American Express receipt later confirmed Oct. 15 as the date of the Jockey Club dinner."[51]

But when Larry testified before the House task force, he offered a different version and said "his father spoke with William Casey by telephone on the morning of Sunday, October 19. . . . Larry Casey recalls that he also spoke with William Casey during that telephone call and based on the clarity of the connection believed it to be a local call."[52]

There was nothing to corroborate Larry Casey's memory. There were no questions about whether "the clarity" of the phone call was such that it could definitively place Casey in the Washington area. Because Larry said his father and his uncle talked about having a midday meal that day, the discussion suggested "that Casey was in the local area on Sunday."[53]

And that was it.

Of course, none of this addressed the question of whether Bush was in the loop about what Casey was up to. About whether he knew what was going on. After all, both men were vaunted spymasters, and Bush had headed the CIA himself under President Ford.

Which was why I couldn't help breaking into a grin when I learned the details about their dinner together in Washington on July 30—just two weeks after the Republican National Convention but, more important, the day after the Madrid meetings in which Casey had first told the Iranians he wanted to delay the hostage release. Whatever Casey and Bush may have discussed, we can be certain of only one thing: Whoever booked the restaurant had a sense of humor. It was called the Alibi Club.

Chapter Nine
The X-Files

In the face of these inconsistencies in the congressional reports, Parry doubled down on the story, and almost two years after the House report was released, he found himself in an office off the Rayburn House Office Building's parking garage. More specifically, he was in what once was a women's bathroom, staring at a trove of October Surprise documents.

By 1994, Parry had already committed a significant part of his career to the story in one form or another—some ten years, including his work on Iran-Contra. More important, though, the congressional investigations were simply too flawed to let them go unstudied—regardless of whether the media was interested in them. "He just went back to digging some more," said his wife, Diane Duston.[1] "He just never stopped. Ever."

One of the first things Parry noted after the task force report was released was that several international leaders, including Palestine Liberation Organization (PLO) chairman Yasir Arafat and Israeli prime minister Yitzhak Shamir, came forward saying Congress had gotten it wrong. Arafat said that senior Republicans had traveled to Beirut in 1980 seeking avenues to the Iranian leadership, while Shamir confirmed the conspiracy in a May 1993 interview.[2]

Furthermore, after reading the report closely, it had become increasingly clear just how hard Hamilton's task force had worked to dismiss any evidence that ran counter to their narrative. Such was the case with Alexandre de Marenches, the former head of French intelligence and a very close friend of Casey's. De Marenches privately ridiculed the House task force findings, which included the testimony of David Andelman, a former CBS News and *New York Times* reporter who coauthored de Marenches's biography, *The Fourth World War: Diplomacy and Espionage in the Age of Terrorism.*[3]

"Casey was the only CIA guy de Marenches could ever trust," Andelman told me.[4] "[De Marenches] said the CIA couldn't keep the secret, so he never shared anything with them. But Casey was different."

A fellow World War II veteran who shared Casey's profound distaste for Jimmy Carter, de Marenches said that Carter had in effect disbanded his covert intelligence service and in doing so had achieved "a job which the other side could not have done, even if it had worked for decades."[5]

"Under Carter," de Marenches later wrote, "the Americans committed voluntary suicide, the consequences of which are irrevocable."[6]

Given his relationship with Casey, his distaste for Carter, and the fact that the Paris meeting would have taken place in his backyard, de Marenches's perspective should have been of high importance to the committee. According to the House report, "Andelman told the Task Force that during the course of ninety hours of interviews with de Marenches between late 1988 and late 1991, de Marenches . . . acknowledged setting up a meeting in Paris between Casey and some Iranians in late October of 1980."[7]

When I interviewed Andelman in 2024, he described de Marenches as "one of the savviest spies I've ever run into—a master, a master spy. I mean, he was the Henry Kissinger of spying."[8]

"When I tried to grill him on [the October Surprise meetings in Paris]," Andelman told me,[9] "he basically dismissed it. 'It's all bullshit,' he said. 'I arranged a meeting. I set up a room.' And French intelligence would never set up a room where they couldn't actually find out what was going on in that room. It was surveilled."

For all the insight Andelman's testimony offered into how the meetings in Paris were set up, House investigators brushed it aside as having "little probative value" because "it would have been very embarrassing" for de Marenches to admit that he knew nothing about it.[10] They seemed to think de Marenches was just showing off.

Similarly, the task force buried the testimony and statements of others who supported the October Surprise, including Jamshid Hashemi; President Abolhassan Bani-Sadr; the statements and writings of foreign minister Sadegh Ghotbzadeh; former Iranian defense minister Ahmed Madani; and intelligence agents tied to Israel, France, and the United States, Ben-Menashe among them.

The task force's dismissive treatment of Bani-Sadr was particularly noteworthy in that it treated the man who was the president of Iran when the October Surprise was taking place as if he was a distant observer who had come up with a wild conspiracy theory to rationalize his subsequent overthrow. "Bani-Sadr claims to have hearsay knowledge of the alleged meetings in Madrid by virtue of information obtained essentially contemporaneously from a variety of sources close to Khomeini. None of these sources of information actually participated in the events," the House task force concluded.[11]

In 2016, when I interviewed Bani-Sadr myself, he told me that the information in that last sentence was false. Bani-Sadr was a very active player involved in trying to stop the October Surprise and told me in considerable detail meetings with Ayatollah Khomeini, Khomeini nephew Reza Pasandideh, and other players on the Iranian side.

The task force report added, "Bani-Sadr could offer no direct evidence that the matters under review actually occurred."[12]

I also knew that to be false. And I couldn't help but notice that the task force report had cultivated its own special brand of pretzel logic. On the one hand, it said Bani-Sadr's testimony should be disregarded because he *wasn't* closely involved, and in another part argued that it should be disregarded because he was too closely involved and had a self-interest at stake. Having been impeached, having survived assassination attempts, and having been forced into exile, they reasoned, he had been affected personally by the October Surprise and therefore could not be trusted.

Most perplexing of all, however, was the fact that whatever one thought of Bani-Sadr, he *had* brought documents—but the House task force didn't bother to examine them. If you thought about it, there had to be a paper trail of some sort. Assuming there was a deal between Iran and the Republicans, there had to be an Iranian side to the story, so far largely untold. There had to be paperwork. Receipts from hotels, air travel, restaurants. There had to be arms deals. Cargo ships and planes. Who knows what Bani-Sadr had?

If flaws like these could be discovered merely from reading the published congressional report, imagine what one might find with access to the raw data that had been left on the cutting-room floor. No one, Parry noted, had bothered to examine the integrity of the investigation itself, or listen to the few opposing voices in it.

And that was how, on December 20, 1994, Bob Parry found himself at the Rayburn House Office Building, the biggest of three huge structures on Capitol Hill serving the House of Representatives. He took the elevator to a subbasement, and then snaked his way through a musty underground garage until he reached the exit ramp on the building's south side. To the right, behind Venetian-blind-covered windows, was a small, locked office, inside of which were a few desks, cloth-covered partitions, disused phones (landlines, of course), and an antiquated, rumbling copying machine.

At the rear of the office was an abandoned ladies' room that had been repurposed and was now used as a storage room. The task force's taped boxes sat against the wall, under an empty tampon dispenser that still hung from the salmon-colored tiles.

There was no one else there, and Parry began ripping the tape off the boxes and poring over the files. Not only did he find unclassified notes and documents about the task force's work, but he also found "secret" and even "top secret" documents that had been left behind, apparently in the haste to wrap up the investigation.

He had found the motherlode. Nirvana under the tampon dispenser.[13]

Parry, however, didn't want to alert the suspicions of the polite staffer for the House International Relations Committee in the next room—especially since he was going to copy classified documents. Committee rules allowed Bob to photocopy only a handful of documents at a time, so he scribbled notes down in his notepad for some documents and read the most important passages into his tape recorder for others.[14]

Then, when he was ready to use the photocopy machine, Parry volunteered to do it himself. Not only did that ingratiate him with the congressional staffer, but it also gave him a bit of privacy and kept the staffer from interfering. Since many of the documents were classified and stamped SECRET, Parry put an unclassified paper on top of the whole batch, so it would be the only page that was visible. Immediately below it, but not visible, were the classified documents that had the most historical significance.

Still, he was allowed to take only so many pages per visit, so he returned again and again over the next few weeks. Before long, he had amassed a significant archive of documents that challenged the task force's findings. He referred to them as "the X-Files," after the popular TV show. But nothing about this trove of documents evoked tinfoil-hat conspiracies. They were government documents that included classified material from the FBI, documents supplied by former Iranian president Bani-Sadr, from Russian intelligence, and much, much more. Some of them were highly relevant, and yet the House task force had, in effect, thrown them away.

From it all, Parry excavated the true story of the committee's work, making it increasingly clear just how much evidence this bipartisan group of lawmakers had overlooked in order to say that the October Surprise didn't occur.

One of the most astonishing documents Parry unearthed was a file that was received by the task force on January 11, 1993, just two days before its final report was issued. At the time, Washington was preparing for the January 20 inauguration of Bill Clinton as the first Democratic president to take the White House in a dozen years. The House task force had put the final touches on its October Surprise investigation, having already determined that there was "no credible evidence" to support the allegations.

The file in question contained a cable from Moscow in response to a query in October from Lee Hamilton to Sergey Vadimovich Stepashin, chair of the Supreme Soviet's Committee on Defense and Security Issues, about the October Surprise.[15] At the time, Stepashin, who later served briefly as prime minister of the Russian Federation, had a position that was roughly equivalent to being head of the Senate Intelligence Committee. The Soviet Union had just dissolved ten months earlier, and relations between the United States and the newly formed Russian Federation, led by President Boris Yeltsin, were relatively friendly—friendly enough that Russia was willing to share intelligence with the United States.

According to the documents, the Soviet reply was prepared by Nikolay Kuznetsov, secretary of the subcommittee on state security, who apologized for the late response. A six-page translation of it was quickly sent to Hamilton. The Soviet report came to exactly the opposite of the task force's conclusion.

The Soviets stated as fact that Casey, George Bush, and other Republicans had secretly met with Iranian officials in Europe during the 1980 presidential campaign. "William Casey, in 1980, met three times with representatives of the Iranian leadership," the Russians wrote.[16] "The meetings took place in Madrid and Paris."

At the Paris meeting in October 1980, "R[obert] Gates, at that time a staffer of the National Security Council in the administration of Jimmy Carter, and former CIA director George Bush also took part," the Russians said. "In Madrid and Paris, the representatives of Ronald Reagan and the Iranian leadership discussed the question of possibly delaying the release of 52 hostages from the staff of the US Embassy in Teheran."[17]

Both the Reagan Republicans and Carter Democrats "started from the proposition that Imam [Ruhollah] Khomeini, having announced a policy of 'neither the West nor the East,' and cursing the 'American devil,' imperialism and Zionism, was forced to acquire American weapons, spares and military supplies by any and all possible means," the Russians wrote. According to the report, the Republicans won the bidding war, and the arms shipments were carried out by Israel, often through private arms dealers.

By the time the Russian report arrived on January 11, 1993, however, the task force had already sent their report to the printer for release two days later.

When Parry later asked task force chair Lee Hamilton, he told him, "I don't recall seeing it."[18]

At home, Parry put together a summary of what he had discovered in the X-Files and began to pitch one editor after another. But no one would touch it. The October Surprise was so taboo that even left-wing publications recoiled when he breached the subject.[19]

Once he had distilled all his findings, Parry circulated the X-Files as a 138-page self-published paperback and published them on the internet as an eight-part series over a three-month period in early 1996. "That gave him an outlet," said Diane.[20] "It was important to him psychologically to get something out."

Not that many people noticed. In September 1996, an alternative newspaper in Los Angeles, the *LA Weekly*, published an article about Bob's findings on page thirty-six.[21] But other than that, a search of LexisNexis and Newspapers.com databases shows that not one single newspaper or broadcast outlet in the United States saw fit to disseminate Parry's discoveries.

So, no one picked up his stories. "Of course, he was mad about it," said Diane.[22] "But he understood the politics of it. It had been debunked, and everyone had turned against it as a conspiracy theory. But he never gave up. He was a family man, so he had kids and responsibilities, and we had a good marriage, so there was a lot that kept him grounded."

"He wasn't able to do the work that he wanted to do," said Sam Parry, his oldest son. "And he was also very inspired by I. F. Stone, the great journalist who had gone independent and started his own newsletter. I remember Dad talking about that being a model for him."[23]

So Parry began a newsletter. Initially, it was called *IF Magazine*, in honor of Stone, and later *American Dispatches*. Parry had written a couple of stories for *The Nation*, and in lieu of payment, had been given their mailing lists. Every other Friday, he and Sam would sit in their basement folding newsletters, stuffing them into envelopes, and putting stamps and mailing labels on them. But the costs were prohibitive, and it was short-lived.[24]

At the time, the internet was still very much in its infancy. But thanks to the first widely used web browsers, Netscape Navigator and Internet Explorer, millions of people were logging on for the first time and building their own websites. "So, I said, you can scan the documents and post them on this thing called the World Wide Web," recalls Sam.[25] And that was the origin of the *Consortium News* website (www.consortiumnews.com). Parry got to work with his son Sam building *Consortium News* into an ongoing concern, finally putting the October Surprise on the back burner.

In 1996, when money got tight, Diane, who had been a fellow reporter at the Associated Press when they met, found a better paying job in marketing. Bob's four children—Sam, Nat, Liz, and Jeff—were also supportive. Sam and Nat pitched in to help Parry pursue the stories he wanted without being tethered to institutions that wouldn't run them. In 1999, he published *Lost History: Contras, Cocaine, the Press, and "Project Truth,"* about the high price paid by journalists investigating Iran-Contra and other related scandals. In 2004 and 2007, he took on the Bush dynasty in *Secrecy & Privilege: Rise of the Bush Dynasty* and *Neck Deep: The Disastrous Presidency of George W. Bush,* the latter cowritten with Sam and Nat. Later, after Bob's death, Nat compiled and edited *American Dispatches, a Robert Parry Reader,* with a forward by Diane.

It wasn't until 2011 that Parry made another crucial discovery about the October Surprise, when, in response to his various FOIA requests, the George H. W. Bush Library in Texas made available 4,800 pages of previously unreleased documents revealing how Bush's inner circle in the White House handled the October Surprise allegations as the 1992 presidential campaign got underway.[26] So, on July 12, 2011, Parry cashed in his frequent flier miles and flew from Reagan National Airport in Washington to Houston, Texas. There, he rented a car and drove ninety miles to College Station, home of Texas A&M University and the George H. W. Bush Presidential Library.[27]

As he scrutinized these new pages from the Bush White House, Parry turned up something of grave importance concerning Bill Casey. Until that point, the focus on Casey and Madrid had always centered on his alibi—either in London or Bohemian Grove.

Parry had effectively eliminated those alibis, but in doing so he had merely proved that Casey couldn't be accounted for. They did not prove he was in Madrid. He *could* have been in Madrid, or he could have been somewhere else.

Unless, of course, one could finally find documentation showing that Casey really *was* in Madrid in July 1980? That would in effect be conclusive evidence that the October Surprise actually took place.

Even Lee Hamilton had been thinking along those lines, and, as a result, in the fall of 1991, the House task force sent a request to the Bush White House and State Department for any documents that might provide evidence of Casey's location on those fateful days in the summer of 1980. American officials at the embassy sometimes kept records of prominent Americans passing through town. It was worth a try.

In response to the task force request, the State Department searched diplomatic cables from the Madrid embassy in the summer of 1980. Edwin D. Williamson had been installed as the State Department's legal adviser, the highest-ranking legal position in the department, working under Secretary of State James Baker, President Bush's consigliere and lifelong friend. The White House Counsel's office had also brought in a new lawyer, Chester Paul Beach Jr., who spent much of his career as an attorney for the United States Navy but transferred to the White House in 1991 to handle the seemingly never-ending Iran-Contra investigation. "When Lee Hamilton geared up and issued requests for information and documents about the October Surprise, I was asked to take it on because I was already working on Iran-Contra," Beach told me.[28]

On November 4, the same day that both *Newsweek* and *The New Republic* were publishing stories "proving" that Casey could not have gone to Madrid, Beach ended up on the phone with Ed Williamson discussing the same topic. More precisely, they were discussing which documents should be turned over to Congress and who should make those decisions—the White House or State Department. More specifically still, Williamson was concerned with the disposition of an embassy cable concerning Bill Casey's whereabouts in Madrid in 1980.[29]

Beach—an innocent naïf when it came to the October Surprise and a newcomer in the White House—was only concerned with the protocols. "I was talking to somebody who in my judgment was the highest lawyer in the government beyond maybe my own boss, counsel to the president," he told me.[30] "I'd never met this guy [Williamson], but I knew who he was by his name and his title. And this was a new issue for me. I knew nothing about the whole October Surprise set of allegations. The one thing I came away with was the State Department wanted to handle the document requests. And that was fine with us."

In the interests of documenting the conversation accurately, Beach wrote a memorandum for the record noting that the State Department had discovered material that was "potentially relevant to the October Surprise allegations."[31] Of particular importance, he noted, was a July 1980 cable from the US embassy in Madrid, which, as Beach phrased it, read, "Bill Casey was in town, for purposes unknown."

In other words, Bill Casey *had* been in Madrid when the October Surprise meetings took place. Even the Bush White House said so. It was beyond dispute. And Parry had just uncovered the memo that proved it in the Bush library's document dump.

Two days after Beach's memo, on November 6, White House Counsel C. Boyden Gray, Beach's boss, arranged an interagency strategy session to discuss how to contain the congressional investigation into the October Surprise, with an eye toward protecting President Bush's reelection hopes in 1992, according to Kai Bird in his book about the Carter presidency, *The Outlier*.

The "October surprise" was "of special interest" to President Bush, Gray told Bird, and it was essential that there be "no Surprises to the White House."

Then, he added, somewhat ominously, "This is partisan."[32]

And because it was partisan, in 1992 Lee Hamilton and the October Surprise Task Force were never told that the Beach memo existed.

On Thursday, June 6, 2013, Hamilton responded to a document that Parry had emailed him including the memo in question.

"We found no evidence to confirm Casey's trip to Madrid," Hamilton told Parry. "We couldn't show that. The [Bush-41] White House did not notify us that he did make the trip. Should they have passed that on to us? They should have because they knew we were interested in that."[33]

To say the Bush White House should have passed it on was an understatement. The document proved the one thing that everyone from all sides agreed was of utmost importance: Casey was in Madrid. When Hamilton was asked if knowledge about Casey's presence in Madrid might have changed the task force's dismissive October Surprise conclusion, he said yes, because the question of the Madrid trip was key to the task force's investigation. "If the White House knew that Casey was there, they certainly should have shared it with us," he added.[34]

Once again, it seemed Hamilton expected that the Republicans would play by the rules. Once again, they didn't.

GIVEN THE MOUNTAIN OF EVIDENCE THAT HAD BEEN DIScounted, ignored, or outright dismissed, the House committee's findings were at best incomplete, and at worst damaged goods. So in late September 2016, I made a side trip from Paris to Versailles to interview former Iranian president Abolhassan Bani-Sadr.

Long exiled to Paris, the former Iranian president had given several interviews—to the *Miami Herald*, the *New York Times*, Bob Parry and *Frontline*, to the House task force, and more—in which he claimed the Khomeini regime had made a secret deal with the Republicans. But there had been very little follow-up by either congressional investigators or journalists. Lee Hamilton had brushed him aside. I wanted to hear the story.

Over the course of four hours, he explained, in depth, how he learned about the October Surprise while he was president of Iran, how he tried to stop the conspiracy, how he survived three assassination attempts by militant clerics, and, finally, how he fled the country.

He also told me that Lee Hamilton had interviewed him in 1992 as part of the congressional investigation into the scandal, and Bani-Sadr had recounted, chapter and verse, everything relating to it that transpired in Iran. More specifically, Bani-Sadr said he had told Hamilton how he found out about secret meetings between the Republicans and hardline mullahs in the summer of 1980.[35]

Ultimately, Bani-Sadr told me, Hamilton found the story so chilling that he didn't know what to do. "It would be very dangerous if we accepted such a thing," Hamilton told Bani-Sadr. "If we say such a thing happened, that means the last three presidential elections were not legitimate. The cost of accepting that is too heavy."

"Yes," replied Bani-Sadr. "But the price is much heavier if you don't tell the truth to Americans. Then, you really endanger democracy."[36]

Part II
Cold Case

Chapter Ten
Casey's Network

In the fall of 2022, I caught an early-morning train from New York's Penn Station to Union Station in Washington, crossed the Potomac River to Arlington, Virginia, and went to the home of Diane Duston. Bob Parry had died almost four years earlier, of pancreatic cancer, and Diane, his widow, had generously offered me access to his archives.

Over the next day and a half, I wriggled my way back and forth through the crawl space under the Parry-Duston house, carried one cardboard packing box after another upstairs, rummaged through the files, and, with Diane's permission, of course, took whatever I thought might be relevant. Diane also gave me a thumb drive with twenty-three gigabytes of Bob's files on the October Surprise and related issues.

As soon as I returned home to Brooklyn, I unpacked and dove in. I had brought back with me as much as I could carry—sixty or so pounds' worth of white looseleaf binders, black looseleaf binders, brown cardboard accordion folders, and the like—all stuffed to the gills with government documents. Most valuable of all was the thumb drive, which included, among other things, photocopies and PDFs of the X-Files, audiotapes and rare videotaped interviews with key figures in the October Surprise, and so much else—that is, roughly 678,000 pages of documents per gigabyte—that when I put together an inventory of the documents, even that was mind-numbing.

Now, with Parry's archive in hand, my plan was simply to combine my own work with Parry's and those of other investigators in hopes of answering the most elusive October Surprise question of all: How did Bill Casey do it?

This marked the first time in decades that the October Surprise would be my sole focus, but I had not ignored it completely over the years. In 1992, after *Newsweek*, I had pursued the October Surprise with stories in the *Village Voice* and the *Washington Post*. With Murray Waas, I cowrote "In the Loop" for *The New Yorker*, a story about how then vice president (and former CIA director) George H. W. Bush was sent on a mission by then DCI Bill Casey to deliver strategic military intelligence to Saddam Hussein to escalate its bombing deep inside Iranian territory.[1]

But none of this was enough to make a living. And so, for a while at least, the October Surprise was not much more than a hobby. When it came to rebuilding my career, one obstacle I faced was Bud McFarlane's libel suit against me. When I took the stand, McFarlane's lawyer, Forrest Hainline, apparently unaware that I'm Jewish, insinuated that my work was anti-Semitic, presumably because it exposed Israel's role in the Iran arms trade.[2] In 1994, a federal judge in Washington threw it out of court, citing lack of jurisdiction. The judge also ruled that McFarlane did not show that the article was published with "actual malice," an essential element in proving libel.[3] But that wasn't the end.

Later that year, McFarlane appealed to the US Court of Appeals for the DC Circuit. It also found in my favor, noting, as a Seton Hall Law School journal put it, "that there was no evidence to suggest the material in the article was false."[4] Even after losing his appeal, McFarlane tried to take his case to the US Supreme Court, which ended it once and for all in 1996 by denying cert and refusing to hear the case.

Now I could finally start to repair my reputation. Newspapers from coast to coast had reported that I was being sued for millions of dollars—not helpful when you are trying to restart your career—and now I thought I might get a taste of vindication. As I stepped down from the witness stand, I surveyed the courtroom to see if there were any reporters there. But by this time, the press seemed to have lost interest in the October Surprise entirely, so there was only one—Bob Parry.

Even with my name cleared, I still struggled to get my career back on track. A year and a half later, I reluctantly caved into financial pressures, sold my Upper West Side co-op, yanked up stakes, and moved to Boston as the editor in chief of *Boston Magazine*. Over the following five years or so, I spent most of my time trying to revitalize a tired city magazine before moving on to writing books.

Although just about everyone else had largely forgotten the October Surprise, I never really put it aside completely. I kept in touch with Martin Kilian, Gary Sick, and various other October Surprise buffs who shared new developments in a dark corner of its history that America didn't want to acknowledge. In 1998, I trekked out to Michigan, the home of Don Albosta, a former Democratic congressman who investigated covert operations by the Republicans in the 1980 campaign. He gave me thousands of pages of files, which I stashed away for safekeeping. His report, whose full name was "Unauthorized Transfers of Nonpublic Information During the 1980 Presidential Election," was sometimes referred to as the Albosta Report, and it represented the first serious investigation of the Reagan-Bush campaign.

I also continued to reach out to many of the names in and around the case, seeing who might be willing to talk now that more time had passed, and quite frankly, people were dying off. Part of me wanted to get to as many people as I could before their stories disappeared forever. There had to be at least one guilty conscience out there who was willing to provide a deathbed confession.

By this point, I felt one of the central questions about the October Surprise had been settled. With regard to Casey's alleged presence in Madrid, I thought the preponderance of evidence was clear. When you combined Jamshid Hashemi's account with the Soviet report placing him in Madrid, and the State Department cable placing him in Madrid "for reasons unknown," to multiple other sources, I was convinced that Casey was there. And if Casey was in Madrid, then the October Surprise really did happen.

Yet there was a bigger question looming over everything. If the October Surprise happened, *how* did Bill Casey pull it off? This was the question I hoped to answer as clearly as I could.

For all the drawbacks of pursuing a trail gone cold with the passage of time, there were a few advantages as well. Because scrutiny of us was so intense back in 1991, we were always playing defense in our investigations, fending off challenges by Republicans and neoconservative operatives who were trying to knock down the story.

Over the years, however, some of our most persistent nemeses had fallen by the wayside. Among them was Steven Emerson, who had repeatedly attacked Parry, Sick, Kilian, me, and the October Surprise in *The New Republic*, the *Wall Street Journal*, CNN, *Nightline*, and elsewhere. In the years since, Emerson had been widely discredited by charges of plagiarism, fabrication of phony FBI files, and multiple reports in which he wrongly blamed Arab Americans or Muslims. According to the *New York Times*, Emerson's 1991 book *Terrorist* was "marred by factual errors . . . and by a pervasive anti-Arab and anti-Palestinian bias."[5] Similarly, his 1994 PBS video, *Jihad in America*, was criticized in *The Nation* for "creating mass hysteria against American Arabs."[6]

Emerson's errors were not merely a question of a few careless mistakes. There was a pattern. In 1995, Emerson wrongly identified Muslims as the perpetrators of the Oklahoma City bombings that killed 168 people and were committed by white supremacist Timothy McVeigh. In 2013, on C-SPAN, he incorrectly blamed the 2013 Boston Marathon bombings on a Middle East terrorist.[7] In 2015, he falsely asserted, on Fox News, that Birmingham, England, was "a totally Muslim city," after which British prime minister David Cameron said he "choked on his porridge" because Emerson was so "clearly an idiot."[8] Later, Emerson was named by the liberal Center for American

Progress as one of the top five Islamophobia propagandists in this country.[9]

Why the barrage of falsehoods? According to the *Jerusalem Post*, Emerson's fictional reports were the product of his "close ties to Israeli intelligence." Victor Ostrovsky, who defected from Mossad and has written books about Israeli intelligence, referred to Emerson as "the horn"—because he championed Mossad talking points.[10] Proving beyond a shadow of a doubt that he was an Israel asset would be impossible—Emerson wasn't talking—but it sure seemed to me as if we had been at least partially undone by an Israeli disinformation operation. With Emerson and company on the sidelines, it finally might be possible to tell the story as it should be told.

In addition, I could now safely ignore disinformation from the likes of Oswald LeWinter and others, and, instead, go back and pick facts—verified and verifiable facts!—from the House and the Senate investigations into the October Surprise, official investigations of Iran-Contra and BCCI, Parry's archives, FBI wiretap transcripts, and the hundreds of people I had interviewed in the United States, Israel, Iran, and France.

Now, it was possible to reconstruct Casey's network, to lay the stories from these disparate sources on top of one another like the anatomical transparencies in a medical textbook, to reveal a secret spy network that assaulted the body politic.

As soon as Casey took over the Reagan campaign, the tone changed—subtly, at first. The hostage issue was at the top of Casey's agenda, and he got to work on it behind the scenes.

Even though it was springtime in an election year, the magnitude of the Desert One catastrophe meant that President Carter had to devote his full efforts to the hostage crisis, at the expense of campaigning. But Carter's Rose Garden strategy also had the unintended consequence of isolating him and focusing America's attention on the failure of Desert One and our shared national humiliation.

On the surface, Casey's campaign operated well within the boundaries of acceptable political discourse. After expressing sympathy for those who died trying to rescue the hostages, Ronald Reagan, who was very much the GOP frontrunner but had not yet sewn up the nomination, waited a few days and then finally attacked President Carter's handling of the Iranian crisis as "a national disgrace."[11] He said this despite earlier having urged the administration to apply "extreme pressure" to Iran that might even have to "touch on a threat of force."[12]

"We support the president in seeking to save the hostages," Reagan said at a news conference while campaigning in Texas. "And we deeply regret that this mission failed. But as I have been saying for some time, specific action to bring the hostages home was long overdue."[13]

On occasion, when Carter had a press conference to update the American people on the hostage issue, as he did before the Wisconsin primary, Casey demanded that the Reagan campaign be given equal time under the FCC regulations* to counter what he saw as "an obvious partisan announcement."[14] It was the start of Casey's work to paint Carter as a president manipulating the hostage issue to his political advantage.

But the real action was behind the scenes. In April, not long after he became campaign manager, Casey put together a group of approximately sixty prominent foreign policy advisers from academia and various think tanks to provide guidance to the campaign on key foreign policy issues. This group was in turn divided into smaller working groups, one of which was called the October Surprise Group.[15]

---

* Until it was abolished in 1987, the Federal Communications Commission's "fairness doctrine" policy required the holders of broadcast licenses both to present controversial issues of public importance and to do so in a manner that fairly reflected differing viewpoints.

Unlike other subgroups on the foreign policy side of the campaign, the names of "advisers" participating in the October Surprise Group were unlisted.

Chaired by Richard V. Allen, Reagan's top foreign policy adviser and a close associate of Casey's, the October Surprise Group had been created to anticipate any eleventh-hour surprise Carter might pull (such as the release of the hostages), prepare appropriate responses, and inoculate the electorate against the emotional appeal of such an event by asserting repeatedly that Carter was planning the hostage release as a cynical political ploy. The group included among its members Richard Allen, Fred C. Ikle, Charles M. Kupperman, John R. Lehman Jr., Thomas H. Moore, Robert G. Neumann, Eugene V. Rostow, Laurence Silberman, William R. Van Cleave, and Seymour Weiss.[16]

As Parry reported on his website, that list made it into the task force report, but other, more sensitive information was omitted, including material noting how former CIA personnel who had worked with Bush's presidential campaign "became the nucleus of the Republican intelligence operation that monitored Carter's Iran-hostage negotiations for the Reagan-Bush team."[17]

When I asked Richard Allen about the October Surprise Group, he described what they did in more innocuous terms and recalled for me a discussion he had with Reagan strategist Dick Wirthlin about the hostage issue, warning that Carter could strike a last-minute deal with Iran.[18] "Wirthlin said, 'Well, we may be having a little surprise here in October.'

"And I said, 'That's it! It's the October Surprise. And we're going to now deploy that term in the campaign. I want *all* the senior people to use the words 'October surprise.'"

Allen saw it as an amusing meme that could be recycled throughout the campaign. "A good newsman would jump on it and say, 'What do you mean by that?' And I'd just shake my head or say you'll have to think about that yourself. It kept the mystery alive, which is exactly what I wanted to do. It turned out to be an enormously successful strategy, so I would say it in my interviews during the campaign of 1980."[19]

Shortly after Casey created the Reagan Campaign's October Surprise Group, Allen told me his team began to receive daily staff reports from Carter's National Security Council, reports that National Security Adviser Zbigniew Brzezinski later said were "extraordinarily sensitive," and that presumably came from disaffected staffers in the Carter administration.

But even Allen, a close friend of Casey's, was out of the loop when it came to the spymaster's darker machinations and was relegated to fending off dozens of over-the-transom volunteers. "We had tips coming in from all over the place about the release of the hostages," Allen told me.[20] "I know because I was sitting in the cockpit behind the wheel. There were countless self-starters who wanted to get involved."[21]

As for the rest of Casey's machinations, Allen didn't have a clue. "I had a very warm and deep relationship with him over many years until his death," Allen told me.[22] "But I can say that he was secretive. He didn't mess around. He had his own cutouts and private channels of communication which I didn't begrudge him. Everyone does, especially when you get to positions of high importance."

ORDINARILY, CAMPAIGN MANAGERS OF PRESIDENTIAL CANDIDATES do not spend their spare time overseeing clandestine networks, participating in secret meetings with rogue operatives all over the world, or making illegal arms deals with a hostile foreign power. But Casey did. And understanding his network—who was in it, how it came to be, and how it aided the October Surprise—was crucial to showing how the great spymaster pulled off one of the most extraordinary covert operations in American history.

To make this happen, Casey needed arms dealers who were willing to breach the American embargo against Iran and were able to do so without getting caught. He needed high-level officials in Iran and Israel who could assess Iran's military needs and coordinate them with Israeli arms supplies. He needed someone to arrange for highly secure meeting spaces somewhere in Europe. He needed weapons, and to ship the weapons, he needed cargo jets and ships and pilots and captains. Sophisticated as Casey was, he couldn't have done any of this alone.

Part of the mystery behind Casey and his network was that he had *never* been in the CIA prior to leading the agency for Reagan. In the thirty-five years since his glory days in the OSS, he had been a tax lawyer, written books, and had run both the SEC and the Export-Import Bank. Nevertheless, he had never really left the intelligence world. He was wired into Langley, but because he had never officially been with the Agency, there was no public record of exactly what he'd been doing all that time. Casey liked it that way. He worked off the books.

At almost every stage of his career, Casey had managed to discover new assets for his network that might become invaluable later, and one of the most vital was Alexandre de Marenches. Dating back to his OSS days, Casey had established a close friendship with de Marenches,[23] the director of the Service de Documentation Extérieure et de Contre-Espionnage (SDECE), the French counterpart of the CIA, which had been of enormous long-term value. After all, as de Marenches's coauthor, David Andelman, told the House task force, it was de Marenches, a ferocious Cold War hawk like Casey, who later set up and provided security for secret meetings in Paris in October 1980 between Republican operatives and emissaries from the new Iranian government.

But de Marenches's long-standing ties to Casey were not the only thing that made him of interest. Because de Marenches shared Casey's disgust at how the Pike Committee, the Church Committee, and CIA directors James Schlesinger* and Stansfield Turner had weakened American intelligence, the Frenchman also saw opportunity. De Marenches knew the CIA was so hamstrung that disgruntled operatives at the highest levels of the intelligence world had begun to ply their trade elsewhere. Hundreds of freelance operatives from all over the world—Israel, Iran, France, South Africa, and more—were ready, willing, and able to deliver payback to the Carter administration.

With all of these former spies available for off-the-books operations, de Marenches helped put together a covert alliance of intelligence services that became known as the Safari Club. In an exceptionally candid 2002 speech to fellow alumni at Georgetown University, Prince Turki bin Faisal Al Sa'ud, who succeeded his uncle Kamal Adham as the Saudi intelligence chief, explained that in 1976, "your intelligence community was literally tied up by Congress. It could not do anything. It could not send spies, it could not write reports, and it could not pay money. In order to compensate for that, a group of countries got together in the hopes of fighting Communism and established the Safari Club."[24]

The Safari Club's original members included Adham; Gen. Nematollah Nassiri, the head of Iran's brutal intelligence service, SAVAK, under the Shah; their counterparts in Egypt, Morocco, and more. The CIA was represented by Ted Shackley, a former Bush protégé from its Directorate of Operations. Similarly, Miles Copeland Jr., another fabled ex-CIA officer, referred to the Safari Club as his "private CIA."[25] Copeland was notable because he had been a key operative in Operation Ajax in 1953.

The group took its name from a luxurious resort in Nairobi, Kenya, owned by billionaire Saudi arms dealer Adnan Khashoggi, where they first met in 1976. Its purpose was to share information and

---

* Stansfield Turner eliminated the jobs of hundreds of operatives at Langley, but during his six months as DCI under Richard Nixon, James Schlesinger, who was known as Nixon's axe man, earned more than his share of enmity at Langley when he reduced staff by 7 percent in what became known as the Schlesinger Purge.

to counter Soviet influence. As a result, when purged CIA officers or other rogue covert operatives needed financing for their clandestine ventures, they went to then-Saudi intelligence chief Kamal Adham and his nephew, Prince Turki, who served as his deputy. Adham was also a major shareholder in the BCCI, which in addition to becoming the notorious bank of choice for drug cartels and arms dealers, was also funding covert, off-the-books CIA operations in 1976 while Bush was the head of the CIA.[26]

The Safari Club was not the only source of operatives for Casey. In the sixties, Casey's close associate John Shaheen had taken on energy consultant Roy Furmark as an associate. As Furmark's son, Erik, told me, his father in turn had[27] developed close long-term working relationships with Adnan Khashoggi, who was known as AK in the Furmark household, and other arms dealers.[28] At times, he served as a trusted intermediary for Casey himself.[29] Furmark would also end up working in Cyrus Hashemi's London office. Meanwhile during the Nixon administration, as a State Department official and as head of the Export-Import Bank of the United States, Casey had developed a friendship with Jack Shaw, a former State Department official who had expertise in the intelligence world and could be another cutout for Casey.[30] At the Export-Import Bank, Casey had also okayed loans enabling the Shah to spend billions of dollars buying American arms. As a result, Casey had far more than a passing interest in Iran. He was wired. He knew the players—arms dealers, arms procurement officers, and fixers, as well as the Shah's operatives who had stayed behind in Iran.

Another man Casey turned to was Robert Sensi, who had first met Casey in the seventies, when he worked as a sales manager for Bahrain's Gulf Air and later Kuwait Airways.[31] When Casey became DCI in 1981, Sensi worked for him in the CIA, and was later convicted of stealing more than $2.5 million from Kuwait Airlines and sentenced to six months in jail.[32] (He maintained that he had been authorized to spend the money by a member of the Kuwaiti royal family, who was a top official at the airline.)[33]

According to Larry Kolb's book *America at Night*, Sensi had developed a reputation among diplomats and Arab VIPs as a fixer who was "adept at solving problems with the INS, customs, local police, just the guy to arrange theater tickets and private shopping tours for wives or to discreetly procure prostitutes or about anything else for their husbands once the wives were out on the town."[34]

All in all, Sensi was exactly the kind of guy Bill Casey was likely to tap. He spoke passable Arabic and Farsi—enough at least to navigate the world of intelligence in those cultures. And, most important, he knew the right people in Iran. "It just kind of evolved," Sensi told me.[35] "I had met a lot of Iranians during the time of the Shah. I knew a lot of people in his inner circle."

According to Sensi, Casey rigorously observed the best practices of intelligence tradecraft. When it came to serious discussions about operations, "Casey never spoke on the phone," said Sensi.[36] "Casey kept everything very compartmentalized. He never wanted the left hand to know what the right was doing."

Sensi had found his way into Casey's orbit by way of Robert B. Carter, the convention manager for the Republican National Convention in Detroit who functioned as a low-profile deputy of sorts to Casey. He was also a close friend of Sensi and provided the introduction with Casey. "[Carter] connected me to Casey, and then I connected Casey to Iranians," said Sensi.[37] "He always maintained a very close personal friendship with Casey, and he was with him all the time. *All* the time. He traveled with Casey. He was with him in Washington a lot. Bob Carter was very close to him. He was one of the closest people to Casey."

It was not lost on me that Sensi and Bob Carter were completely ignored in both the House and Senate investigations.* The inescapable conclusion was that neither legislative body had bothered to

---

* Sensi was not mentioned in either report. As for Robert Carter, he was cited in the Senate investigation as a deputy of Casey's who "had no knowledge that Casey traveled to Europe during the 1980 race and doubted the campaign director had the time to do so."

scrutinize Casey's private network of arms dealers and intelligence operatives. They were largely in the dark about the fact that, even before he joined the Reagan campaign, Casey had a nascent intelligence operation that, when activated, could become extraordinarily powerful.

Of all these connections, the single most important relationship in that network was Casey's enduring friendship with John Shaheen. Shaheen was conspicuous by his relative absence in two of the most significant books about the former CIA director: *Casey*, the biography by Joseph Persico, and *Veil* by Bob Woodward. But, according to Richard Manning, a close friend and former attorney of Shaheen's, Shaheen was Casey's principal collaborator in the October Surprise.

"They were great patriots, the last of the macho OSS guys," Manning told me in 1992.[38] "John loved that spy stuff so much that I have no doubt he knew damn near everything Bill Casey knew. Casey was his very close friend. John was the guy who could do stuff behind the scenes. He was part of the network. I was in Paris with John in the summer of 1980, at the Plaza Athenée, and it would surprise the hell out of me if he didn't stay up all night long calling all over the world."

What Manning told me flew in the face of the conclusions of the House October Surprise Task Force, which dismissed out of hand the notion that Casey used John Shaheen as an intermediary to work with Cyrus Hashemi. "At no time did Cyrus indicate to [Elliot] Richardson that Cyrus had prior contact with Casey," the task force reported.[39] "Conversely, at no time did Casey, in his conversations with Richardson, indicate that he had prior contact with Cyrus."

As if Casey, Cyrus Hashemi, and Shaheen—virtuosos in the world of espionage—would give the game away so easily.

In fact, Manning was not the only source who saw Shaheen as Casey's key operative. Among others, Jamshid Hashemi, Elliot Richardson, and Shaheen himself all attested to the importance of the relationship between the two men. "What I know is what he [Cyrus] has told me, that for many years he's been cooperating with Mr. Shaheen," said Jamshid, in a videotaped interview with Parry.[40] "That was in the end of 1979. He was very open about it. . . . They were as best possible friends as anybody could be."

PERHAPS NOTHING UNDERSCORED THE LONG-STANDING RELATIONSHIP between Cyrus and Shaheen quite as clearly as Shaheen's oil refinery up in Newfoundland.

Like Casey, Shaheen was very much wired into the powers that be. Having grown up in Tampico, Illinois, as a boyhood friend of Ronald Reagan,[41] he became close to Richard Nixon, who served as his lawyer and later appointed him ambassador to Colombia. After the war, Shaheen first made a fortune by starting a company that sold life insurance through vending machines in airports all over the country[42] and selling it to Mutual of Omaha.[43] Then, as president of Macmillan Ring-Free Oil, he had put together a mini-empire valued as high as $250 million as a maverick oil producer in the early seventies.[44]

Another of his companies, Shaheen Natural Resources Company, armed with legal counsel provided by Casey and his law firm, Rogers & Wells, spent years pursuing an eccentric and ambitious project in a tiny coastal hamlet in Newfoundland. By any standards, it was an unusual business proposition, involving as it did the construction of an enormous crude oil refinery at a remote Canadian settlement known as Come By Chance, population less than 250, on the southern coast of Newfoundland's Placentia Bay.

Shaheen first appeared on the Newfoundland scene in 1960 at a time when its prime minister was Joey Smallwood, a famously gullible

On November 4, 1979, thirteen days after the United States admitted the exiled Shah to America, hundreds of Iranian students seized the American embassy and detained fifty-two Americans as hostages for 444 days. The hostage crisis had begun.
Historic Collection/Alamy

On the first day of the crisis, militant students blindfolded the hostages in a humiliating spectacle in which the United States came to be characterized as a pitiful helpless giant.
Bettman/Getty Images

In 1953, Mohammad Mossadegh, the democratically elected prime minister of Iran, shown here in a 1951 rally, was deposed in a CIA-planned coup d'état after he vowed to nationalize Iran's oil industry.
AP Photo

The CIA's Kermit "Kim" Roosevelt Jr. and his associates used the US embassy in Tehran to plan Operation Ajax, the 1953 coup that overthrew Mossadegh and installed the Shah's brutal regime. Subsequently, the embassy was known as a "den of spies" among anti-Shah activists. AP Photo

Exile's return: In early 1979, not long after the Shah fled Tehran, the Ayatollah Ruhollah Khomeini, a powerful cleric who had been living in exile, prepared to return to Iran from his temporary home in Neauphle-le-Chateau, France.
Sergio Gaudenti/Getty Images

Henry Kissinger (*left*), a close friend of Shah Reza Pahlavi (*right*), joined members of the so-called Rockefeller Group in lobbying President Jimmy Carter to admit the Shah to the United States rather than make him search for refuge.

Keystone Press/Alamy

President Carter and the Shah in the Oval Office, about two years before the Iranian Revolution. Admitting the Shah to the United States for medical treatment ignited the hostage crisis, and quickly proved to be Carter's worst mistake as president.

Everett Collection Historical/Alamy

Iranian president Abolhassan Bani-Sadr, at the podium in November 1979, had a long-term relationship with Ayatollah Khomeini, who initially supported his presidency. But before long, Khomeini betrayed the man he had once thought of as a son.

Arnaud de Wildenberg/Getty Images

Gary Sick (*right*) served as the Iran specialist on President Carter's National Security Council during the hostage crisis. Eleven years later, after he began to unravel the October Surprise, he said, "You take events you know very well and strip off a layer and suddenly there is a whole different world." AP Photo

Operation Eagle Claw: On April 24, 1980, the catastrophic attempt to rescue the hostages in Iran left eight American servicemen dead. Rolls Press/Getty Images

Bill Casey: Part James Bond, part Mr. Magoo. Even before the hostage crisis, master spy Casey had assembled a secret intelligence network that included arms dealers, Israeli intelligence operatives, corrupt bankers, and a host of operatives to set up secret meetings and oversee illegal arms shipments. The Carter administration didn't have a clue.
Alon Reininger/Contact Press Images

The cutout: Oilman John Shaheen's close friendship with Casey dated back to their heyday in the Office of Strategic Services (OSS). As the intermediary with arms dealer Cyrus Hashemi and other operatives, Shaheen was Casey's chief go-between during the October Surprise.
AP Photo

Even before Cyrus Hashemi (*left*) approached the Carter administration to help negotiate the release of the hostages, he was a double agent who had been secretly working with Casey's pal John Shaheen. Cyrus's brother, Jamshid Hashemi (*right*), joined him in orchestrating arms sales to Iran.

Casey's man in Aman: Yehoshua Saguy, the director of Israeli Military Intelligence, confirmed that Ari Ben-Menashe worked for his unit. Saguy communicated regularly with Bill Casey in 1979 and 1980, even though Casey was not in the US government.
SA'AR YA'ACOV/
National Photo Collection of Israel

Rogue Israeli intelligence operative Ari Ben-Menashe confounded journalists and congressional investigators alike with his often-dubious tales of intrigue. In the end, however, he offered a window into illicit arms sales to Iran.
Ben Rushton/
Getty Images

Elliot Richardson, one of the only heroes of Watergate, helped sound the alarm about the October Surprise. "If it happened, it was despicable," he said. "Compared to the October Surprise, Watergate was an innocent child's frolic."
Janet Fries/Getty Images

No reporter did more to get to the bottom of the October Surprise than Bob Parry, whose discovery of Congress's discarded files revealed the House investigation to be little more than a whitewash.
Diane Duston

Rep. Lee Hamilton (D-IN) led the House task force investigating the October Surprise that produced the final report (*right*). Hamilton's leadership resulted in many probative documents being discarded. They were missing until Bob Parry found them in an abandoned ladies' room in a subbasement of the Rayburn House Office Building.
Maureen Keating/CQ Roll Call/AP Photo

on Calendar No. 634 102d Congress, 2d Session H. Rept. No. 102–1102

United States House of Representatives
102d Congress, 2d Session

JOINT REPORT
OF THE
TASK FORCE TO INVESTIGATE CERTAIN ALLEGATIONS CONCERNING THE HOLDING OF AMERICAN HOSTAGES BY IRAN IN 1980
("October Surprise Task Force")

Lee H. Hamilton, Chairman
Henry J. Hyde, Ranking Republican Member

January 3, 1993—Committed to the Committee of the Whole House on the State of the Union, and ordered to be printed

Washington, DC

After Congress cracked down on the CIA with the Church Committee and the Pike Committee, French spy chief Alexandre de Marenches, an old pal of Casey's, helped put together a covert alliance of intelligence services that became known as the Safari Club. It was named after the Mount Kenya Safari Club in Kenya. Lion/Alamy

De Marenches (*right*) also helped set up meetings in Paris to finalize terms for the October Surprise. Later, in 1983, he met with President Ronald Reagan in the White House. Eraza Collection/Alamy

In the summer of 1980, Ben Barnes (*left*) and John Connally (*center*) met with Egyptian president Anwar Sadat as part of Connally's effort to delay the release of the hostages on behalf of Casey. Courtesy Ben Barnes

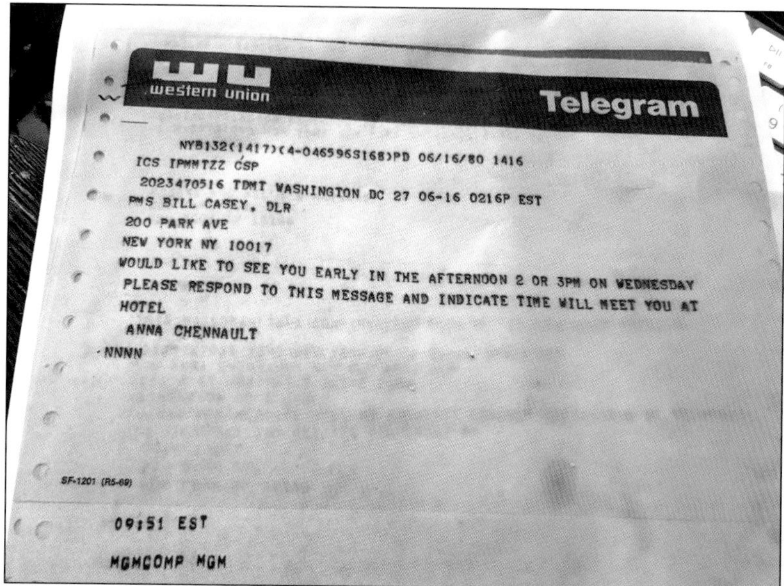

western union

Telegram

NYB132(1417)(4-046596S168)PD 06/16/80 1416
ICS IPMMTZZ CSP
2023470516 TDMT WASHINGTON DC 27 06-16 0216P EST
PMS BILL CASEY, DLR
200 PARK AVE
NEW YORK NY 10017
WOULD LIKE TO SEE YOU EARLY IN THE AFTERNOON 2 OR 3PM ON WEDNESDAY
PLEASE RESPOND TO THIS MESSAGE AND INDICATE TIME WILL MEET YOU AT
HOTEL
ANNA CHENNAULT
NNNN

SF-1201 (R5-69)

09:51 EST

MGMCOMP MGM

In June 1980, Casey set up a secret meeting with Republican lobbyist Anna Chennault, who had helped the Nixon campaign sabotage Lyndon Johnson's attempt to end the Vietnam War via peace talks in Paris. By hijacking American foreign policy just before the 1968 election, Chennault's operation prefigured the October Surprise. William J. Casey Archives, Hoover Institute, Stanford University

Casey's counterpart in the October Surprise negotiations in Madrid in late July was Mehdi Karroubi, a powerful Shi'ite cleric who was negotiating for Khomeini.
Atta Kenare/Getty Images

Robert Sensi, one of Casey's fixers, said that in August 1980, he helped set up a second set of meetings for Casey in Madrid. When asked if the October Surprise happened, Sensi replied, "Absolutely."
Courtesy of Robert Sensi.

The odd couple: Both men served as directors of the CIA, but Bill Casey and George H. W. Bush were cut from very different cloths. Casey, a Fordham grad whose father was a Tammany Hall bureaucrat, was a master spy, going in a million compartmentalized directions at once. Bush, a patrician Yalie, made sure any role he might have played was shrouded in secrecy. This photo was taken in February 1981, shortly after Bush took office as vice president and Casey became director of the CIA. Ronald Reagan Presidential Library

The Carter administration's most promising outreach to resolve the hostage crisis was through Palestine Liberation Organization (PLO) leader Yasser Arafat, shown here in 1979 with Khomeini (*above*). Casey operative Jack Shaw (*left*), whose ties to the spymaster dated back to the Nixon administration, served as yet another cutout and intervened in an attempt to disrupt President Carter's overture to Arafat.

History and Art Collection/Alamy (*above*); courtesy of the Gerald R. Ford Presidential Library (*left*)

	Monday 28 July				Tuesday 29 July				Wednesday 30 July			
Name	I Opening	II China	Lunch	III Russia	IV Secret Operations	V Roosevelt & Churchill	Lunch	VI Italian Campaign	VII Ultra	VIII Relations with the French	Lunch	IX Science
Barnett	✗	✗	✗	✗	✓	✗	✗	✗	✓	✗	✗	✗
Blumenson	✓	✓	✓	✓	✓	✓	✓	✓	✓	✓		✓
J. Casey	✓	✓	✓	✗ Came at 4pm	✓	✓	✓	✓	✗	✗	✗	✗
Crowl	✓	✗	✓	✓	✗	✗	✗	✗	✗	✗		✗
Ballek	✓	✓	✓	✓	✓	✓	✓	✓	✗ ✓	✓	✓	✓
C. de Bussy	✗	✗	✗	✗	✗	✗	✗	✗	✗	✗	✗	✗
Deutsch	✓	✓	✓	✓	✓	✓	✓	✓	✓	✓		✓
Funk	✓	✓	✓	✓	✓	✓	✓	✓	✓	✓		✓
L. Gaddis	✓	✓	✓	✓	✓	✓	✓	✓	✓	✓	✓	✓
Daniel Kevles	✗	✗	✗	✗	✗	✗	✗	✗	✗	✗	✗	✗
Kimball	✓	✓	✓	✓	✓	✓	✓	✓	✓	✓		✓
Maurice Matloff	✓	✓	✓	✓	✓	✓	✓	✓	✓	✓		✗

The alibi that fell apart: Here's the controversial chart that *Newsweek* and *The New Republic* used to falsely discredit the October Surprise by showing, supposedly, that Casey could not have been in Madrid. Jonathan Chadwick took attendance at the infamous OSS reunion in London in July. Note the light pencil marks next to Casey's name—indicating he was expected to attend—as opposed to ink marks. Also see the notation: "Came at 4 pm."

The author with former Iranian president Abolhassan Bani-Sadr in Versailles in 2016. When asked if he thought the October Surprise was still important, even after so many years, Bani-Sadr said, "You have to write it. If not, it will happen again." Craig Unger

In a 2014 interview with the author in Tehran, Mohsen Rafighdoost, a founder of the Islamic Revolutionary Guard Corps (IRGC), denied that the October Surprise took place and said Iran would never have traded arms with Israel. However, one Iranian source said that Rafighdoost, who reportedly had a key role in arms procurement at the time, accompanied one of the arms shipments to Iran that was a payoff for the October Surprise. Craig Unger

Betrayal: Bani-Sadr, shown here with Khomeini in February 1980, had been the Ayatollah's choice for the presidency and had expected Iran would become a secular democracy. But before long, he said, Khomeini became addicted to power and turned Iran into an Islamist theocracy. Historic Collection/Alamy

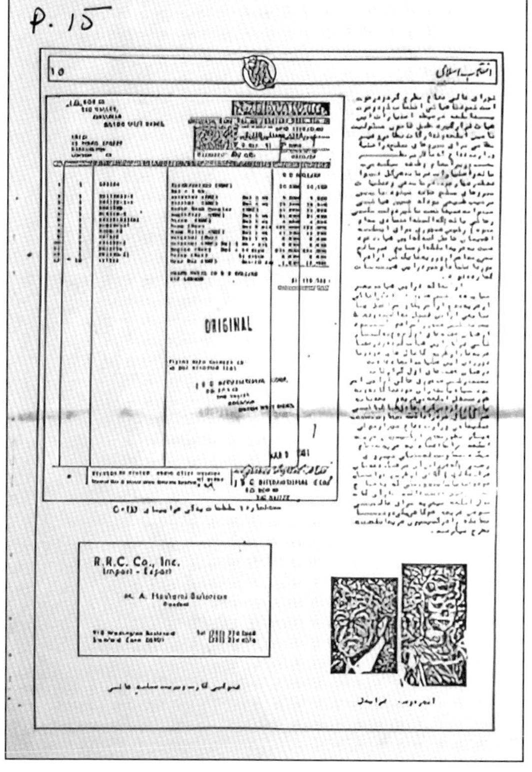

P. 15

۱۵ انقلاب اسلامی

ORIGINAL

R.R.C. Co., Inc.
Import - Export

The receipts: Never-before-published invoices discarded by the House task force and rescued by Bob Parry show sales of weapons from Mohammad Ali Hashemi-Balanian—aka Jamshid Hashemi—to Iran. According to Gary Sick, the arms shipments are "definitively" tied to "one of the arms dealers who was 'playing both sides' in Casey's plan." Parry Archive

On October 4, 1980, a month before the election, Bush and Reagan confer after being briefed on the Iran-Iraq war by CIA Director Stansfield Turner.
Bettman/Getty Images

Reagan surged ahead after the one and only presidential debate between him and Carter, on October 28. Later, it was revealed that Carter's debate preparation papers had been stolen by the Republicans. The perpetrator? According to James Baker, it was Bill Casey.
AP Photo

Even as Reagan took the oath of office on January 20, 1980, the hostages were still in Iran. Moments later, they were released. *The Onion* later lampooned the coincidence as one of the great events of the twentieth century: "Hostages Released; Reagan Urges American People Not to Put Two and Two Together." Reagan Presidential Library

Unidentified hostages arrive at Rhein-Main Air Base in Frankfurt, West Germany, after their release from Iran. AP Photo

While Carter retired to Plains, Georgia, Reagan, here with former hostage Bruce Laingen, basked in the glory of the hostages' return. AP Photo

With Reagan as president, Casey was finally officially in charge of the nation's intelligence apparatus. Here, in 1982, he is accompanied by Reagan waving to CIA employees after signing a bill protecting the identity of CIA agents. Bettman/Getty Images

On January 30, the hostages' return was celebrated in a ticker-tape parade in New York that marked Reagan's "new morning in America." Although it was founded on a treasonous conspiracy, the Reagan-Bush victory gave birth to a new era of conservatism.
Dennis Brack/Alamy

politician who was prepared to back virtually every economic and industrial development in Newfoundland, feasible or not, no matter the cost. In the 1960s, entrepreneurs looking for a handout flocked to Smallwood in droves. John Shaheen was at the front of the line.[45]

As John C. Crosbie, a minister in Smallwood's administration, put it in his memoir *No Holds Barred: My Life in Politics*, "Smallwood was like Play-Doh in the hands of Shaheen."[46] Obsequious to a fault, Smallwood essentially gave away the store to Shaheen in the form of an agreement to finance his refinery that was "completely one-sided" and of "little economic benefit" to Newfoundland.[47]

In 1973, Shaheen opened the refinery to great fanfare by having the *Queen Elizabeth II* ocean liner sail into Come By Chance harbor with 1,000 dignitaries on board enjoying an extravagant party in the tiny village by the sea.[48] Three years later, it became one of the largest bankruptcies in Canadian history, leaving some $500 million in debts.[49] John Shaheen was at the helm of an enterprise that by every measure was a monumental failure.

When conventional sources of credit dried up, the Senate report noted, "Shaheen turned to Cyrus Hashemi, then a London and New York banker, for high interest loans to re-finance the project."[50] The relationship between the two men, and the fact that it predated the hostage crisis, I believed, was a crucial part of the October Surprise.

In the end, there were many unanswered questions about Shaheen's refinery and the complex litigation surrounding it. Over the years, Shaheen kept trying to bring the refinery back to life and went to Casey for advice on it, Manning told me.[51] At various times billionaire dictators, exiled Iranian royalty, and corrupt banks circled around the Come By Chance refinery.

Now, with the Iran hostage crisis and the subsequent embargo on Iranian oil, Come By Chance faced even greater challenges, but Shaheen still wanted to revive it—even during the hostage crisis. According to Manning, none of it made sense. "I didn't think John had the money," he told me.[52] "I *knew* the oil refinery could never be resurrected. It *couldn't* make money." Even if Shaheen put together some temporary solution, he said, it would fail before long.

Before I left my interview with Manning—this was back in 1992—he gave me a 3.5-inch floppy disk in a hard, blue plastic shell that was loaded with files full of lawsuits and countersuits and depositions regarding the Come By Chance refinery.

Most strikingly, the documents, backed up by Jamshid, revealed something of the scope of Shaheen's business relationship with Cyrus. "For many years, he [Cyrus] had been cooperating with Mr. Shaheen," Jamshid said in a videotaped interview with Parry.[53] "He was very open about it. On the few occasions I was present with Shaheen speaking to my brother, it seemed they knew each other very well. They had shared business and political interests in Lebanon, and my brother was helping Shaheen with a refinery in Canada."[54]

That was no small matter. When I first started on the October Surprise, a widespread assumption was that Casey's operation started *after* he took over the Reagan campaign in early March 1980. If that were the case, Casey would have had to transform a complete stranger into a double agent overnight.

But the reality was that Cyrus Hashemi wasn't a stranger at all. At a minimum Shaheen knew him quite well, had done business with him, and kept Casey very much in the loop. The implications of this were huge. It meant that in November 1979, when Cyrus first approached the Carter State Department to help resolve the hostage crisis, he was already wired into Casey's network.

In other words, Hashemi had been a mole all along.

This was William Casey's and John Shaheen's dominion and it had all been assembled before the hostage crisis had even begun. "[Casey and Shaheen] had networks all over the world," Manning told me. "I believe they honestly wanted the hostages home as soon as possible. But they hated Jimmy Carter. The Iranians hated Jimmy Carter. The Israelis hated Jimmy Carter. And there was no way the hostages could be returned while Jimmy Carter was president."[55]

Chapter Eleven Double Agents

THE EVIDENCE THAT SHAHEEN'S TIES TO CYRUS PREDATED the hostage crisis was a game changer. It was at the heart of everything—both the task force's failure to do a serious investigation and the October Surprise itself. When I reviewed the task force report, it was staring them in the face and they refused to see it.

I went back to Elliot Richardson's interview with Parry and listened again. "It's quite clear that Hashemi was a person capable of playing more than one role simultaneously and seeming quite convincing to his audience, whatever it was," Richardson said. "What I know now is certainly not wholly inconsistent with the possibility that he could have been playing a double or triple game."[1]

And since that was the case, John Shaheen must have been the cutout, the middleman. It was all starting to make sense. For Casey to be in direct contact with Cyrus would have been laughably poor tradecraft. But Shaheen, a fellow OSS veteran, had been his pal for years. And, as Jamshid said, he had known and worked with Cyrus for years. Using a cutout was basic Tradecraft 101, but somehow the task force didn't take it as a serious possibility—even when it was investigating a master spy like Casey.

In any case, the fact that Cyrus Hashemi had worked with Shaheen before the hostage crisis was fundamental to Casey's entire operation and that meant it was essential to put all of Cyrus's efforts under the microscope. Since Cyrus was part of the Carter administration's secret back-channel discussions with Iran, one had to ask if he was sharing Carter's secrets with Casey. Was he simply stringing Carter along in a bid to help Casey? Or was he trying to play off two potential sellers—the Carter administration and the Republicans—in an effort to get the best deal.

During the first two months of the hostage crisis, Cyrus appeared to diligently court militant clerics and moderates alike, on behalf of the Carter administration, in search of an Iranian partner to help resolve the hostage crisis. Before long, he had established his bona fides by showing he had access to highly placed officials in the new Khomeini regime and that he had a grasp of the still-evolving calculus at work in the newly created Islamic Republic of Iran.[2]

On December 3, 1979, Cyrus had met in New York with former attorney general Ramsey Clark, who had briefly tried to intervene with Iran on behalf of Carter. According to FBI documents, he gave the impression of being "akin to a moderate/liberal Democrat who was unimpressed with Republicans . . . He believed the hostage situation was damaging to Iran."[3]

A report of the meeting was forwarded to Deputy Secretary of State Warren Christopher, including a more detailed summary of what would be needed to win the release of the hostages.

Then, on January 2, 1980, nearly two months into the crisis, Harold Saunders, Carter's assistant secretary of state for Near East Affairs, met in New York with Cyrus Hashemi. Also present were Cyrus's attorney, Stanley Pottinger, and Cyrus's brother, Jamshid Hashemi.[4] Jamshid agreed to attempt to set up a meeting between representatives of the State Department and one of Khomeini's relatives they knew, namely, the Supreme Leader's nephew, Reza Pasandideh.[5]

In the State Department, Hal Saunders was not terribly sanguine about reaching out to Pasandideh, but he still thought it was worth a shot.[6] Cyrus got things underway by having Pasandideh's father, Ayatollah Morteza Pasandideh, ask Ayatollah Khomeini, his brother, for his blessing on this overture.[7] Then, it was just a matter of waiting.

Behind the scenes, the dynamic between the brothers created an additional layer of tension. Cyrus discreetly indulged himself with high-stakes gambling and high-priced escorts but kept the dark side of his life well hidden from view, presenting himself as a sophisticated professional without giving the game away. Jamshid was more down-to-earth, "talkative, good-natured, friendly, and full of shit, but in an inoffensive way," as one associate put it, in an off-the-record conversation.

After Jamshid left the room, Cyrus was known to roll his eyes and remark that he loved his sibling—in fact, they were stepbrothers[8]—but he could never tell if Jamshid really knew what he was talking about. Jamshid also had a secret life and was known to work under various pseudonyms,* but in the United States, he watched Cyrus take charge, listened, and generally did as he was told. In the end, Cyrus didn't fully trust Jamshid, but that didn't stop the two brothers from doing business together.

Now that he was watching his brother in action in the US for the first time, Jamshid saw that John Shaheen had long played an important role in Cyrus's life. To Jamshid, Shaheen had a certain mystique.[9] He could navigate the corridors of power at Langley and introduce Jamshid as someone who could help solve the hostage crisis or establish a dialog with Khomeini.[10] But any misgivings Jamshid had about Shaheen vanished when the maverick oilman obtained a visa for Jamshid on a moment's notice. "In those days, for an Iranian to get a visa in a matter of hours, it would have been a miracle," he told Parry.[11] Shaheen had done it instantly.

But the hostage issue wasn't the only reason the Carter administration was meeting with the Hashemis. The new revolutionary government in Iran was putting together its first presidential election, and the Hashemi brothers were backing Iran's minister of defense,

* Jamshid Hashemi used a number of aliases, among them Mohammed Ali Balanian, Mohamed Balanian, Mario Cabrini, Abdula Hashemi, Abdullah Hashemi, Mohammed Ali Hashemi, Jamshid Khalaj, James Khan, and Jamshid H. Naini.

Adm. Ahmed Madani, as a relatively moderate, pro-West candidate for president. "When I came to this country, I had actually come for the purpose of getting funds for Madani's campaign to become the president of the country," said Jamshid.[12] "Now, Cyrus told me, the American government wanted to talk to me before I go back." That meant that the CIA was interested in Madani, and they needed to talk to the Hashemis.

So, according to the House task force, on January 5, 1980, the Hashemis had another meeting with US government officials, this time in London.[13] Cyrus Hashemi was there as himself, but the other two people said to be at the meeting were not who they claimed to be. Jamshid introduced himself as Mohammad Ali Balanian, one of his many aliases.[14] The third man went by the name of Charles Kalligan and was introduced as someone who worked for the "White House Coordinating Committee."[15] But Kalligan was really the cover name for Charles Cogan, chief of the Near East and South Asia division of the CIA's Directorate of Operations.

The purpose of the meeting was to discuss the so-called second prong of the Carter administration's relationship with the Hashemis.[16] At the time, Madani supported the release of the hostages and he appeared to be a viable presidential candidate for the upcoming elections later in January. Internal CIA documents touted Madani as "one of the most prominent, and, potentially, effective of the Iranians opposing the dominant clerical leadership,"[17] and the CIA hoped that when the dust settled from the Revolution they could have a friendly face in Iran's presidency. Finally, Cyrus promised the CIA that if Pasandideh's mediation didn't work and if Madani were not elected president, Madani would lead a military operation to release the hostages.[18]

Consequently, the Agency eventually gave $500,000 total in cash (about $2 million in 2024 dollars) to the Hashemis in support of Madani's campaign.[19] Just weeks after he first reached out to the Carter administration, Cyrus Hashemi had created one of the most important channels between Washington and the new government taking shape in Tehran.

Still, that didn't mean that the administration took everything he said at face value. Even in its earliest dealings with Cyrus, the State Department's Iran Working Group expressed "a shadow of suspicion that [Hashemi was] serving his own personal interests."[20]

And, sure enough, by late February, the CIA discovered that only a small portion of its money had gone to the Madani campaign. Most of it was eventually returned, but CIA officials concluded that Jamshid was, according to the House task force report, a "trafficker in intelligence to whomever would buy it," and "dishonest and untrustworthy beyond belief."[21] On January 25, Madani had lost the presidential race to Abolhassan Bani-Sadr, so he had no clout whatsoever. So the CIA realized its Hashemi gambit was a bust, and terminated contact with the Hashemis because they were not "proving able to achieve the accomplishment of hostage release."[22]

The Carter administration was making no progress. "We seem to be negotiating primarily with ourselves," Sick wrote in a memo to Brzezinski.[23] "People go to Tehran, listen to various officials who speak only for themselves, then come back, and ask us to meet hypothetical demands with absolutely nothing coming from the other side."

Consequently, even though the CIA had dropped the Hashemis, the State Department continued the relationship in the hope that they could reel in Reza Pasandideh and produce some kind of breakthrough.

Yet, nothing happened. Day after day. Carter's approval rating sank, from 58 percent at the end of January, when America rallied around a president desperately trying to bring our boys home, to 43 percent in mid-March, and to 39 percent by the end of the month.[24] Clearly, the return of the hostages was crucial to Carter's reelection, but it seemed like there was nothing they could do.

By March, Casey, freshly installed as campaign manager for the Reagan campaign, sprang into action. At the time,

Jamshid Hashemi was still in Washington, staying at the Mayflower Hotel, about half a mile from the White House. As he explained in the videotaped interview with Parry, on March 21, Jamshid was in his hotel room when two men knocked at the door. He was not expecting a visitor but when he opened the door, Jamshid said, "Mr. Casey came in, and he wanted to talk to me."[25] The two men had never met before, and Jamshid had no idea who Casey was.

Casey was reportedly accompanied by his associate, Roy Furmark, the energy consultant, who had worked with Shaheen and Casey for years and had also worked in Cyrus's London office. He had helped Shaheen on the Newfoundland oil refinery and he often acted as a go-between with high-level arms dealers, including Saudi billionaire Adnan Khashoggi.[26]

Casey, rumpled as usual, started to talk about politics, but Jamshid cut him short.

"I don't know who you are," he said.[27]

Then, Jamshid called his brother Cyrus, who explained that Casey "was an important figure in Republican politics, and that contact with Casey could prove worthwhile."[28]

Jamshid passed the phone to Casey. He spoke briefly with Cyrus, then said goodbye to Jamshid, and left.

Jamshid's first contact with the fabled spymaster had lasted just a few minutes, and it raised one very serious question. The Hashemis had been working with the Carter State Department for months to bring home the hostages, so what the hell was Cyrus doing with Ronald Reagan's campaign manager?

Later that day, according to the Senate report, Jamshid said he traveled to Cyrus's home in Wilton, Connecticut, to celebrate Now Ruz, the Persian new year.[29] When he got a private moment with his brother, he finally confronted Cyrus.

"We are now here trying to release the hostages from one side and trying to do something, whatever in our little capacity we could do," Jamshid said, according to his deposition. "And you're talking to the Republicans. How come?"[30]

"We shouldn't put all our eggs in one basket," Cyrus replied. "You don't understand American politics. I've been longer here and I know how to deal with the people and never mind. Don't bother about these things."

He finally explained that if Republicans won the next presidential election, it would be useful to have ties to Casey and John Shaheen. Later, Cyrus told Jamshid that "it had been the wish of Mr. Casey to meet with somebody from Iran."[31]

Shortly afterward, it became clear precisely what that meant, and Jamshid began getting directives to arrange meetings in Europe for Casey—not Carter.[32] "That's when I started getting on this work of inviting both Mehdi [Karroubi] . . . and Hassan . . . to come indirectly to Madrid," Jamshid told Parry. "I contacted them by telephone from here [London]. We had scramblers. He [Hassan] had a scrambler and I had a scrambler. Other times I used to fly to different cities in Europe [to contact him]."[33]

The next time Jamshid saw Bill Casey was several months later—in Madrid.

Chapter Twelve
Eagle Claw

As April began, nothing was panning out for the Carter administration. Cyrus Hashemi's efforts to set up meetings with Reza Pasandideh had not come to fruition. In the end, the Hashemis had done nothing for Carter but waste time, which added to the mounting sense of desperation. Carter had cultivated a congenial discourse[1] via back channels with President Bani-Sadr, but that was of no value whatsoever because Khomeini delegated the task of resolving the hostage crisis to the Majlis, the Iranian parliament, a body that would not even be seated until a second round of voting in May. Bani-Sadr had such a fragile hold on power that he was in no position to deliver the hostages.

Doing nothing was increasingly untenable. With oil and arms embargos already in place, on March 19, Gary Sick had proposed setting a deadline of April 15 after which, if a settlement had not been arranged, the United States would "take unilateral action to disrupt Iran's economy" via a blockade implemented by "mining the key ports of entry" in the Persian Gulf.[2] But even that was not certain to yield a positive result and risked damaging US relations with other Gulf states. As a result, Sick said, "We should use the intervening time before the deadline to get in place the elements of the best rescue operation we can mount. This could be needed as a fallback if the Iranians begin threatening the lives of the hostages as bargaining leverage."[3]

Meanwhile, in late March, as the Wisconsin primary approached, Carter nursed one last hope that there might be some positive movement in the negotiations. In the early-morning hours of April 1, Iranian president Bani-Sadr announced that the American hostages would be separated from the militants and put in the care and protection of the Khomeini government. That might not have sounded like earth-shattering news, but it represented real progress. The Islamist militants who had seized the hostages were not even part of the government, and therefore were useless as negotiating partners. However, if the Khomeini regime controlled the hostages, Iran would finally be in a position to negotiate seriously.

More important, Bani-Sadr's words were also part of a prearranged code, an innocuous but mutually agreed upon phrase between the United States and Iran that was meant to trigger a series of positive responses between the two presidents.

Now that Bani-Sadr had done his part, it was time for Carter to do his. So at 7:13 a.m., an unusual time for a presidential press conference, it was Carter's turn to describe Bani-Sadr's words as "a positive step."[4]

And that was it. In theory, at least, Carter had signaled that the United States was ready for direct talks to take place.

There was just one problem. In Iran, the president could be overruled by the Supreme Leader, Ayatollah Ruhollah Khomeini—and that's exactly what happened. "We were informed by President Bani-Sadr later that the Ayatollah Khomeini had reversed the decision, and the hostages would not be released," Carter later said.

Initially, Carter had thought of a rescue as a last resort, but by this time, the White House had realized how little power Bani-Sadr held under Khomeini. Diplomacy had failed.[5] On April 7, Carter formally terminated official diplomatic relations with Iran.[6] At a National Security Council meeting on April 11, Carter finally gave the green light. He was ready to act.[7]

Prior to its authorization, Operation Eagle Claw had not been the only rescue plan under consideration. According to Ben-Menashe, one of the first meetings on a possible rescue took place in December 1979, shortly after the hostages were seized, not at the Pentagon, but at the Georgetown home of Miles Copeland Jr.[8]

Copeland was a former member of the OSS and CIA who had been instrumental in the Operation Ajax coup in Iran, which brought the Shah to power in 1953. His good ole boy affect notwithstanding, Copeland was a famously accomplished Arabist who hid his mastery of the Arabic language under a honey-sweet Alabama accent.* He had also been a close personal adviser to Egyptian leader Gamal Abdel Nasser. All of which had long made him persona non grata in Israel.

Given Israel's distaste for Copeland, it was all the more striking that, among those gathered at his house that December, was Deputy Director of Mossad David Kimche, as alleged by Ben-Menashe. Copeland was apparently joining forces with the Israeli spymaster Kimche, who later became famous as the key Israeli official overseeing covert arms sales to Iran during Iran-Contra.[9] That alone was a noteworthy reminder of how the hostage crisis had reconfigured the Middle East.

"Copeland was disgusted with Carter's handling of the situation," Ben-Menashe told me.[10] He dismissed Carter as someone who was imprisoned by his own naïve, guileless Sunday school morality. Copeland offered a similar assessment to Bob Parry, later saying Jimmy Carter's sin wasn't stupidity. It was worse, he told Parry. "Carter was a Utopian. He believed literally that you must do the right thing and take your chances on the consequences. He told me that. He literally believed that."[11]

As Copeland and his colleagues saw it, rather than playing Boy Scout by cracking down on the Shah's human rights abuses, Carter should have come to the aid of America's steadfast friend. "There were many of us—myself, along with Henry Kissinger, David Rockefeller,

* The Copeland family had a colorful history in the music world as well. In the forties, Miles had a brief career as a big band trumpeter who played with Benny Goodman and Glenn Miller. His son, Stewart Copeland, was the drummer with Sting and the Police, and Miles Copeland III managed the band.

Archie Roosevelt in the CIA at the time," Copeland said. "We believed very strongly that we were showing a kind of weakness, which people in Iran and elsewhere in the world hold in great contempt."[12]

According to Ben-Menashe, there was at least one other person attending Copeland's meeting who was of special interest to me: John Shaheen.[13] After all, if Shaheen was privy to anything Copeland had in the works, Bill Casey was almost certainly aware of it as well.

And yet, for all intents and purposes, Miles Copeland and company were merely patriotic Americans, former intelligence officers, who were doing their best to bring back the hostages. Copeland said his hostage rescue plan grew out of a request from the State Department to come up with something that would break the logjam with Iran.[14] Even Ben-Menashe saw these initial overtures as benign. "The whole thing didn't start out as a scheme to delay the hostages," he told me.[15] "It became that later on. At first it was normal undercurrent diplomacy. The motive was to arm the Iranians so they could fight the Iraqis."

Ben-Menashe added that "Kimche understood that it was in the interests of the United States as well to arm Iran against the Iraqis. But he also understood that there was no way for America to supply arms to Iran without the help of a third party."[16]

And that meant Israel.

Sometime in late December, Shaheen had approached the Carter White House with a proposal to rescue the hostages—likely the same plan concocted by Copeland and company.[17] It was to be under the authority of Gen. Arteshbod Gholam-Ali Oveissi, formerly the commander of the Iranian armed forces under the Shah. Oveissi had since moved to New York but he supposedly had one hundred Iranian fighters in place in Tehran who would execute the operation.*[18] After

---

* According to the House report (page 143), Shaheen got his proposal to the White House with the help of Leonard Wrench, a mutual friend of Shaheen and Charles Kirbo, a senior adviser to President Carter. Kirbo, in turn, mentioned Shaheen's proposal to Carter, and, at Carter's request, subsequently raised the matter with CIA Director Stansfield Turner. It is unclear whether Shaheen's proposal was an outgrowth of the meetings with Miles Copeland.

Shaheen's proposal was vetted by both the Carter White House and the CIA, an Agency official said he found Shaheen's proposal "well-intentioned," but nevertheless persuaded Shaheen to drop the project because it was impractical.[19]

But Copeland wasn't through, and, by early spring, he and other disgruntled operatives began to take matters into their own hands. To that end, Copeland, then sixty-five, called several of his most distinguished colleagues to another meeting at his Georgetown home on Saturday morning, March 22, 1980. Among them were Kermit Roosevelt Jr. and his cousin, Archibald Roosevelt Jr., both of whom played key roles in Operation Ajax and had been a part of the Rockefeller Group's Project Alpha to bring the Shah to the United States.[20]

Copeland's assemblage in March was not "an official group"—in the sense that they were no longer part of the CIA. A bit long in the tooth for covert ops, they were all in their sixties by then. Despite having long since retired from the CIA, they still kept their hands in the intelligence business. Yet those assembled, with all their connections to the 1953 coup and the glory days of what the CIA had achieved in Iran, were so distressed by the Carter administration's failure to resolve the hostage crisis that they had put together their own plan with Steven Meade, former chief of the CIA's Escape and Evasion Unit, who was also at Copeland's home and who specialized in rescue operations.

In his memoir *The Game Player*, Copeland explained what followed his March 22 meeting. "Steve [Meade], Kim [Roosevelt], some CIA old-timers whose names I am forbidden to reveal, and I got to together on a plan that would almost certainly have worked."[21] According to Copeland's account, the plan called for the CIA to enlist "Iranian-appearing" operatives near the embassy "in police or army uniforms claiming that they only wanted to move the hostages to more secure locations, not to free them"[22] because an attack was imminent and authorities had to disperse the hostages to several different locations. The entire operation was to be a ruse in which all movements "appear to be mere relocations of the hostages instead of a rescue."[23] All this was to be facilitated by "innumerable disinformation ploys," by the infiltration of enough CIA assets "to take out the leaders and disorient the others," and sophisticated techniques "of mob creation, control, reversal, and neutralization."[24]

Copeland told Parry that copies of the plan had been sent to both Richard Nixon and Henry Kissinger.[25] In the end, however, it was turned down by the Carter administration even though it had been endorsed by the CIA.[26] Why the plans never became operational is unclear, but perhaps it was because Operation Eagle Claw was already underway. In any case, as Operation Eagle Claw approached its launch date, there was good reason for Carter to fear a security breach.

Even though his rescue plan had been quashed, on April 20, Copeland wrote a piece in the *Washington Star* putting forth the idea of implementing a covert operation in which helicopter-borne commandos rescued the hostages.[27] The timing of this piece—coming just four days before the actual rescue attempt—was troubling. One Carter administration official told the *Washington Post* that the next day the story was "picked up and carried in Iranian newspapers as though it was the official American rescue plan."[28] In other words, thanks in part to Copeland's article, the Iranians were now on high alert.

On April 22, two days before the scheduled operation, a radio broadcast in Tehran revealed a CIA plot to rescue the hostages. "They didn't mention the Copeland piece," CIA Director Stansfield Turner told me.[29] "But we assumed the two were related. We were terrified at first but came to the conclusion that it was worth going on with the operation." He added that Copeland's scheme bore some resemblance to one of several actually being worked on by the administration.

Meanwhile the Republicans had been able to collect information on it without lifting a finger. Reagan foreign affairs adviser Richard Allen, a close ally of Casey's, had even been contacted by an anonymous man who met him on a park bench and offered up all sorts of highly confidential details that only a handful of people in the White House knew.[30]

Clearly people were talking about Eagle Claw far beyond the walls of the Oval Office.

It is hard to overstate the devastation wrought by the Eagle Claw catastrophe. Eight American servicemen died trying to carry out a mission that had been ordered by President Carter, and it would be an understatement to say that he took the loss in a deeply personal way.

Reagan mourned the loss of US service members, but behind the scenes the Republican campaign was thrilled.[31] The entire country had become a captive audience to a spectacle that was seared deeply into the American consciousness, in which the United States had become a pitiful, helpless giant, a spectacle that would forever be identified with Jimmy Carter.

BECAUSE THE FAILURE OF OPERATION EAGLE CLAW CAME TO have such profound consequences on the election, I wanted to give it more scrutiny in light of all I'd learned. For years, the disaster of Operation Eagle Claw was thought of as purely Carter's failure to bear. Yet given how porous secrecy on the operation was—and how many current and former CIA officers loathed Carter—it was worth understanding the operational risks and whether these leaks played a role in the operation's demise. After all, this was a top-secret mission, yet its security had been breached repeatedly.

In February 2023, I ended up on the phone with Joel McCleary, who had served as treasurer of the Democratic National Committee and deputy assistant to the president during the Carter administration. As president of the Sawyer-Miller Group, a legendary political consultancy, McCleary oversaw international strategic advisory work for fourteen prime ministers and presidents. Over the years, his political work brought him into close contact with the intelligence community in exotic locales all over the world.

During the Carter administration, McCleary told me, he had become friendly with a British intelligence operative named Timothy Landon who was helpful in developing an American arms depot off the coast of Oman, the tiny, oil-rich sultanate strategically located at the mouth of the Persian Gulf.[32]

Landon was an extraordinary character—an adventurer, in the grand old British colonial tradition, who became known as the "Lawrence of Arabia" of Oman. It was a reputation he earned in Oman, in 1970, when he played a key role in the British-backed coup that dethroned Sultan Saeed bin Taymur and replaced him with his son, Qaboos bin Said Al Said. The son had befriended Landon when the two young men trained together at the Royal Military Academy, Sandhurst. Once Qaboos was enthroned, Landon became his "consigliere," as *The Guardian* reported, and helped transform Oman from a primitive agrarian state into a modern industrial state fueled by vast new oil revenues, all while he was brokering lucrative oil and arms deals.[33]

Landon played the Great Game of politics as if Rudyard Kipling were keeping a very close eye on him, and he played it to win. "Tim was a man who always had his eye to the main chance," said John Beasant, author of *Oman: The True-Life Drama and Intrigue of an Arab State*, in an interview with the *Globe and Mail*. "What he did do through his advisory to Qaboos in fashioning a modern state, which primarily meant establishing a modern navy, army, and air force, meant that he was able to make huge amounts of money through the arms deals he brokered on behalf of the Sultan."[34]

By the time he died in 2007, Landon had put together a fortune of 500 million pounds sterling (nearly $1 billion in 2024). A soldier of fortune who had hit the big time, he had become richer than the Queen—or so it was said.[35] And he had done so nearly in total secrecy. He was the stuff of legends, and he was known as the White Sultan.

Not long before his death, in 2007, Landon called McCleary and invited him to Faccombe, the renowned 4,250-acre hunting estate Landon owned in Hampshire, England. The two men had an unusual friendship. They had become pals when McCleary was in the Carter administration and Landon was briefly helping them. His role, according to McCleary, was to help the United States in "developing an arms depot that we had off the coast of Oman."[36]

Friendly as they were, Landon and McCleary had very different politics. Landon, McCleary told me, "was never a pro-Carter person."[37] And McClearly also knew that Landon was no Cub Scout. There were all sorts of wild stories about Landon brandishing a pistol on the steps of the Sultan's palace in Muscat. Some of those tales were exaggerated, no doubt. But Landon had staged coup d'états. He was an arms dealer. He was a tough guy, and he had the bullet wounds to prove it. The deposed sultan of Oman, Saeed bin Taymur, on his deathbed, said that his greatest regret in his life was "not having had Landon shot."[38]

For most of his life, the *Guardian* reported, Landon was "a somewhat shadowy figure" whose visibility was inversely proportional to his growing notoriety as an arms dealer and oil broker.[39] In London, to maintain his desired anonymity, Landon was driven around in his own black cab. He enjoyed a congenial and lucrative working relationship with Zimbabwe strongman Robert Mugabe, whose brutal policies of torture, jailing, and compulsory disappearances caused the deaths of at least ten thousand civilians.[40]

Unaware of Landon's antipathy toward Jimmy Carter, McCleary built a relationship with him that was animated in large measure by their mutual interest in Buddhism. As a board member of the International Campaign for Tibet, McCleary had served as an adviser to the Dalai Lama.[41] In fact, one day around 2005 (McCleary did not recall the date), Landon called McCleary and asked for an introduction to him.[42] Before long, McCleary and Landon had flown to Switzerland where, according to McCleary, Landon had an audience with the Dalai Lama that "was very emotional. You could tell something was on his conscience. There was obviously a lot on his mind."[43] McCleary had wondered if Landon was confronting his own mortality.

McCleary didn't learn any more until a year or two later, when Landon called again. This time, he was more explicit about why he wanted to see McCleary. By this time, Landon had been informed he was dying of lung cancer. He invited McCleary to spend a few days with him at Faccombe because he wanted to make a deathbed confession.

Once McCleary arrived, there were beautiful dogs running around and servants galore, and they sat down to have a drink. It was a very emotional scene, McCleary said, and he was stunned by what Landon said. "He was just getting very sick, and he said, 'You know, I wanted to apologize.'"[44]

McCleary was puzzled. Apologize? For what? If Landon had in some way breached their friendship, McCleary was completely unaware of it.

"Do you know why I wanted to see you?" Landon asked.

"Why is that?" McCleary replied.

"Well, I have something to tell you, something that has been on my conscience."

Tim was obviously plagued by something that had gone on in his life, McCleary told me.

"Joel, I really liked you and [Carter aide] Tom Beard," Landon said. "But you know, I always felt badly by the fact that you know, that I was part of blocking the rescue operation."[45]

McCleary was stunned. "I almost fell out of my chair," he told me.

When it came to the 1980 presidential election, Landon said, he did *not* feel bad about sabotaging Carter's campaign. That wasn't the point. Carter was a lousy president who deserved to lose, he said.

What he really felt guilty about, he said, was that in doing so he had betrayed his friends, McCleary and Beard.

Exactly what role Landon played was not entirely clear, but McCleary did learn that Landon had very close ties to the Agency—especially the people who had been purged in the midseventies by James Schlesinger and Stansfield Turner. As McCleary told me, "I think all [Landon's] contacts [in the CIA] were with all those people who were fired by Stansfield Turner."

Specifically, McCleary said, Landon was close to Theodore "Ted" Shackley, the fabled spy in the Directorate of Operations of the CIA who oversaw the notorious Phoenix program, which had been set up to capture or kill suspected Viet Cong leaders.[46] According to Leslie Cockburn's *Out of Control*, he was responsible for "the murder of tens of thousands of Vietnamese civilians on the grounds that they were part of what the CIA claimed was a Vietcong infrastructure."[47]

According to *Blond Ghost*, a biography of Shackley by David Corn, when Bush had been head of the Agency, he made a point of trying to protect Shackley among others from the inquisition of the Church Committee.[48] But once Jimmy Carter became president and appointed Stansfield Turner director of Central Intelligence, Shackley saw the writing on the wall. After Turner purged 820 agents in the Directorate of Operations, Shackley hung on for another year, and then resigned.

Shackley, however, was not out of the game. Over the next few years, he shared his mastery of covert operations with the Safari Club members, corrupt banks like BCCI, and all the other components necessary for sophisticated off-the-books covert operations and providing intelligence to the Reagan-Bush campaign.[49] To that end, in the X-Files, Parry had uncovered notes from the Reagan-Bush campaign tying Theodore Shackley to the campaign's efforts in Iran.[50]

"Landon knew these guys and he was close to them, and they'd been involved with Iran," said McCleary. "And they were involved in making sure Carter's attempts to negotiate with Iran failed."

McCleary left his visit with Landon with far more questions than answers. When it came to specifying exactly what that role was, however, Landon was frustratingly vague. "He was very careful about what he said," McCleary recalled.[51] "I was so stunned by it, I didn't know how to follow up."

Landon died in 2007. His ties to Shackley automatically raised questions, but even more notable was the fact that Landon was based in Oman. One of the staging areas for Operation Eagle Claw had been the strategically located US base on the tiny island of Masirah, off the coast of Oman, just across the Strait of Hormuz from Iran.

In the end, there was just one takeaway that was certain: Landon had told McCleary he had been involved in the October Surprise. "I can definitively say without reserve that he apologized and admitted to having a role, a significant role, in what unfolded. He was a major player in Oman, and he acknowledged having been involved in the October Surprise."[52]

McCleary's story about Landon came to mind in late 2023, when I was rummaging through thousands of documents in Parry's archives, and I discovered a never-before-published letter to Parry written in July 2014 that made some astounding allegations. It was written by Mustafa Zein, a Lebanese businessman who, in CIA-speak, was known as an "access agent." In this case, that meant that Zein was one of the few people with ties to the CIA who had cultivated close relationships with the leadership of the PLO and Hezbollah.

As a result, Zein was of special interest to the CIA during the hostage crisis. At the time, Yasser Arafat had very close ties to Iran, having successfully negotiated the release of thirteen female and African American hostages on November 19 and 20, 1979. According to the hostage takers, they were released in solidarity with oppressed minorities and out of respect for "the special place of women in Islam."[53] He had also helped retrieve the bodies of the eight Americans who had died at the Eagle Claw rescue attempt in April.[54] No one had had more success in achieving results than Arafat. If he was lucky enough to help win release of *all* the hostages, Arafat hoped, Washington might bestow official recognition on the PLO.[55] As a result, when Robert Ames, the Near East director of the CIA, began building a network of valuable secret contacts, Mustafa Zein was exactly the kind of person he was looking for.

A talented linguist who was highly skilled at navigating the smoke and mirrors of the Middle East, Ames died in April 1983 when a suicide bomber attacked the US embassy in Beirut. The story of how he developed extraordinarily deep relationships with key Middle Eastern operatives and cultivated Arafat in 1980 is told in Kai Bird's *The Good Spy*. Bird is the Pulitzer Prize–winning author of *American Prometheus: The Triumph and Tragedy of J. Robert Oppenheimer*. Ames was such a good spy that Bill Casey, who was CIA director at the time he was killed, called him "the closest thing to an irreplaceable man."[56]

One of Ames's greatest accomplishments as a spy was to open a discreet back channel to the PLO through Zein at a time when doing so was both dangerous and difficult. As one of Ames's CIA colleagues put it in *The Good Spy*, "Zein was Ames's Sancho Panza for the next fourteen years."[57]

Zein's letter raised far more questions than it answered, but what it does contain is rather sensational, as is a manuscript he left with Parry that consists of his unpublished memoirs. In the latter, Zein refers to John Shaheen as "my friend and close associate"[58] and recalls the one and only time Shaheen introduced him to Casey. "I found him [Casey] extremely intelligent but always in a hurry as if being chased or chasing to catch a departing train at the last minute," Zein wrote. "He had a habit that immediately turned me off, mumbling his words, which made it hard to understand him, and spewing spit like April showers when he talked! The man, as intelligent as he was, did not seem aware of his disgusting habit and the effect it had on people."[59]

Shaheen had been born in the United States, but his background was Lebanese, and, according to Zein, he felt enough kinship to open up to Mustafa. "He loved to tell stories of the old days of the OSS during the war, and he felt that history was repeating itself in the secret campaign that was being waged by Casey against President Carter! He loved to talk about Casey's exploits in recruiting very high officials in the CIA, the Pentagon, and even in the National Security Council and in the White House to work for Casey and supply him with the latest moves of the Carter administration!"[60]

According to Zein's memoirs, Shaheen "was given the task by Casey to keep a close eye on Iran through his Iranian business associates. Also, Casey was receiving information from the National Security Council member, working secretly with him. It detailed a rescue mission, drawn by the CIA and the Pentagon combined, to free the hostages."[61]

The mission to which Zein was referring was Operation Eagle Claw, and in his letter to Bob Parry, he noted that it was "Ames who told me he suspected something going on, especially during the Operation Eagle Claw operation of rescuing the hostages in Tehran that failed because of the failure of two helicopters."[62]

Beyond that, Zein's letter does not specify the exact nature of Ames's suspicions, but Zein was acutely aware of the larger forces at work. "Bob wanted this operation to succeed," he wrote, "but Casey wanted [it] by all means possible to fail and he succeeded."[63]

The letter is written in Zein's fluent but flawed English, replete with misspellings and typographical errors, and absent the context necessary to fully understand what he is saying. But it offers an unusually intimate peek into the world of counterterrorism. Among other subjects, Zein writes about one of his most prized sources, Imad Mughniyeh, the infamous terrorist who is said to have been behind the 1983 US embassy bombings in Beirut that killed eighty-three people (including Bob Ames), the Marine Corps barracks bombing in Beirut later that year that killed more than three hundred people, and the 1984 kidnapping, torture, and death of Beirut CIA station chief William Buckley.[64]

A longtime friend of Ames, Buckley had arrived in Beirut at a time when the Shi'ite population had become radicalized. He was said to be successfully rebuilding the network that had been destroyed by the bombings, when, on March 16, 1984, he was kidnapped as he left his apartment house on his way to work. His kidnapping meant, in effect, the end of the line in terms of the United States having a military presence in Lebanon.

Over the next fifteen months, Buckley was tortured and grilled relentlessly. As if to tease the CIA, Buckley's captors sent videos of his interrogation to Langley. According to Gordon Thomas's *Journey into Madness: Medical Torture and the Mind Controller*, Buckley's "words were often incoherent; he slobbered and drooled and, most unnerving of all, he would suddenly scream in terror, his eyes rolling helplessly and his body shaking."[65] There were needle marks that indicated he had been injected with narcotics.

But what *did* Buckley tell his captors? As Tom Clancy and Gen. Carl Stiner wrote in *Shadow Warriors*, "Not long after his capture, his agents either vanished or were killed. It was clear that his captors had tortured him into revealing the network of agents he had established—the source for most of our intelligence on the various factions in Beirut."[66]

In his letter to Parry, Mustafa Zein wrote about what purportedly was the most heinous revelation by Buckley. "Imad Moghniye [*sic*] showed me a tape in which William Buckley the CIA Chief of station in Beirut confessing to may [*sic*] things including the disabling of the two helicopters," Zein wrote, referring to the events that led to aborting the mission.[67]

In his unpublished memoirs, Zein doubled down on the notion that Operation Eagle Claw had been sabotaged. "The greatest shock that shook me from the depths of my heart," he wrote, "was when I heard the confession of William Buckley, the CIA station chief in Beirut who was kidnapped by the Jihad four years later. He confessed that the mission to rescue the hostages in Tehran was sabotaged by 'the off the shelf' organization ordered by Casey! All they had to do was disable one more helicopter, which they actually did and he named the man who saw to it!

"I could not help notice the relief of the pro-Republican supporters when they heard the news of the failure! I saw John Shaheen who really seemed upset and was really angry at some who were celebrating openly!"[68]

The three helicopters that had failed were prevented from completing their mission for three different reasons. One was lost in a haboob, an intense dust storm sometimes prevalent in the Middle East characterized by rapid wind shifts from multiple directions, sudden downdrafts, and massive walls of dust that make navigating a helicopter extraordinarily difficult. One had hydraulic problems. Another had a warning light saying the helicopter rotor blades had lost pressure.

And how credible was Zein? "Mustafa was inclined to see the world through conspiratorial glasses," Kai Bird told me.[69] "But I was able to check out and confirm a lot of what he told me."

However, corroborating allegations that the rescue was sabotaged was another story. Everyone with firsthand knowledge—Bob Ames and Mustafa Zein included—was likely dead. Even if Casey had still been alive, he would have been silent as a vault. In the end, there was no conclusive evidence to support Zein's assertion that Eagle Claw had been sabotaged.

But there was plenty of evidence that Casey was doing everything he could to thwart the early return of the hostages.

Chapter Thirteen
Asymmetry

The aftermath of Operation Eagle Claw left the Carter administration with even fewer diplomatic options. Just when the administration thought relations with Khomeini's regime couldn't get any worse, they did. In Iran, the horrifying reality that the American military had penetrated Iranian territory reawakened the nightmarish specter of America's imperial power seizing control of Iran's destiny as it had in 1953. As a result, any so-called moderate politician in Iran—Bani-Sadr, for example—who wanted to return the hostages and normalize relations with the West knew he had better keep his mouth shut.

In the White House, plans for a second rescue attempt were in the works, but Iran had relocated the hostages and scattered them about to disparate sites so a rescue would be all but impossible. How could they put together another rescue mission if they didn't even know where the hostages where?

In May, Assistant Secretary of State Hal Saunders and Henry Precht, chief of the State Department's Iran Desk, went to Europe for consultations with the French, the Germans, and the British about how their diplomats in Tehran could help achieve a quick solution to the hostage crisis.[1] According to a State Department briefing memo at the time, "They had good talks with the French, the Germans and the British on ways in which their diplomats in Tehran can be helpful in working to persuade the Iranian authorities, especially the clerics, that a quick solution of the hostage issue is in Iran's interest."[2] The idea was to keep lines open to President Bani-Sadr and Foreign Minister Sadegh Ghotbzadeh, while encouraging the Europeans to persuade the clerics to end the stalemate.[3] At the time, however, both Bani-Sadr and Ghotbzadeh were fighting for their political survival—and losing.

Meanwhile Iran's once-powerful military had been gutted by a shortage of spare parts for its largely American- and British-made equipment,[4] leaving Iran increasingly vulnerable to the growing military threat posed by Iraqi dictator Saddam Hussein. If Iraq attacked and took over Iranian oil reserves, that would be a global catastrophe of the first order.

The Carter administration was desperate to get the hostages back; the Iranians were desperate for American military hardware. The conditions for an arms-for-hostages deal made more sense than ever before, and yet public opinion in each country was such that neither side could be caught cutting a deal that gave the other side what it wanted.

In many ways it was a study in the realpolitik needed to execute American foreign policy. The very thing that would have allowed Carter to resolve the crisis—finding a covert way to send arms to Iran—went against his foreign policy principles. Carter's moral sensibility had been a crucial factor in helping him negotiate the Camp David Accords between Israel and Egypt, but in a crisis such as this, it impeded his ability to negotiate with Iran using the only leverage he had: military hardware. Compounding the limitations of his position was the animus, both open and secret, that the intelligence establishment felt toward Carter. Even if Carter had been willing to trade arms for hostages in secret, it seemed likely that those opposed to him would make sure nothing stayed secret for long.

It was an impasse that Bill Casey was all too happy to exploit. For his part, Casey knew that covert deals such as what the hostage crisis required weren't just a part of American foreign policy—they were the backbone of it. Sometimes you had to get your hands dirty, and that was fine as long as no one found out. Keeping it secret was one of the defining aspects of American power in the twentieth century. The bottom line was that no one could ever know.

In the end, Carter and Casey were playing by very different sets of rules—and that gave Casey a huge advantage.

CASEY'S NETWORK WAS BOTH WIDE AND DEEP, BUT BECAUSE the Hashemis were double agents who were also working for the Carter administration, they were Casey's single most vital weapon. According to Gary Sick's *October Surprise*, by this time, Cyrus had come up with two possible Iranians he knew who might be able to help get the hostages released.[5] One was Mehdi Karroubi, one of the most powerful clerics in Khomeini's inner circle. Jamshid had become friendly with Karroubi when both men served on a committee founded after the Revolution to monitor Iran's radio stations.[6] The other was Reza Pasandideh, Khomeini's nephew, whom the Hashemis had approached in January after they first met with the State Department. For five months, there had been no discernible progress in setting up the meeting, but now, in July, Pasandideh had finally been cleared by Khomeini to meet with representatives of the Carter administration in Madrid.

By this time, even though the State Department had lost its enthusiasm for the Hashemis, it was still so desperate that it had to take seriously anyone with even the slightest shred of credibility in Tehran.[7] Pasandideh was of interest because, according to Cyrus, he had been against the hostage taking from the beginning. His father, Morteza, was Khomeini's brother and was known as Ayatollah Pasandideh.

Until 1921, to the extent Khomeini and his siblings shared a surname, they were known as "Hindi"—from India—because their grandfather came from there. But after the 1921 Persian coup d'état, Reza Shah ordered all Iranians to take a surname. Ruhollah took the name Khomeini—from Khomeyn, a town in the Markazi province of Iran. His brother Morteza chose Pasandideh—which means "pleasant."[8]

Now that moderates were in such disfavor, Pasandideh, thanks to his familial relationship, was one of the few people who could talk to Khomeini about such matters.[9] The State Department needed to contact the powerful clerics close to Khomeini and, at the time, this was their best opening.[10]

The only problem was that, unbeknownst to the Carter State Department, the Hashemis were part of Casey's operation, and Casey too had asked Cyrus to set up a meeting with Iranian officials who would be in a position of authority regarding the hostages. That meant Casey was in the know, and Carter wasn't.

And, like any good bazaari, Cyrus also knew that the only thing better than having a buyer for your rug was to have two buyers. So, yes, Cyrus had gotten clearance for Pasandideh to meet with Carter administration representatives. But he had also gotten clearance for *both* Pasandideh and Mehdi Karroubi to meet with Casey. And that was just the start.

The bidding war got underway in late June when Cyrus told his attorney, Stan Pottinger, to inform the State Department "that Pasandideh was prepared to meet an American representative in a European city."[11] Madrid was chosen, a favored destination for Iranians, in part because Spain required no visa. Meeting with Pasandideh was potentially a major breakthrough, but, according to one knowledgeable source, Hal Saunders declined to attend. Instead, he authorized Pottinger to go to Madrid as a representative of the Carter administration who had no formal authority to speak for the United States, but was expected to assess Pasandideh's credibility.[12] Saunders told the State Department's Working Group that he would brief Pottinger with "just enough to give him some innocent but cogent questions" to determine whether there was anything to be gained from the Pasandideh overture.[13]

Just before the Madrid meeting, as a warmup of sorts, Pottinger met Adm. Ahmad Madani—the man who had been the Carter administration's preferred candidate for the Iranian presidency—at

Cyrus's home in London. After losing the presidential election to Bani-Sadr, Madani had fled to West Germany, but, according to one professional associate who wished to remain anonymous, he was still an imposing presence. Cyrus saw him as a true Iranian hero who one day might help shape Iran's future. Thanks to a nasty auto accident he and his wife, Homa, had just survived, Cyrus was on crutches, and stood upright, leaning against them, for most of the evening.[14] The source added that no one present had any real information about the hostages' well-being; instead, Cyrus talked about the political rivalries between President Bani-Sadr and Muhammad Beheshti, the chief justice of the Supreme Court of Iran, who was, after Khomeini, the second most powerful man in Iran.[15]

More important, there was little, if any, talk about Pasandideh or the meeting they were about to have. Cyrus had suggested he was a bit of a hot dog who was trying to leverage his blood relationship with Khomeini into money or political clout. To the extent that he mentioned Pasandideh's name, it was not with approval.[16]

As I researched the July 2 meeting in Madrid between Pottinger and Pasandideh, I triangulated between the House and Senate October Surprise investigations, State Department documents, and various other sources, discovering new details and conflicting accounts each time I made another pass.

For starters, according to one observer, the meeting took place at the Madrid Plaza—not the Hilton, as the joint task force reported.[17] (The Senate's Special Counsel report got it right.) Both the task force and the Senate reported that those attending the meeting included Reza Pasandideh, Mahmoud Moini Eraghi, Stanley Pottinger, and Cyrus Hashemi.

In the end, however, it was not even clear who was present. According to one associate, having received threats saying he had been bought off by the United States, Cyrus was particularly uneasy about being seen with American officials—particularly after one of his colleagues in Iran had been taken to the roof of an office building and shot.[18] Because he was still on crutches as the result of the auto accident he'd had, the associate said Cyrus didn't even attend—an assertion contradicted by both the Senate and House reports.[19]

According to another version, Jamshid was there instead of Cyrus, under a pseudonym, registered as Mohammad Ali Balanian Hashemi.[20] Various accounts conflict, but Jamshid testified before the Senate investigation that he chartered a private airplane to take Cyrus and Pottinger from London to Madrid and back again.[21]

It was a hot summer afternoon in Madrid when they got to the Plaza Hotel that day. Pottinger, Pasandideh, and, possibly, Jamshid Hashemi joined Dr. Moini Eraghi in a hotel conference room and sat down with participants on both sides of the table. Moini, an Iranian lawyer also known as Max Moini, was Pasandideh's brother-in-law, and served as legal adviser to the Iranian embassy in the United States.[22] According to a deposition by Stanley Pottinger, even before things got underway, Moini indicated that Pasandideh was very uneasy about meeting with a representative of the US government and required some reassurance before going ahead.[23]

According to the task force report, once the meeting got underway Pasandideh said that his "close relative"—that is, Ayatollah Khomeini—knew he was in Madrid, as did Bani-Sadr.[24] He added that he was there as Bani-Sadr's emissary, and that Khomeini's "key people" wanted to end the crisis. With a little bit of luck, this meeting would help achieve those ends. Bani-Sadr was now ready to start talks in Europe to resolve matters, State Department records noted, adding that included "the release of the hostages."[25]

Unfortunately, according to Moini's deposition in the Senate report, the meeting got off to a bad start when it became clear that the American and Iranian parties had different expectations. Apparently Pasandideh had anticipated receiving a letter from President Carter at the meeting to take back to Iran.[26] When that failed to materialize, Pottinger testified that there was a discussion about how to initiate contacts between the United States and Iran, at the end of which they decided that then secretary of state Ed Muskie should write a letter to President Bani-Sadr.[27]

When the conversation came to an end, for reasons that were unclear, according to the Senate report, "Hashemi dictated to Moini a message for Pasandideh. Pasandideh appeared pale and nervous, and asked Moini if that was all he was to receive; the conversation broke down and the two sides separated after a handshake."[28]

And that meant the meeting had been an abject disaster. The bottom line was that six months after the Hashemis had tried to set up the meeting, they had spent less than an hour with Pasandideh—twenty minutes, one source told me—and it had gone nowhere. They were back to square one.

Nothing more clearly underlined the failure of this outreach than the memo Secretary of State Muskie wrote to President Carter summarizing it the next day. Informing the president that Pasandideh "claimed to be acting as Bani-Sadr's emissary," Muskie added that there was a "consensus among Khomeini, Bani-Sadr, Pasandideh's father [Khomeini's brother], and Pasandideh himself that the time has come to end the crisis. Pasandideh said that Bani-Sadr is seeking through these talks to develop a proposal to put before the Parliament. He reportedly believes that a majority of the Parliament will support him on this issue."

The memo concluded that "Bani-Sadr was now interested in beginning talks in Europe between his representative and a U.S. representative, to discuss a possible settlement, including release of the hostages."[29]

Sadly the Muskie memo was full of errors. In fact, Pasandideh was not an emissary of Bani-Sadr's. The two men, Bani-Sadr later told me, had not even met.[30] Moreover, the idea that there was a consensus between Bani-Sadr and Khomeini and his aides could not have been further from the truth. Finally, the suggestion that Bani-Sadr could get a majority in Parliament to support him betrayed a deep-seated ignorance of the bitter ongoing battles in Iran between militant clerics and the more liberal secularists.

The meeting had produced no breakthrough of any kind or even a path forward. Nothing hard or specific had been decided. At best, it could be said that the Hashemis had proven their bona fides in terms of their connections to the Khomeini regime.[31] Otherwise, it was a complete bust. Pasandideh returned to Tehran. There were scores of unanswered questions, not to mention conflicting versions of what happened. To get more, I would need to get the Iranian side of the story.

Chapter Fourteen
Overdrive

AT ABOUT 10:00 A.M. ON A WARM SEPTEMBER DAY IN 2016, I arrived at the gare de Montreuil train station in Versailles, and walked about a mile to number 5, rue Général Pershing. In addition to having been, under Louis XV, the capital of the most powerful kingdom in Europe, Versailles, with its magnificent royal palace and gardens, had evolved into the chic and wealthy bedroom community it is today, just about ten miles west of Paris's center. Bani-Sadr's home was about two miles from the palace.

I entered a large, sturdy building behind some hedges lining the avenue. This was where Bani-Sadr had lived and worked since the early eighties, but it was neither a real home nor a real office. Only later did I learn that, after fleeing Iran in 1981, Bani-Sadr took his own flat in Versailles near a school.[1] But, given the power and reach of his Iranian foes, his neighbors forced him to move, lest they end up as collateral damage in a terrorist attack by Islamic fundamentalists.

I was greeted by Mahmood Delkhasteh, a London-based author, journalist, and academic, who appeared to be in his forties and was Bani-Sadr's frequent coauthor and interlocutor. He had helped set up my interview with the former Iranian president, and had agreed to translate my English-Farsi conversation with Bani-Sadr.

Then eighty-three, Bani-Sadr wore a pale blue shirt opened at the neck, untucked, a black blazer, and dark horn-rimmed glasses. He had an impish, almost angelic smile, his face framed by a crown of curly gray hair. I found him to be unimposing and unassuming for a man who had walked the world stage as head of state for the world's biggest Islamic republic, one of the most powerful regional players in the world.

Later, I came to see him as the Iranian counterpart of Jimmy Carter in at least one important regard. Both men were religious fundamentalists—Carter, a born-again Christian; Bani-Sadr, a Shi'ite Muslim. But neither carried with him the reactionary political baggage that often went hand in hand with their faiths. Both men were thoughtful, humane, idealistic, and intelligent—qualities that had propelled them to such lofty positions. But once they got there, they were both relatively weak and ineffective when it came to wielding power—and their foes went in for the kill.

A highly regarded Koran scholar, Bani-Sadr nonetheless believed in secular democracy and had hoped to replace the Shah's brutal monarchy in Iran with something more akin to the policies of former Iranian prime minister Mohammad Mossadegh, whom he so revered. They were admirable sentiments, but, as I quickly learned when I started investigating, his militant adversaries—Khomeini and the Islamist clerics who supported him—would have none of it.

I sat down in a sparsely decorated living room with Delkhasteh and Bani-Sadr and went to work. Because he had fled Iran after all his belongings had been confiscated, Bani-Sadr had no possessions with him whatsoever when he first arrived in France. After his more than three decades living there, the room still had few personal touches—a reflection, perhaps, of what it means to be a political exile. It occurred to me that even though I'd fended off a lawsuit for my work on the October Surprise, I'd gotten off easy compared to Bani-Sadr. He had been betrayed by a man he revered—the Supreme Leader, Ayatollah Khomeini, no less.

At the heart of Bani-Sadr's story was his relationship with Khomeini, who had been close friends with Bani-Sadr's father. At his father's funeral, Bani-Sadr had a particularly warm conversation with Khomeini, and cemented a bond that passed into its second generation.[2] Khomeini said that Bani-Sadr became "like a son" to him, and the two men developed a long-distance father-son relationship of sorts, with Bani-Sadr in Paris and Khomeini in Najaf, a sacred pilgrimage site for Shi'ite Muslims. Khomeini had been an attractive figure to Bani-Sadr—and to tens of millions of Iranians—in that he had courageously spoken out against the Shah's brutal repression at considerable personal risk. By the same token, Khomeini saw Bani-Sadr as someone he could trust—a devout Shi'ite Muslim who had been in exile during the Shah's reign and was the son of a good friend.[3]

In 1978, Khomeini moved to Neauphle-le-Chateau, France, about twenty-five miles outside Paris, and met regularly with Bani-Sadr, who lived ten minutes away in Versailles. On February 1, 1979, a month after the Shah fled Iran for good, Bani-Sadr accompanied Khomeini on his return to Tehran where they were greeted by more than five million people cheering in the streets. (This was the plane ride to Tehran to which I had been invited but passed up.) Immediately afterward, the Shah's government collapsed.

A year later, on January 25, 1980, Bani-Sadr won the presidency, overwhelmingly, with 76 percent of the vote—a margin that was highly misleading in terms of his fragile hold on power. Before long, the father-son relationship between him and Khomeini—the bond that was so vital to his political power—began to deteriorate. When they had been in France, before returning to Tehran, Bani-Sadr had assembled a list of twenty basic principles that were essential to building a secular democracy in Iran, and Khomeini seemed to approve of them. But as soon as Khomeini saw millions cheering him in the streets, he changed. "When we got to Iran, he immediately showed signs that he was not going to hold to those principles," Bani-Sadr told me.[4]

Amidst the tumult and chaos of the times, Bani-Sadr saw Khomeini become addicted to power.[5] Among other alleged "crimes," the Ayatollah attacked Bani-Sadr by name for using stationery left over from when the Shah fled a few months earlier. In late June, Khomeini decreed that if anyone was found to be using the Shah's imperial stationery, he would be treated like a heroin trafficker and shot.[6]

THEN, ON JULY 5, 1980, IN THE MIDST OF THE TEMPESTUOUS early months of Bani-Sadr's presidency, Reza Pasandideh[7] asked for a meeting with President Bani-Sadr on "a very important" subject. He had just returned from the Madrid meeting with Stan Pottinger, and he wanted to give Bani-Sadr his report.

Bani-Sadr's account of what happened next was astonishing in several regards. First, he told me that at the time of the July meeting, he had never even met Pasandideh before. In other words, the story that Pasandideh told Pottinger in which he said he was there as Bani-Sadr's emissary and that they were close friends was complete fiction. Furthermore, when Pasandideh sat down in Bani-Sadr's office, he told the president a story that was equally false. As Bani-Sadr explained it to me, Pasandideh said he was in Spain on vacation just a few days earlier, the Americans "accidentally" got in touch with him to discuss the hostage situation.[8]

Bani-Sadr couldn't believe what he was hearing.[9] From the beginning, he had felt the hostages should be released immediately, but he was in no position to overrule Khomeini and the militant clerics. Nevertheless, Bani-Sadr had established back-channel communications with the Carter administration through friendly diplomats in Germany and Switzerland. Both Bani-Sadr and Carter had urgent political imperatives calling for a quick resolution to the hostage crisis. For Carter, of course, it was the election. And from Iran's side, Bani-Sadr wanted to resume relations with the United States so Iran would be properly equipped to fend off a belligerent Saddam Hussein.

Pasandideh had no ties whatsoever to the German and Swiss back channels, and the meeting he described in Madrid, Bani-Sadr told me, was "totally disconnected to ongoing negotiations."[10]

When Pasandideh said the Americans "accidentally" contacted him, he was lying, of course, and Bani-Sadr knew it. A repressive theocracy had just seized power in Iran, and the idea that Khomeini's nephew, Reza Pasandideh, would be idly moseying around Madrid and just happen to run into operatives of the Great Satan—that just didn't pass the smell test. Highly sensitive as it was, this kind of meeting would have required approval from the highest authorities in Iran. "There is no way Pasandideh could have gone there without Khomeini's permission," Bani-Sadr told me.[11]

From the start, Bani-Sadr had felt that nothing was more antithetical to Iranian interests than holding on to the hostages. Thanks to the hostage takeover, more than $11 billion in Iranian money had been frozen in the American banking system. Japan and Portugal banned all oil imports from Iran. Denmark, Britain, West Germany, France, Italy, and Canada all, in one way or another, curbed diplomatic and economic relations with Iran.[12] When the Shah had been in power, Iran was able to turn to its American benefactors whenever it needed weapons. As the threat of war from Iraq grew, Iran's need for spare parts from the United States for its military became increasingly dire.

And as for the fifty-two hostages, so long as they were captive, their fate had become the tipping point in multiple narratives arcing through the Middle East, part of a complex political calculus involving two adversarial countries—both led by incumbent presidents who were holding on to power by the thinnest of threads. If the hostages were released before the November elections, the polls showed, Jimmy Carter's likely victory would mean continuity in terms of America's leadership. Similarly, the fates of Khomeini's Islamic Revolution and Bani-Sadr's presidency—indeed, the balance of power in the Middle East—depended on the outcome.

With so much at stake, Bani-Sadr said, nothing was accidental. He didn't believe Pasandideh's story about an accidental unplanned meeting in Madrid. But he wanted to know more.

Then he asked Pasandideh, "Which Americans are you talking about? The Carter administration?"

As Bani-Sadr recounted the story, Pasandideh didn't give Bani-Sadr any names, but his response was shocking, nonetheless. "No," he replied. "The Republicans."

But instead of trying to get Iran to release the hostages, Pasandideh said, the Reagan team wanted Iran to delay the release of the hostages until after the American election. That, of course, would redound to Reagan's advantage, and, once they were securely ensconced in the White House, they promised to be friendlier to Iran than Carter had been.

"That was a very dirty thing to do—using the hostages as a weapon to help Reagan win the election," Bani-Sadr said.[13] "And I told [Pasandideh] the outcome could be the election of Ronald Reagan, which would be a disaster for Iran and for the rest of the world. I told him we can't negotiate with them. The Democrats are in power. And if we made a deal with them [the Republicans], it would help Reagan's chances, which would be terrible for Iran."

As president, Bani-Sadr kept his followers informed through a regular column he wrote for *Enghelab Eslami* (Islamic Revolution), his Tehran newspaper. After his meeting with Pasandideh, Bani-Sadr considered telling all of Iran what was going on, but he was constrained because Pasandideh had insisted that his life would be in jeopardy if Bani-Sadr revealed that the Reagan-Bush camp was trying to delay the hostage release.

That night of July 7, 1980, he took the first step, and wrote about it in a memo he later sent to the House task force.[14] "I decided to expose the Secret Deal with Republicans in a public speech. I wrote in the Column [in *Enghelab Eslami*]."

Initially, Bani-Sadr said, he had thought Khomeini knew nothing about Pasandideh's duplicitous machinations.[15] He wrote about it obliquely, deliberately omitting Pasandideh's real name, not revealing the details of the nascent agreement, but threatening to go public with it.

And so, an elaborate cat-and-mouse game between Khomeini and Bani-Sadr began to unfold. "Khomeini kept on promissing [*sic*] to do something about it on the one hand, and at the same time breaking those promisses [*sic*]," Bani-Sadr wrote in a memo to the task force.[16]

Before long, he realized that Pasandideh's meeting could not possibly have taken place without Khomeini's authorization and that Khomeini had almost certainly given Pasandideh the thankless task of trying to bring Bani-Sadr on board.

Nevertheless, Bani-Sadr wouldn't budge. He tasked his staffers with investigating the October Surprise and asked them to document it as much as possible. He met with undisclosed sources who kept him informed about the ongoing talks between the Republicans and the mullahs.[17]

Discussions with cabinet members about the "secret deal" sometimes went on until nearly 4:00 a.m. On July 20, Bani-Sadr talked to two members of the Majlis about the October Surprise, and wrote about it—again, obliquely—that day: "I talked to him about the 'Secret Deal' . . . I told him we have act [*sic*] soon and fast, before . . . this devilish Plan [*sic*] is implemented."[18]

Knowing that Bani-Sadr might be resistant to dealing with Reagan's team, Pasandideh raised the ante. "He said if you are not ready to make a deal with the Republicans, they'll make a deal with your opponents, the IRP," Bani-Sadr told me, referring to the hardline clerics of Khomeini's Islamic Republican Party.

Pasandideh added one last threat to Bani-Sadr, the meaning of which was unmistakable. "He told me that my refusal of their offer [to work with the Republicans] would result in my elimination," Bani-Sadr told me.[19]

Elimination. This at a time when the Islamic Republic had revived the practice of public executions, which often took place by firing squads or hangings from mobile cranes mounted on trucks, which served as makeshift gallows. It gave Bani-Sadr pause for thought.

So now, just five months into Bani-Sadr's tenure as president, it was becoming clear that as a covert operation, the

October Surprise was a twofer: Both Carter and Bani-Sadr were being undermined from within. In effect, team Casey in the United States and the Islamic Republican Party were working together to make sure Ronald Reagan beat Carter in the US election. Their deal also had the effect of solidifying Ayatollah Khomeini's position as the ruler of Iran and eliminating the pesky irritants of Bani-Sadr and secular democracy.

When I interviewed him in Versailles, Bani-Sadr described what transpired as "a creeping coup," in which, bit by bit, Khomeini and his followers robbed Bani-Sadr of his dwindling presidential powers. The very same Republican hardliners who so decried militant Islamism were doing everything in their power to make certain that an Islamist theocracy was securely installed in Iran.

Impossible as it was to square the various contradictory accounts of Pasandideh's July 2 Madrid meeting, one huge question loomed unanswered: who was there? One knowledgeable source told me that nothing about Reagan or his campaign had been discussed at the meeting, nor was anyone associated with Reagan in attendance.[20]

But Pasandideh had said there were Republicans. "Pasandideh said only that the interlocutor was apparently working for Carter and actually working for Reagan," Bani-Sadr told me.[21] "Pasandideh told me that the Reagan team wanted to work with me."

Given that Stanley Pottinger was a registered Republican who happened to be temporarily helping the State Department for the Carter administration, some observers speculated that perhaps he was secretly working for the Reagan campaign, that he was a double agent.

But there was no evidence to support such conjecture. Moreover, Pottinger* was decidedly out of favor with the Reagan-Bush camp. In addition to having served a stint in the Carter Justice Department,

* According to Watergate reporter Bob Woodward, Pottinger was the only person to figure out that Watergate source Deep Throat was Mark Felt, the associate director of the FBI. Pottinger kept the secret until 2005, when Felt finally went public with the news.

according to my source, he had taken liberal positions on school busing, affirmative action, and other issues that were anathema to the Reaganites.[22] Moreover, at the time, his longtime girlfriend was Gloria Steinem, the feminist icon who was a lightning rod for right-wing Republican activists.

There were other possibilities. Perhaps Jamshid was there—not saying a word, according to one observer—and he was the one Republican operative Pasandideh mentioned. Or Cyrus. Or maybe there was another side meeting in Madrid that day with a different cast of characters. No one seemed to know.

But in the end, one thing was clear about what took place in Madrid that first week of July 1980: somewhere in the morass of contradictory evidence, a hideous act of betrayal had taken place.

Meanwhile, whatever role Casey might or might not have had in the episode, he was not idle. At the end of June, he had taken off for a short trip to London and Paris, where he dropped by to meet with his old friend French intelligence chief Alexandre de Marenches, head of the Safari Club.

Chapter Fifteen
Interference

Of course, the Hashemis were not the only avenue Carter was pursuing to resolve the hostage crisis. The State Department and the CIA were also working multiple channels for any possible opening that could lead to a breakthrough. Unfortunately, Casey was always one step ahead, outmaneuvering them at every turn.

Early on in the hostage crisis, on January 9, 1980, in a memo to National Security Adviser Zbigniew Brzezinski, Gary Sick had noted that another opening to Tehran was through PLO Chairman Yasir Arafat, who was "eager to help resolve the crisis."[1] Initially, such overtures amounted to little more than a prescription to hurry up and wait. But the Arafat outreach had not been abandoned, and, at Langley, Robert Ames's most highly prized connection was with Mustafa Zein. (Kai Bird told me he had heard that Zein had died, but I was unable to corroborate that.)[2]

To be clear, as Bird reported in *The Good Spy*, in working with Ames, Zein was not a CIA agent—or at least not a paid one. "Mustafa Zein never received any monies for his efforts," one CIA agent testified in court. "The basis for Mr. Zein's collaboration with the Agency has been his desire for the United States to comprehend and sympathize with the Arab and Palestinian perspective on the situation in the Middle East."[3]

With Zein as a resource, Ames and the CIA established direct contact with Arafat and PLO intelligence chief Ali Hassan Salameh for the first time. It was a highly significant intelligence breakthrough for the Carter administration.[4]

Indeed, reaching out to Arafat was so promising that throughout the early spring of 1980, Secretary of State Cyrus Vance was in contact with him almost every day.[5] There was still a chance that Arafat would make the journey to Tehran, but he was reluctant to do so until he was confident of success. And from the Carter administration's point of view, obviously, it would not be a good thing if Bill Casey found out about its communications with Arafat.

But in order to make a deal with Iran, Casey knew he also had to stop Jimmy Carter from making one first. Acquiring intelligence from within the Carter camp was just the first step. He then needed operatives who could act on that intelligence and, in so doing, disrupt any progress Carter had made with Iran.

To that end, according to *The Good Spy*, Casey relied on Jack Shaw, the former associate from the Nixon administration who was helping Casey raise funds for Reagan. In addition to his positions in the Nixon administration, Shaw had served as a State Department official in the Ford administration, as an executive at Booz Allen Hamilton, and as senior fellow at the Center for Strategic and International Studies.[6]

It started innocently enough in the summer of 1980 after Zein decided that meeting Shaw might be worthwhile because he was likely to have a significant position on the National Security Council if Reagan won the election.[7] After their first meeting, a cat-and-mouse game ensued between the two men, in which they felt each other out. Much of it was secretly taped by Zein, and, in one unusually candid conversation, Shaw confided that he knew Bill Casey well. He added that, thanks to Casey, he also knew that Zein was the secret back channel through which Ames communicated with Arafat.[8]

Then came the kicker. When Zein disclosed that Arafat was still trying to secure the freedom of the remaining hostages, according to *The Good Spy*, Shaw asked if Arafat could be encouraged to hold off until after the presidential elections. After all, he argued, a strong president like Reagan would be better for the Palestinians than a weakling like Carter.[9] "Shaw made himself very clear and outright that Casey wanted me to convince Arafat to stop his efforts," Zein later wrote in his 2014 letter to Parry.[10] If Arafat obliged, Zein was told, the PLO would have "very grateful friends" in the White House.

Shaw later provided a more innocent explanation of what happened, acknowledging that the meetings with Zein took place but asserting that he had not been "approached directly by Casey on this."[11] Often working indirectly, he told Bird, Casey's "modus operandi was to bounce the cue ball off several billiard balls to get a job done without his fingerprints on it."[12] Shaw seemed to be saying that Casey wasn't tasking an operative. He was merely having a harmless conversation with an associate. But in the end, of course, Jack Shaw *was* a Casey operative. Zein even went to Shaheen for confirmation of that—and says he got it.[13]

Several days after meeting with Shaheen, Zein passed on the information to Arafat himself. Then, according to *The Good Spy*, Zein wrote Arafat a memo: "Double your efforts to release the hostages because the coming administration, if the Republican ticket wins, has a devil in it. Reagan and Bush are decent men, but the maestro who is conducting the orchestra . . . cannot be trusted."[14]

Kai Bird's account was not the first to assert that Casey had mounted an operation to block Arafat's attempts to release the hostages. In fact, in 1988, a *Playboy* magazine article by Yippie activist Abbie Hoffman and Jonathan Silvers reported that Arafat's chief spokesman, Bassam Abu Sharif, said that in the summer of 1980 he was approached by a Reagan backer and close friend who "asked that I contact the chairman [Arafat] and make the request. . . . We were told that if the hostages were held, the P.L.O. would be given recognition as the legitimate representative of the Palestinian peoples and the White House door would be open for us."[15]

Abu Sharif didn't seem to know the name of the man in question, but said he was "one of Reagan's closest friends and a major financial contributor to the campaign. . . . He kept referring to him as

Ronnie. . . . He said he wanted the P.L.O. to use its influence to delay the release of the American hostages from the embassy in Tehran until after the election."[16] Later, on Parry's *Consortium News*, the Reagan emissary was identified as John Shaheen, who had grown up in Tampico, Illinois, with his boyhood friend Ronnie Reagan.[17]

In 1996, Arafat himself had confirmed the Republican efforts to sabotage an early hostage release in a private meeting with President Carter in Gaza City. Historian Douglas Brinkley was present at the time and wrote about it in the fall issue of the scholarly journal *Diplomatic History*.[18] "There is something I want to tell you," Arafat told Carter.[19] "You should know that in 1980 the Republicans approached me with an arms deal [for the Palestine Liberation Organization] if I could arrange to keep the hostages in Iran until after the [US presidential] election."

THERE WERE PROBABLY ONLY A HANDFUL OF ASTUTE OBSERVers who noticed it, but if Casey's Arafat operation sounded familiar, it was because something very similar had happened before. Indeed, twelve years earlier in the 1968 presidential campaign between Hubert Humphrey and Richard Nixon, the Nixon campaign feared that incumbent president Lyndon Johnson might engineer a Vietnam peace initiative to give Humphrey a last-minute boost over Nixon just before the election.

At the time, William Safire was a Nixon speechwriter, and his old pal Bill Casey was also a Nixon aide. "I have no notes to verify this," Safire wrote in 2002, when he was a *New York Times* columnist, "but can recollect [Casey] saying often that he suspected that Lyndon Johnson would 'pull an October surprise'—some Vietnam peace initiative—to help the Democrat Hubert Humphrey defeat Nixon in the closing days of the tight campaign."[20]

Though many people claimed credit for originating the term, Safire's account may well have documented its first use.

But the larger point is that in 1968, Nixon operatives intervened in affairs of state in a manner that closely prefigured the 1980 October Surprise. Once a tightly held secret that was dismissed as a bizarre conspiracy theory, the Anna Chennault Affair, as it is sometimes known, is now extraordinarily well documented thanks to tape recordings and memos in the LBJ Presidential Library in Austin, and the Miller Center at the University of Virginia in Charlottesville. It has been written about at length in Ken Hughes's 2014 book, *Chasing Shadows: The Nixon Tapes, the Chennault Affair, and the Origins of Watergate*, and Lawrence O'Donnell's *Playing with Fire: The 1968 Election and the Transformation of American Politics* in 2017, among others.

There were a number of parallels with 1980. As the 1968 presidential season got underway, antiwar demonstrations erupted across America, and President Lyndon Johnson, under fire for prosecuting the war in Vietnam, took the highly unusual step of announcing that he would not seek reelection. In April, Martin Luther King Jr. was assassinated, leading to riots in more than 110 American cities. Bobby Kennedy, the leading contender to win the Democratic presidential nomination, was killed in June. In August, the Democratic National Convention in Chicago devolved into a chaotic police riot. As protests against the Vietnam War raged on through the summer, blood flowed in the streets, not just in the United States, but in Paris, Prague, and all over the world. Meanwhile, during the heated presidential race between Richard Nixon and Hubert Humphrey, President Johnson initiated talks in Paris with North Vietnam in hopes of ending the war.

But then, Nixon went to work. Publicly, he took the high road and told supporters that it would be inappropriate for him to comment on the latest developments in the Paris Peace Talks. "Neither [my running mate] nor I will destroy the chance of peace. We want peace," said Nixon at a Madison Square Garden rally immediately after Johnson's speech.[21]

But behind the scenes, Nixon secretly deputized GOP operative Anna Chennault to intervene on his behalf and talk directly to the powers that be in South Vietnam. A prominent Republican and a leading force in the US China Lobby, Chennault was the widow of famed US Army aviator Claire "Old Leatherface" Chennault, and a powerful Washington society hostess who had cultivated a network of influential politicians.

Richard Nixon himself had designated her as "the sole representative between the Vietnamese government and the Nixon campaign headquarters," as she wrote in her 1980 memoir, *The Education of Anna*. "Anna is my good friend," Nixon said when he introduced her to Bui Diem, the South Vietnamese ambassador. "She knows all about Asia. I know you also consider her a friend, so please rely on her from now on as the only contact between myself and your government. If you have any message for me, please give it to Anna and she will relay it to me, and I will do the same in the future."[22]

As Election Day neared, the North Vietnamese suddenly made last-minute concessions to the Democratic administration in Washington. In response on Halloween Night, October 31, just five days before the election, Johnson began a historic bombing halt of North Vietnam. Potentially, that was Nixon's nightmare, a 1968 version of Carter freeing the hostages—day after day of headlines promising the imminent end of the Vietnam War by the Democrats.

But on October 31, just hours after the bombing halt was announced and the Paris Peace Talks were about to begin, campaign aide John Mitchell, who later became Nixon's attorney general, phoned Chennault. "Anna, I'm speaking on behalf of Mr. Nixon. It's very important that our Vietnamese friends understand our Republican position and I hope you have made that clear to them," he told her.[23] "Do you think they have decided not to go to Paris?"

The rationale behind her mission was essentially the same as the one that the Republicans used twelve years later for the 1980 October Surprise: Tell the South Vietnamese (or, in 1980, the Iranians) *not* to participate in the negotiations proposed by the Democratic administration. If South Vietnam does take part in the peace talks, Democratic nominee Hubert Humphrey will likely win the November election. But if they don't go along—and if South Vietnam boycotts the Paris Peace Talks—the Republicans will win, and when that happens, newly elected President Nixon will give them a much better deal than the Democrats would.

One of the people facilitating these top-secret contacts between Nixon and Chennault, however reluctantly, was Richard V. Allen, then a thirty-two-year-old foreign policy adviser.[24] In a 2024 interview, Allen told me that the moment he met Chennault, he loudly voiced his apprehension about her—almost certainly within earshot of his pal and mentor, fellow Nixon aide William J. Casey. "After I met with her half a dozen times, I said, 'No, no, no, don't touch this person.' Very early on, I saw big damn trouble. I smelled a rat. I did meet with her a number of times. I still gave her a wide berth. I only did it to keep RN happy. Otherwise, she would be banging on the door of [Nixon secretary] Rosemary Woods all day long."[25]

Chennault's machinations were hidden from the general public, of course, but President Johnson had his suspicions, and a week before the election he had the FBI wiretap the South Vietnamese embassy and tail Chennault.[26] According to *Chasing Shadows*, the first FBI report on the embassy noted that at 7:30 a.m. on October 30, an unidentified woman called South Vietnamese ambassador Bui Diem, who recognized her by her voice and told her to come by that day.

Sometime that afternoon, Madame Chennault visited the South Vietnamese embassy in Washington for about half an hour.[27] According to the FBI, "Mrs. Anna Chennault contacted Vietnamese Ambassador Bui Diem and advised him that she had received a message from her boss (not further identified) which her boss wanted her to give personally to the ambassador. She said the message was that the ambassador is to 'hold on, we are gonna win' and that her boss also said, 'Hold on, he understands all of it.' She repeated that this is the only message. 'He said please tell your boss to hold on.'"[28]

After Chennault delivered her message, South Vietnamese president Nguyen Van Thieu instantly went along with it. So, on November 2, just three days before the US elections, the front-page of the *New York Times* announced, "Thieu Says Saigon Cannot Join Paris Talks Under Present Plan."[29]

As a result, during this last week of the presidential campaign, the Paris Peace Talks completely fell apart.[30] And when it came time to vote, the American people were in the dark about what really happened. Thanks to Nixon's unseen machinations, to voters, it appeared that the Democratic administration of Lyndon Johnson was so incompetent it couldn't even get America's South Vietnamese allies to the bargaining table.

The length of time it took for this deception to spill into the open—as well as the fact that Nixon ultimately left office in disgrace for his role in a *different*, more memorable, election-related deception—blunted the significance of this revelation for many Americans. But make no mistake, this was not just another political dirty trick. As characterized by the late Richard Holbrooke, who had been attached to the Paris talks as a diplomat, "The Nixon people . . . massively, directly, and covertly interfered in a major diplomatic negotiation, probably one of the most important negotiations in American diplomatic history."[31] Defense Secretary Clark Clifford said Nixon had violated the Logan Act of 1799, which makes it a crime for a private citizen (which Nixon was at the time) to obstruct US government diplomatic negotiations. Senate Minority Leader Everett Dirksen, the Republican senator from Illinois, and Lyndon Johnson agreed that what Nixon had done was an act of "treason."[32]

For Nixon, though, the ruse worked brilliantly. On November 5, Nixon won the presidency with a plurality of 512,000 votes, less than one percentage point. In the Electoral College Nixon won 301 electoral votes, compared to 191 for Humphrey, and 46 for third-party candidate George Wallace. In the wake of Nixon's victory, the war continued for six more years, resulting in another twenty thousand unnecessary American deaths, not to mention millions of Cambodian, Laotian, and Vietnamese casualties.

In 1968, President Lyndon Johnson had become suspicious of Nixon's personal involvement. Johnson, however, decided the revelations were too explosive to go public, but that the tapes and documents he acquired could have enormous political value down the road. And that was exactly what Nixon was afraid of.

In fact, according to memos by LBJ's national security adviser Walt Rostow, Nixon regarded the Anna Chennault Affair[33] as so explosive that his efforts to contain it ultimately led to the scandal that caused his downfall. According to *Chasing Shadows*, once Nixon became president, he feared that revelations about the Chennault Affair might hurt his 1972 reelection campaign, so he assembled a team of burglars—the so-called White House Plumbers—to break into the Brookings Institution in hopes of stealing any tapes or documents the Democrats had regarding the crime Nixon and Chennault committed in 1968. After breaking into the office of Daniel Ellsberg's psychiatrist, in an attempt to discredit the man who leaked the Pentagon Papers, the Plumbers zeroed in on a target that had strategic importance to the Democrats, specifically, a large residential-office complex in the Foggy Bottom neighborhood of Washington, DC. It was known as the Watergate.

Today, anyone who doubts that such skullduggery took place can read about it in Hughes's book or Lawrence O'Donnell's *Playing with Fire*, or listen online to a series of fascinating audiotapes about it in the archives of the Miller Center's Presidential Recording Program—including a phone call of Lyndon Johnson confronting Richard Nixon on the subject.

But at the time in question millions of American voters were completely oblivious to a blockbuster news story that might well have changed the outcome of the presidential election. Though it is now widely accepted by historians, news about the Chennault Affair dribbled out slowly over the years. In 1980, Chennault wrote about it herself in her memoir, *The Education of Anna*. In 1983, it was written about in Seymour Hersh's *The Price of Power: Kissinger in the Nixon White House*,[34] Stephen Ambrose's 1989 biography of Nixon,[35] and referred to in passing by the *New York Times* and the *Los Angeles Times*.[36] In 2009, after the release of LBJ's secret tapes, the History News Network posted an article, *Did Richard Nixon Commit Treason in 1968? What the New LBJ Tapes Reveal*.[37]

By the time it was fully revealed, the story landed as just another example of Nixonian politics at work. It was old news, and it wasn't terribly shocking at that: the man who had already been disgraced by Watergate had been involved in yet another scandal. Ho-hum. Cynicism about Nixon's criminal behavior had already been baked into the public's perception of him. The Chennault Affair didn't move the needle. It just confirmed what people already thought about Nixon.

When I asked Richard Allen if Casey was in on the Chennault Affair, he said no, that Casey was overseeing Nixon's research. But Casey knew about it.[38] And if there was a lesson to be learned about the Chennault Affair, it was this: Nixon had, in effect, gotten away with it—a treasonous act, no less. Watergate was a different story, but for the Chennault Affair, he had paid no price. There was no accountability.

I discovered in Casey's personal files at the Hoover Institute at Stanford that he had scheduled meetings with Anna Chennault in June 1980.[39] In light of the above, that can only raise the tantalizing, unanswered question of whether they were comparing notes with regard to the 1980 October Surprise.

Of course, thwarting the Arafat initiative was just one of the many tricks Casey had up his sleeve, and in the aftermath of the RNC, he went into overdrive. Now that the Reagan-Bush ticket had been forged, there were plenty of ambitious pols sniffing around for cabinet posts in their upcoming administration, and Casey knew exactly how to put them to work. Among them, one of the most notable was John Connally, the former Democratic governor of Texas who had switched parties, made an enormously costly but disastrous run for the Republican nomination, and had then thrown what little support he had to Reagan. According to his close friend and protégé Ben Barnes, himself the former lieutenant governor of Texas, Connally resolved to help Reagan beat Carter and "in the process . . . make his own case for becoming secretary of state or defense in a new administration."[40]

Barnes told his story to Peter Baker of the *New York Times* in March 2023 at a time when Jimmy Carter, then ninety-eight, was in hospice care, and Barnes decided it was necessary to set the record straight while the former president was still alive.[41]

The story had strong echoes of Zein's interactions with Jack Shaw regarding Arafat. According to a knowledgeable source, Connally's office prepared logistics for the trip via a Gulfstream corporate jet owned by Superior Oil, a large independent oil company of which Connally was a board member and in which Casey was a major investor.[42] Then, on July 18, the day after the RNC ended, Connally and Barnes took off for Jordan, Syria, Lebanon, Saudi Arabia, Egypt, and Israel.[43] At the time, Connally was no stranger to the world of Arab billionaires. In 1977, he joined forces with Saudi billionaire and BCCI front man Ghaith Pharaon among others to buy Main Bank of Houston.[44] According to the *Times*' account, at each stop, Barnes recounted, Connally met with regional leaders and, Barnes said, delivered "a blunt message to be passed to Iran: Don't release the hostages before the election. Mr. Reagan will win and give you a better deal."[45]

Barnes said that he didn't figure out what Connally's mission was until he opened his mouth at their first meeting with an Arab leader.[46] "Look, Ronald Reagan's going to be elected president and you need to get the word to Iran that they're going to make a better deal with

Reagan than they are Carter," Connally said, according to Barnes.[47] "It would be very smart for you to pass the word to the Iranians to wait until after this general election is over."

Several years earlier, historian H. W. Brands, a University of Texas professor who happened to know Barnes, wrote a similar account of the trip in his biography *Reagan: The Life*.[48] Brands wrote that when he followed up by researching Connally's papers at the LBJ Library, he "also discovered a memo of a phone call from Nancy Reagan at the Reagan ranch to Connally on the trip."[49]

The bottom line, according to Brands, was that Ronald Reagan was aware of Connally's mission.

According to the *Times*, "shortly after returning home, Mr. Barnes said, Mr. Connally reported to William J. Casey."[50] Barnes also said he joined "Connally in early September to sit down with Mr. Casey to report on their trip during a three-hour meeting in the American Airlines lounge at what was then called the Dallas/Fort Worth Regional Airport."[51]

Barnes added that the whole point of Connally's trip was to tell Iran to hold the hostages until after the election. "I'll go to my grave believing that it was the purpose of the trip," he told the *Times*.[52] The tipoff was the airport meeting with Casey, in which Ben Barnes was treated to the spectacle of seeing the silver-maned, anvil-jawed Connally debriefed by the mumbling and bumbling master spy who so eagerly awaited his report. What Connally did could not have been mere "freelancing," Barnes said, "because Casey was so interested in hearing as soon as we got back to the United States."

Chapter Sixteen The Wire

By the time Connally returned from his mission to the Middle East, Casey had already been in Madrid with the Hashemis and Ayatollah Mehdi Karroubi and his brother Hassan. This, of course, was the infamous set of meetings on July 28 and 29 Jamshid had recounted, the meetings that supposedly never took place because Casey was in London, as *Newsweek* and *The New Republic* reported, or because he was in Bohemian Grove, California, as the task force concluded. Once the other alibis were discredited, however, it became clear the Madrid meetings really *had* taken place.

Jamshid Hashemi, warts and all, had provided the most complete account of the meetings, avowing that Casey had finally cut to the heart of the matter and broached the idea of *delaying* the release of the hostages, asking if they could be freed to Reagan *after* the election. If that happened, Casey added, the Republicans would arrange for the release of Iran's frozen assets and the military equipment that had been held up.

In stark contrast to the confusion and ambiguity that had followed Stan Pottinger's July 2 meeting with Pasandideh, the Iranian contingent walked away from their meetings with Casey understanding exactly where he stood. After all, Mehdi Karroubi, a highly placed member of the Majlis, the Iranian parliament, had not even been present at Pottinger's meeting, but the Hashemis had arranged for him to be at Casey's. And Casey did not waste the opportunity, laying out in clear terms what he was offering.

In broad terms, the conditions had been set for a deal between the Republican and the mullahs. Details and various protocols and logistical questions were yet to be resolved, but by and large, it seemed Iran was ready to make a deal with Bill Casey.

When the Madrid meetings were over, Mehdi Karroubi immediately returned to Tehran to consult with Khomeini,[1] after which he asked Jamshid to set up another meeting with Casey in Madrid a couple of weeks later. According to Sensi, Casey soon asked him to make arrangements for follow-up meetings on August 11 and 12.[2]

Sensi was an obvious choice. He spoke decent Farsi and had worked comfortably in Iran for several years, dating back to around 1976, when, he told me, he helped resolve a long-standing claim between Ingersoll Rand, the American multinational, and the National Iranian Oil Company and ran a front company for the CIA.[3] He was wired and knew some of the most powerful players in Iran.

Sensi also happened to adore Casey. He loved Casey, he told me, because he always had half a dozen crazy schemes in the works simultaneously and nobody could say no to him.[4] There were fake identities, disguises, and passports galore. For the next meetings in Madrid, Sensi told me, Casey traveled on a phony passport under the name of Daniel O'Neill and wore a blond wig that was "the color of Donald Trump's hair."[5] Nobody fucked with Casey. "He had so much going on that his right hand didn't know what his left was doing," Sensi told me. "He had the balls of a giraffe."

Within the context of Casey's operation, Sensi told me that he was merely a gofer. "My role was nothing, really," he said.[6] "I was just a bit player. But I knew my way around and could get access to people in Iran that not that many people had."

This time, according to Sensi, the Iranians sent another Shi'ite cleric close to Khomeini, Ayatollah Mohammad Reza Mahdavi Kani,[7] who served as secretary of the Guardian Council, and was soon to be appointed minister of the interior and later became prime minister. Sensi described Ayatollah Kani as "a very practical man" who saw the United States as "a necessary evil."

"They finalized whatever missing elements there were from the Karroubi meeting," Sensi told me.[8] "They had to make sure that the hostages were going to be held until after the election, and that the Israelis would sell them military hardware."

Finally, I asked Sensi if all this meant that the October Surprise had taken place. "One hundred million percent," he replied.[9] "Absolutely. Unequivocally. And you can quote me."

THE ILLICIT ARMS TRADE TO IRAN WAS FINALLY GETTING started. However, unbeknownst to Casey and the Hashemis, people were watching what they were up to. And not just anyone. It was the FBI.

The Bureau's interest dated back a few weeks earlier to July 22, 1980, when Ali Akbar Tabatabai was shot and killed at his home in Bethesda, Maryland.[10] Not long afterward, according to the House task force, "the FBI heard from a reliable source that [Cyrus] Hashemi had instructed that Tabatabai be assassinated and had financed the operation through his bank."[11] Consequently, the FBI applied for and got an order under the Foreign Surveillance Intelligence Act to bug Cyrus's office and put wiretaps on his phones.

The FBI's suspicions about Cyrus's role in the assassination were off base, but the House task force noted that its surveillance revealed Hashemi to be "engaged in other intelligence activities, including the illegal procurement of military equipment for Iran."[12] So between September 1980 and February 1981 the FBI recorded more than twenty thousand conversations involving the Hashemis, on some 550 tapes, totaling roughly two thousand hours.[13] Capturing phone calls taking place in the office of Cyrus's bank, the First Gulf Bank & Trust on West Fifty-Seventh Street in Manhattan, and on Cyrus's phone lines,[14] the wiretaps recorded conversations between Cyrus Hashemi and Stanley Pottinger about how to help the State Department obtain the release of the hostages, conversations between Cyrus and Speaker of the Majlis Hashemi Rafsanjani about the status of Iran's frozen assets, and a conversation in which Cyrus boasted—truthfully or not—about his close friendship to William Casey.[15]

I'd known about the FBI tapes for years—in fact, I wrote about them in the *Washington Post* in 1992.[16] Not having listened to them myself, I held my judgment in reserve, but some investigators saw them, potentially, at least, as being the Rosetta Stone of the October Surprise, the key that would unlock all its secrets. After all, Casey, Cyrus Hashemi, John Shaheen, and other key figures had died by the time I started investigating, but here the FBI had caught many of them on tape.

I was particularly interested in Cyrus's calls with Shaheen.[17] In 1992, I had filed a Freedom of Information Act request to get the FBI transcripts, but by the time my request was fulfilled, many months later, I had already moved on to other projects. When they arrived, I put them in storage for safekeeping. And there they sat undisturbed for nearly twenty-five years. However, in 2016 my apartment was destroyed when it was flooded with hundreds of thousands of gallons of water. By the time I surveyed the damage the next day, a hazmat crew had already disposed of my precious documents.

Now, with Parry's thumb drive, I was thrilled, but not surprised, to discover that Parry understood their importance as well. In the end, the wiretaps provided documentary evidence of something far more important than a few hundred million dollars' worth of illegal arms sales. They proved that Cyrus Hashemi had been a mole, a double agent, when he first approached the Carter administration. That meant when Cyrus met with Carter administration officials in the State Department, the National Security Council, or the CIA, he was ready, willing, and able to reveal its most sensitive secrets to Casey.

In its fragmentary way, the FBI wiretaps provided many of the answers that showed how Casey implemented the October

Surprise—that is, how he secretly orchestrated the transfer of tens of millions of dollars of weapons to a hostile foreign power, how he and his operatives arranged financing for arms transfers, how they oversaw logistics, transportation, security, and lined up cargo ships and more.

Most important, the wiretap summary shows dozens of calls between Cyrus Hashemi and John Shaheen. In other words, Casey's best pal was getting updates from Cyrus on the various developments regarding arms shipments to Iran. Cyrus was on the phone constantly, making calls regarding night-vision goggles for pilots, spare tires for fighter jets, spare parts for helicopter gunships, and the like.[18] In September 1980, there were calls about important meetings being scheduled later in Paris.

There were phone calls to small aircraft manufacturers, aircraft rental firms, hotels, hospitals, gigantic construction firms like Brown & Root, and savings and loans and banks all over the nation. There were calls to Caesar's Palace and half a dozen other places in Las Vegas. There were calls to Tommy's Supper Club in Tulsa, a hangout for oil executives and visiting Arab oil men. There were phone calls to Ghaith Pharaon, the enormously wealthy Saudi who was a key investor in the Bank of Credit and Commerce International (BCCI). And of course, there were calls to various powerbrokers in Iran as their new government took shape, including allies of the Ayatollah and more moderate forces.

For some time, I had assumed that John Shaheen was Casey's chief cutout, and that Casey had been working with the Hashemis through his old pal. Now, the FBI wiretaps put to rest any remaining doubts I had. "Based on Shaheen's close relationship with Casey, his knowledge of Cyrus Hashemi's involvement regarding the hostages, and finally his own admission that he spoke to William Casey about Cyrus Hashemi and possibly using him as a conduit with the Iranian government regarding the hostage issue," the FBI noted, "an argument can be made that Shaheen was keeping William Casey apprised of Hashemi's activities regarding the hostages."[19]

Or, as Shaheen told Cyrus, in a conversation about Bill Casey: "We are one team that works together."[20]

THE FACT THAT THE ELECTION WAS HELD ON NOVEMBER 4—exactly one year after the hostages were seized—also meant that the anniversary afforded scores of newspapers, magazines, and broadcast outlets another excuse to trot out countless stories about America's humiliation. Thanks to voters who were dissatisfied with how Carter was handling both the economy and the hostage crisis, Reagan surged into the lead in the early summer and maintained it through most of the summer, according to Gallup polls.[21]

So as October began, the pressure for the Carter administration to get a deal done intensified. Surprisingly, Gallup showed Carter surging back into the lead, 44 to 40, over Reagan, after being behind by no fewer than sixteen points in August.[22] Bringing the hostages home could only cement his advantage.

If there were to be a deal between the Carter administration and Iran, it had to take place before Carter became a lame duck. As Gary Sick put it, "the prospect that Iran would get a better deal from the Carter administration after November 4—regardless of the outcome of the election—was remote in the extreme."[23] That meant that Iran's leverage would vanish as soon as the elections were over. Time was running out.

As a result, in the first half of October, a flurry of new developments and potential scenarios for settling the crisis brought a few rays of cautious optimism to the beleaguered Carter White House. For the first time, it seemed that the Carter administration was now considering possible solutions that might be palatable to Iran.[24] With the United States sitting on several hundred million dollars' worth of

Iran's undelivered military equipment, there was a glimmer of hope that these "frozen assets" could provide a solution.[25]

New proposals centering on this idea of "frozen assets" were being promoted by Gerhard Ritzel, the West German ambassador to Iran. Gary Sick described him in *October Surprise* as "an exceptionally talented ambassador, with a flair for the unconventional."[26] On his own initiative, Sick obtained a letter Ritzel had written to Khomeini that suggested the United States "unfreeze all of Iran's assets" as a means through which Iran could "immediately receive all weapons and replacement parts they ordered and paid for. (SECRET)."[27]

What was so appealing about Ritzel's offering was that it recognized how the Iraqi invasion on September 22 had heightened Iran's need for weapons. The powerful Iraqi military had launched a full-scale attack on Iran by air and by ground, striking no fewer than nine Iranian airfields and attacking the province of Khuzestan.[28] Now that the Iran-Iraq War was a reality, suddenly Iran might not be able to wait until after the election for their arms shipments. Thanks to Ritzel's proposal, Carter could get weapons to Iran, but they could be characterized as "frozen assets."

Iran requested an inventory of military equipment that had been bought and paid for by Iran but was still in the United States.[29] Carter responded promptly, sweetened the pot as much as possible, and offered to deliver as much as $150 million of military equipment. National Security Adviser Zbigniew Brzezinski thought this might do the trick. "By the middle of October, we were even discussing among ourselves the possibility of pre-positioning some of these spare parts in Germany, Algeria, or Pakistan, so that the Iranians could then promptly pick them up with their own aircraft," Brzezinski wrote in his memoirs.[30]

According to Gary Sick, right up through October 15, the administration was receiving daily reports from Tehran that it hoped for an early resolution to the crisis in part because it wanted to obtain military equipment from the United States.[31] To many in the Carter administration, the negotiations with Iran had finally become quite promising.

Though the Carter administration knew little of what the Reagan campaign was up to behind the scenes in October, Casey knew all too well what was happening in the Carter administration. He admitted as much himself in an unusual slipup in front of reporters. On July 15, the day after the Republican National Convention opened in Detroit, Casey and Reagan campaign chief of staff Edwin Meese had met with reporters at a breakfast. Casey, in a rare moment of indiscretion, used the term "intelligence operation" to describe what the campaign was doing.[32] Afterward, one Republican official said Meese was "alarmed" by Casey's use of the phrase, and it was not repeated.[33]

Nevertheless, it truly was an intelligence operation, and the rays of optimism penetrating the Oval Office scared the hell out of the Republicans. "Bush Fears October Surprise from Carter Campaign,"[34] read the headline on the Associated Press's lead story for October 2, 1980. "When you are a president, you do have an ability to shape things to some degree," Bush said. He added that he was referring to the return of the hostages before the election.

But the real dirty stuff went on behind closed doors. As the House task force later discovered, Casey had assembled a network of retired military officers that was overseen by Adm. Robert Garrick, a retired rear admiral from the US Naval Reserve, who was tasked with monitoring possible weapons shipments to Iran in exchange for hostages, an operation which, Casey told his secretary, "was top secret. It's never to be discussed except behind closed doors."[35]

Casey described Garrick as "a self-starter who had his own sources of information."[36] According to Ed Meese, who would later become Reagan's attorney general, Garrick received phone calls about the status of planes from friends who were retired military and kept him informed about any unusual movements of American aircraft in the vicinity of Iran or the Persian Gulf.[37] The movement of large aircraft would likely indicate the possibility of another rescue attempt by Carter.

As the task force wrote, Garrick said he knew that large amounts of spare parts ordered and paid for by the Shah were sitting in piles at US Air Force bases—some $250 million in military material titled to Iran that could be shipped there on short notice.[38] Garrick said, "Someplace along the line the concept was developed that the Iranians may be dealing with Carter's people to say, 'Give us this pile of stuff and we'll give you the hostages.'" As result, while reporting to Casey, he oversaw the retired military officers who were monitoring US air bases for signs indicating the possible movement of spare parts to Iran, or a possible second rescue mission.

Garrick wasn't the only Republican sounding the alarm. According to SECRET classified FBI files that were never released to the general public but were discovered by Parry, Stefan Halper, who was reportedly in charge of collecting information on Carter's foreign policy, wrote a SECRET memo saying just that to Ed Meese.[39] "Apparently, the hostages are going to be released just days before the election," he said, according to the wiretaps.[40] He added that "there is a possibility that the Iranians are attempting to enhance Carter's election chances."

Similarly, on October 15, in a memo marked "Sensitive and Confidential," Richard Allen wrote to Ronald Reagan, Ed Meese, and Casey, saying that "an 'unimpeachable source' had alerted him to the possibility of an impending hostage settlement [by the Carter administration.] 'The last week of October,' the memo said, "is the likely time for the hostages to be released. . . . This could come 'at any moment, as a bolt out of the blue.'"[41]

WITH JUST THREE WEEKS LEFT BEFORE THE ELECTION, THE Republicans were getting scared—and with good reason. Just before the October 28 presidential debate between Carter and Reagan, Gallup gave Jimmy Carter an 8 percent lead among registered voters and a 3 percent lead among likely voters.[42] As the debate approached, Reagan surrogates repeated their mantra about how Carter was manipulating the crisis to his advantage. There was one week left before the election, and if he brought home the hostages now, "it would be curtains," the Associated Press quoted one Reagan strategist as saying.[43]

"I can see it now," one senior Reagan aide told the Associated Press. "Carter cancels the debate next week to fly off on *Air Force One* to greet the hostages in Germany."[44]

As the race tightened, Casey ramped up a broad spectrum of operations. Throughout the final weeks of the campaign, Richard Allen's October Surprise Group held daily meetings with no fewer than ten foreign policy specialists to guard against Carter's supposed October Surprise. At the same time, Casey dispatched various operatives to get internal Justice Department documents on an investigation into the president's brother, Billy Carter*; confidential reports on the Iranian hostage crisis from the Justice Department and Carter's National Security Council; and more.[45]

One of the key figures in Casey's operation had been Bush's national policy director, Stefan Halper. The son-in-law of CIA Deputy Director Ray Cline, Halper set up a complex in Arlington, Virginia, that used former CIA operatives to monitor the Carter administration.[46] All of the men working under Halper later denied participating in covert operations for the Reagan-Bush campaign.[47] And Halper said that the existence of an intelligence network spying on the Carter administration was "just absolutely untrue."[48]

Nevertheless, sensitive documents from the Carter-Mondale campaign repeatedly came into their possession, though Halper later told congressional investigators that he did not know how that could

---

* In the scandal that became known as Billygate, Billy Carter registered as a Libyan agent and accepted $220,000 from Libya, thereby precipitating a congressional investigation.

have happened. In September 1980, Halper sent three memos to Ed Meese. The memos indicated that Halper had sources inside the Carter administration or the Carter-Mondale campaign. Each memo was accompanied by materials from the Democrats.[49]

Halper was not the only one close to Bush who had moles inside the Carter organization. In the latter days of the campaign, Bush's brother, Prescott Bush Jr., wrote three letters to James Baker about Herbert Cohen, a consultant to the Justice Department and FBI.[50] The letters asserted that Cohen had reliable sources on Carter's National Security Council and was ready to expose the administration's handling of the hostage situation. Cohen later objected to the way he was characterized in these letters.

ONE OF THE MOST FAMOUS OPERATIONS ORCHESTRATED BY Casey later became known as Debategate, and it involved the apparent theft of Carter's briefing papers by Republicans before the October 1980 presidential debates. It came to light thanks to a 1984 congressional investigation led by Rep. Donald Albosta (D-MI) that later determined that the Reagan-Bush campaign's "information gathering efforts were *not* limited to seeking materials that could be acquired through public channels."[51] The Albosta Report, as the investigation was known, added that there was "credible evidence" that crimes had occurred—specifically because "the subcommittee found a number of documents and items of information in Reagan-Bush campaign files that were transferred in unauthorized fashion from the Carter Administration or the Carter-Mondale campaign."[52]

The crime in question began some days before the one and only presidential debate between Jimmy Carter and Ronald Reagan, a ninety-minute showdown in Cleveland, when Bill Casey dropped by the campaign office of James Baker.[53] The longtime confidant and campaign manager of George Bush, Baker had impressed Reagan intimates by his success in getting Bush to bow out of the race for the Republican nomination before dealing any unseemly blows to Reagan.

Casey later denied it, but, according to testimony by Baker for the Albosta Report, Casey put a black-bound book on Baker's desk.

"You might want to give this to your debate prep people," Casey said, according to Stuart Eizenstat's *President Carter.*[54]

Ronald Reagan was being prepped for his debate with Carter, and James Baker was integral to the process. This apparent theft created a special problem for James Baker. As a lawyer in Houston, Baker had a reputation as a model of probity. It was said that he gave up litigation early in his career because of the unsavory practices it entailed.[55] Accordingly, Baker made a point of looking the other way during the campaign when "dirty tricks" were put into play.

At the same time, part of Baker's job was to supervise people who prepared the debate briefing books for Reagan.[56] The Albosta Report found that at least thirteen members of the Reagan-Bush team admitted they either received the Carter debate material or saw it at one time or another.[57] One was Baker himself, who, in an affidavit, admitted that he had in his possession "materials apparently intended or designed to be used in the preparations of briefings for President Carter."[58] Baker said he passed the material on to other staffers.

According to one knowledgeable Carter aide, the briefing book had apparently been stolen from the desk of David Aaron, deputy national security adviser under Zbigniew Brzezinski, and was returned after having been photocopied.[59] The source added that the book had been in Aaron's desk on the main floor of the White House. It was unclear who stole it, but several staffers on the National Security Council staff were longtime CIA veterans who had the same antipathy to Carter as most of the folks at Langley. No one in the Carter White House had authorized the transfer of these documents to the Reagan-Bush campaign. The Albosta Report concluded, "The presumption, therefore, is that these materials were improperly taken for use by the opposition campaign."[60]

When the debate did get underway, Reagan initially took the high road when he declined "to say anything that would inadvertently delay, in any way, the return of those hostages." But then he let Carter have it for imposing "this humiliation" on America and called for "a complete investigation" by Congress into Carter's failed diplomatic efforts to win back the hostages.

However, Reagan's most effective gambit was his closing question to voters: "Are you better off than you were four years ago? Is it easier for you to go and buy things in the stores than it was four years ago? Is there more or less unemployment in the country than there was four years ago? Is America as respected throughout the world as it was?"

As rhetoric, it was brilliant in its simplicity. To no one's surprise, later in the week in the aftermath of the debate, pundits began to predict a Reagan victory. The *Christian Science Monitor* added one caveat to that prediction—namely that if the fifty-two hostages were released before the elections, that "might give President Carter what he needs to win."[61]

MEANWHILE, BEHIND THE SCENES, THE HASHEMIS WERE working overtime on behalf of Casey. By this time, Jamshid had become a frequent flier on the supersonic Concorde, jetting to London, Lisbon, Hamburg, London again, and New York.[62] According to the FBI records that had been discarded by the task force, "SUBJECTS HAVE ENGAGED IN MILITARY SUPPLY DEALS TO IRAN SINCE OCTOBER 14, 1980."[63]

The FBI added that subsequently the Hashemis "HAVE BEEN RECEIVING ORDERS FOR WEAPONS AND MILITARY SUPPLIES FROM IRAN AND HAVE BEEN ATTEMPTING TO FILL THOSE ORDERS AND ON SEVERAL OCCASIONS, AAND [*sic*] HAVE IN FACT CAUSED SHIPMENTS WHICH ARE PROHIBITED BY LAW, TO BE MADE TO IRAN."[64]

Another of the FBI's many memos that were ignored by the House task force noted that "Dr. Hashmei [*sic*] and REDACTED are currently engaged in an attempt to obtain repair parts for aircraft, including the F-4, and have held discussions with exporters regarding the purchase of missiles."[65]

Even more specifics of the Hashemis' arms shipments were spelled out in additional FBI memos. On September 23, Cyrus received a call at his West Fifty-Seventh Street office from a man named Harold Tillman, who said he had "a Greek ship captain with $3 million to deposit" in Cyrus's bank, the First Gulf Bank & Trust.[66] According to the FBI documents, Tillman appeared to be referring to a ship that later made several round-trip deliveries of weapons between the Israeli port of Eilat and the Iranian port of Bandar Abbas in the Persian Gulf.

The shipments included 155 mm and 105 mm ammunition, 100 mm tank ammunition, and 106 mm antitank guns and ammo, with a total value of $150 million, according to Sick's *October Surprise*,[67] and because they were illegal, the Greek captain took exceptional measures to minimize risk. Most notably, he changed the name of the vessel every time it docked. "I do know for a fact that the ship had been hired to take certain armaments from Eilat to Bandar Abbas," Jamshid explained in a 1992 interview with Parry.[68] "There was a captain who was a Greek. Every time the ship would go to Bandar Abbas, it would have one name. On the way back, it would have another name. Three times."

Afterward, they took the ship out to sea and sank it. They just blew it up. "Can you imagine one single ship having changed names five or six times during a period of two months. It wasn't worth anything, so it went down as evidence," said Jamshid.[69]

Jamshid speculated that a message from Tillman saying that Cyrus would receive a $3 million deposit from the "Greek ship captain"—was directly related to the sinking of the oft-named cargo ship. "I think this was the cost of the ship which went down," Jamshid said.[70] "It's obvious. Here's $3 million. And there's $3 million."

The fact that the $3 million deposit was being arranged by Tillman, a Houston lawyer who, Parry had reported, claimed to be a longtime friend of then vice presidential candidate George Bush, raised questions about Bush that were difficult to answer.[71] Was Tillman reaching out to Cyrus on behalf of the vice presidential nominee? Did Bush have anything to do directly or indirectly with the arms shipments?

But when it came to tying the Iranian arms shipments directly to the Republican campaign, Jamshid didn't want to tempt fate—especially considering his brother's mysterious death. "I really don't like to talk about this," he told Parry. "You are playing with fire, for God's sake! I'd just like to live a few more years if it is possible. Please. Understand! I've got kids living in America! I don't want them to have an accident!"

Tillman's story and that of the Greek ship captain were partially told in classified FBI documents obtained by the task force, but they were omitted from the House and Senate investigations. Instead, as Parry discovered, they were stored in cardboard boxes in the abandoned ladies' room.

Yet another FBI memo noted that Cyrus was doing business as the First Gulf Bank & Trust, and had "received instructions from Iranian principals in Iran to attempt to purchase military weapons and spare parts for Iran to assist the Iranian effort in the current war with Iraq."[72] It was accompanied by several pages of invoices.

To be clear, all these revelations were contained in the documents discarded by Lee Hamilton's House Joint Task Force. I was stunned. In today's parlance, they had the receipts. And they did nothing with them.

GIVEN THAT THE HASHEMIS WERE ALSO IN CONTACT WITH THE Carter administration, the Greek vessel and the shipments also raised the prospect that the arms shipments were on behalf of the Carter administration and not Casey. But according to documents turned over by Bani-Sadr to me, to Parry, and to the task force, the Khomeini regime had just terminated negotiations with the Carter administration, unilaterally, without even telling Washington.

Indeed, between October 15 and October 20, the Carter administration, which had been enjoying productive talks with Iran, suddenly got nothing more than radio silence.[73] For five days. Both Cyrus Hashemi and Hushang Lavi, another Iranian arms dealer, had been phoning in regular reports to the Carter administration from contacts in Tehran, but that came to a sudden halt. European diplomatic channels went silent. This was followed by the shocking news on October 21—just two days after the meetings in Paris took place—that Iran had shifted its position in the negotiations. Now the country that had spent almost a year trying to obtain military aid abruptly disclaimed any further interest in receiving military equipment from the United States.[74]

To everyone in the Carter administration who was privy to the ongoing talks, that was nuts. That could not possibly be. On September 20, Iraq had invaded Iran's Khuzestan province across a front that was several hundred miles wide, and when Iran poured in reinforcements it soon had to replenish and rearm its forces.[75] Meanwhile, Iran also had to divert forces to a second front to deal with an insurrection by its own Kurdish minority. Iran *desperately* needed military hardware—everyone knew that. Yet suddenly, Iran said it didn't need weapons? How could that possibly be? Unless they'd found another source?

In an effort to ease tensions and aide negotiations, Donald McHenry, the US ambassador to the United Nations, finally took a position on Iraq's invasion of Iran, declaring that the United States was "opposed to the dismemberment of Iran" and that the "the national integrity of Iran is today threatened by the Iraqi invasion."[76] These statements had been crafted to revive the suddenly dormant negotiations about the hostage release—but Iran did not bite.

In early October, after the Iranian parliament was in session, Mohammad Montazeri, a member of the parliament's Hostage Committee, had pushed back against Bani-Sadr's efforts to release hostages. According to documents forwarded to the House task force by President Bani-Sadr, Montazeri "said that those who struck a deal with [the] Reagan Camp do not want a deal with Carter and we do not know what to do and we do not want to be responsible for what happens."[77]

Montazeri's statement was another key document omitted in the task force's final report.

Then on October 10, Bani-Sadr wrote that he had asked Hashemi Rafsanjani, the Speaker of the Parliament, "if they are making preparation for a deal with Carter's rival."[78] Initially, Bani-Sadr did not get a direct answer. But "on October 22, and 23, 1980, Rafsanjani changed his position suddenly, and announced that Iran does not need American arms."

Bani-Sadr knew the only possible explanation was that the mullahs had ruled out making a deal with Carter and were secretly making a deal with Reagan.

Meanwhile, the Carter White House continued to get the same silent treatment. On October 21, the Commission in Iran that was negotiating with Carter went silent. For no apparent reason everything came to an abrupt halt. Cyrus's communications with Iran on behalf of the Carter administration suddenly stopped.[79] According to the FBI wiretap summaries, Cyrus Hashemi told Stanley Pottinger that "problems have arisen with the Commission in Iran regarding the hostages."

The FBI added, "[Pottinger] and [Cyrus] appear to be in the dark as [to] all the ramifications of the matter."[80] Apparently Cyrus was "convinced that somebody has deliberately sabotaged the negotiations, apparently in Iran. CH was of the opinion that one of the Iranian officials who were in NY last week for the UN meeting, sandbagged the negotiations."[81]

By this point, according to one person who knew him, Cyrus was almost certainly in the know about Iran abandoning talks with Carter. On the wiretaps, however, he acted surprised and befuddled. Given Cyrus's ties to Shaheen and Casey, his associate told me that Cyrus happened to be a very good actor who was able to silo his feelings and fake his dismay about Iran's silence.

As Cyrus's wife, Homa, chastised him on the following day, October 22, in a taped call, "It is not possible to be a double agent and have two faces."[82]

Chapter Seventeen
Paris

THE OCTOBER SURPRISE WAS ALLEGEDLY FINALIZED IN THE plush confines of a Parisian hotel—the Ritz or the Raphael, depending on whom you talk to—sometime in the third week of October. "It sounds fantastic," Ari Ben-Menashe told me, "but when I give you all the details, everything will fit into place."[1]

Ben-Menashe claimed he was there as part of the Israeli team that helped put the meetings together. Participants included the Americans, the Iranians, and the Israelis. William Casey and Mehdi Karroubi were principal figures at the sessions. Cyrus and Jamshid Hashemi attended and acted as translators. Iran agreed to delay the release of the hostages until after the election and that Israel would serve as a conduit for arms transfers and spare parts.

Or so the story went.[2]

Ben-Menashe said he arrived on Tuesday, October 14.[3] He and three other Israelis stayed at the Hilton, he told me, adding that all records of their visit had been destroyed. "Everything was cleaned out," he said.[4]

"My job in Paris was basically networking with the Iranians, getting addresses and phone numbers and points of contact in Europe to help with arms deliveries later on," he added.[5]

For the most part, the Israelis were told to keep their distance from the Americans, but during the week there were two meetings with them. "One was at the hotel with the Iranians," Ben-Menashe said. "The same stuff was talked about. It was all about arms shipments, about how they were going to be done, and in what form. We were not really talking about the hostages. That was out of our realm. We were not at that level."[6]

On the other hand, the arms shipments *were* about the hostages.

According to Ben-Menashe's account, there were five Americans at the meetings. Among them, he claimed, were two officials on Carter's National Security Council who later became close to Bush—Robert Gates and Donald Gregg. Gates, who was later appointed to head the CIA by President Bush, was then executive assistant to CIA Director Stansfield Turner. Donald Gregg, later ambassador to South Korea under Bush, was then CIA liaison to the National Security Council.[7] Both Gregg and Gates denied allegations that they attended the Paris meetings.

"The night before the big meeting," Ben-Menashe told me, "two other Israelis and myself went to see Mehdi Karroubi in the Hôtel Montaigne, a very small, inconspicuous hotel used by the Iranians all through the years, not far from the Eiffel Tower. We were there to reassure Karroubi about the arms pipeline."

The next morning before noon, Ben-Menashe said, the principles gathered at the Ritz Paris Hotel. "Karroubi and an aide walked in," Ben-Menashe said. "Then George Bush walked in with Casey and said hello to everybody very politely. Then they walked to the conference room on the upper lobby."[8]

This, of course, was the most explosive allegation made tied to the October Surprise.

At the time I interviewed Ben-Menashe, the spring of 1991, George H. W. Bush was the incumbent president who was up for re-election the following year. With his CIA background, Bush certainly could have aided in the Paris meetings, and his position on the presidential ticket might have provided crucial reassurance if Iran needed it. But why would Bush take the extraordinary risk of dashing off to Paris for a covert operation in the closing days of a presidential campaign? Had Iran demanded his presence? It didn't make sense.

"I go back and forth on George," Carter press secretary Jody Powell told me when I first talked to him in 1991.[9] "What's his soul like? And I have a hard time thinking Bush would come up with this.

But let's say the moving force was Casey, and the games started before Bush is on the ticket. You're George Bush. You've been running against Reagan. You get down to convention time, and it turns out you're the vice presidential nominee.

"After the convention is over, you find out these folks are involved in this really scurrilous shit. Do you say, 'Cut this shit out, or I'm gonna resign from the ticket and denounce you?' That doesn't sound like George Bush. Or do you sort of go along and try to keep your distance? I have an easier time accepting that."

I still found the evidence inconclusive that he was in attendance at the Paris meetings. Parry had raised troubling questions about the Secret Service records that suggested it might have been possible. But that didn't prove Bush was in Paris. There were simply too many conflicting accounts.

On the other hand, it is hard to believe that Bush did not know what was going on. But, like any good skilled intelligence operative, if he was in the know, he left no trace.

WHILE THE SPECIFICS OF THE PARIS MEETING WERE NEVER entirely clear, subsequent events suggested it must have been quite productive. In fact, immediately after the meeting, arms really began to flow to Iran.

The details of how and why that came about were first aired on ABC's *World News Tonight* in August 1981, nearly a decade before the story of the October Surprise burst into public view.

The story came to light in 1981, just after the hostage crisis had been resolved, when a man named Jacques Montanès showed up unexpectedly at the Paris office of Pierre Salinger, carrying a bag full of documents.[10] The former press secretary for President John F. Kennedy, Salinger had helped manage Bobby Kennedy's 1968 presidential campaign and had returned to journalism, his first career, and become Paris bureau chief of ABC News, after the latter's assassination. The arrival of Montanès and his documents was exactly the kind of scenario investigative reporters dream of, but rarely happens.

Montanès was a pilot who ran a company called SETI,[11] which, according to Salinger, "was involved" with French intelligence.[12] To the uninitiated, Montanès's documents might have seemed like nothing more than a jumble of receipts and invoices—boring, dry, and of little value. But as it turned out, Montanès had brought documentary evidence that revealed how and when the arms flow began from Israel to France to Iran in the aftermath of the Paris meetings and under the guidance of French intelligence chief Alexandre de Marenches.

After Montanès dropped off his documents, Salinger knew he was on to something, though he had no clue about the big picture, since nothing about the October Surprise had been reported at the time. He broke the story on ABC's *World News Tonight* on August 21, 1981.[13] His report noted that "the bill of lading for the plane, which flew from Nimes, France, to Teheran, was completely falsified with the tacit knowledge of French government officials. It described the tank motors as tractor and truck motors, the M-60 tank spare parts as parts for trucks, and the F-4 tires as those on compressors."[14]

Coming as it did from a source who was well connected to French intelligence, the documents had details that had never been reported before. It noted that the arms transfers had been facilitated by the French trading company SETI, which was "operating under the protection of a key French intelligence officer and at the height of the worldwide boycott of arms sales imposed on Iran after the taking of the American hostages."[15]

After ABC aired Salinger's story, Israel pushed back and said it was all a lie.[16] But that was just about the only response to it. It was a story that appeared in a vacuum, and, ironically, because the story was reported so early, it was subsequently overlooked in terms of the larger role it plays in the October Surprise narrative.

Moreover, even though these shipments were addressed in some detail by the task force, Lee Hamilton's investigation failed to make the most fundamental connections. It noted SETI's role in the shipments but did not in any way tie SETI to French intelligence or de Marenches.

Montanès had told the task force that Iranian foreign minister Sadegh Ghotbzadeh told him "that he knew of secret contacts between officials connected with the Reagan campaign and representatives of the religious faction in Iran's government."[17]

On September 11, Ghotbzadeh went further, in a letter published in the Iranian newspaper *Enghelab Eslami*: "We know that the United States Republican Party, in order to win the coming election campaign, is trying hard to delay the solution of the hostage issue until after the United States elections."[18]

In 1982, Ghotbzadeh was executed by firing squad for his brave statements. But the task force asserted that it "cannot determine with certainty the underlying basis behind Ghotbzadeh's statements to the press and his letter to the Majlis baldly stating that the Republican campaign was making a concerted effort to bar the hostages' release."[19]

As a result, the task force dismissed both Ghotbzadeh's courageous words and the documentation of Montanès's arms shipments, and concluded that "the purpose [of the SETI arms shipments] was to make money. It never had any connection to the American hostages."[20]

Then, in 1995, when the fervor around the October Surprise had died down, Salinger published a book titled *P.S.: A Memoir*. The book came out in both France and the United States, but a portion of it was deleted in the American edition. Parry obtained a draft of the missing pages and wrote about it on his *Consortium News* website.[21] According to Salinger, the eight paragraphs were deleted from the 294-page book "for reasons of length."

Right.

As it happened, the text that had been expunged from Salinger's book related directly to the October Surprise. Salinger's account offered a blueprint of sorts for how, following the Paris meetings, which allegedly occurred between October 15 and October 20, shipments of arms began to flow from Israel to Tehran via Nimes, France. "The first thing I learned was that during the Iran Hostage Crisis, an airplane had been sent from France with a load of military equipment for Iran," said the draft Salinger sent to Parry.[22] "The United States had declared that any arms went to Iran during the hostage crisis was illegal. [*sic*] But this pile of military equipment which came from the United Kingdom, France, Italy, Spain, and Israel had been flown to Tehran on October 24, 1980, from the city of Nimes. Montanès had accompanied that plane."

Earlier in the summer of 1980, Montanès testified that Charter Masters, a charter firm in France that handled "difficult air cargo orders,"[23] had been in contact with an Iranian arms procurement officer named Ahmed Heidari about an ambitious plan to set up about seventy flights carrying arms to Iran. But the plans fell apart when a $200 million letter of credit from Iran never arrived.[24]

In August, however, Heidari tried again, and went to France with a list of spare parts for F-4, F-5, and F-14 aircraft; radar equipment; and other items. According to Sick's *October Surprise*, his key contact in France was Roger Faulques, a French mercenary whose exotic career began as a maquis fighter in the French resistance during World War II, and continued into the First Indochina War, the Algerian War, and the Congo, among other crises. Heidari says that Faulques made it clear that he could not proceed without approval from French intelligence, and that meant Alexandre de Marenches would have the last word.[25] Given de Marenches's disgust with Carter, that was not a difficult ask, and, according to Sick, in early September, de Marenches's principal deputy, Alain Gagneron de Marolles, gave his approval.[26]

The next step was to develop an itemized procurement list.

Enter Jacques Montanès, who had been asked to join a three-man team in September 1980 to survey Iran's military needs.[27] Given the exigencies of the moment, the work was risky, but the pay was good—$180,000 (nearly $670,000 in 2024 dollars)—for just three months' work. So Montanès and his team went to Iran on September 14, just a week before Iraq attacked Iran. While he was there, he and his associates met with officials from all three branches of the military and put together an extensive list of military hardware needed. It included aircraft tires, large quantities of munitions, motors, and spares for armored cars, tanks, and much more.[28]

According to the House task force, however, after Iran prepared invoices for the arms shipments, the representatives of Bank Markazi—aka the Central Bank of Iran—was "concerned about the absence of collateral or other financial guarantees by SETI to ensure delivery of the purchased equipment."[29]

Without the guarantees, they revoked Montanès's passport, leaving him stuck in Iran for nine months, and when he finally returned to France, he was so incensed that he brought all his documents to Salinger.[30]

Meanwhile, even though Montanès was stranded in Iran, the flow of arms had begun. On October 21, right after the Paris meetings took place, Montanès's documents say, $250,000 was transferred to the Israeli purchasing mission in Paris, followed by another $80,000 for "F-4 tires and spares for TAMPELA [*sic*] mortars."[31] According to Salinger, Montanès's papers included payments made to companies in the UK, Israel, Spain, and Italy, as well as payments for planes to ferry the equipment first from Tel Aviv to Nimes, and secondly from Nimes to Tehran. This was Iran Air Flight 999 from Nimes.

In any case, Montanès had papers documenting the arms sales, and he gave them to Salinger. "I got the papers showing the transfer of $85,027.45 to Kredietbank in Luxembourg for the hiring of a Cargolux aircraft to do the flight from Nimes to Teheran," Salinger wrote. "Two other papers showed the transfer of a total of $330,042.65 to the Bank Hapoalim in Zurich for the mission of the Government of Israel."

The documents did not indicate the source of the funds, but the invoices had been prepared by Ahmed Heidari, the Iranian arms procurement official.[32] Iran, of course, had already paid the United States for the weapons, so in effect, they were paying twice. "Israel may have stepped in to pay for some of the transactions, with the idea that they would be repaid," Sick told me.[33]

Initially, I was unsure how much weight to give Salinger's report. After all, invoices could easily be faked. There was disinformation everywhere. And Pierre Salinger's reputation was not spotless: in 1996, he had bought into a discredited conspiracy theory asserting that when TWA Flight 800 crashed, killing 230 people, it had been brought down by a missile fired from a US Navy ship.[34]

Still, these invoices aligned neatly with the timeline following the Paris meetings, meetings which had not yet been revealed in 1981 when Salinger broke his ABC story. And they weren't the only part of Salinger's investigation that was of interest. As he wrote in his memoir, in 1991, after *Newsweek* eviscerated the October Surprise, Salinger took exception to its conclusions and decided to investigate it further. An opportunity arose the following year, when David Andelman, de Marenches's coauthor and a resident of Paris at the time, told Salinger he was traveling to the US with de Marenches to promote their new book.

"I called him [Andelman] and told him that while he was with Marenche [*sic*] to push him roughly to get the truth about the Paris meeting," Salinger wrote.[35] When Andelman got back to Salinger, he said "that Marenche had finally agreed he organize [sic] the meeting, under the request of an old friend, William Casey."

Salinger added, "There was an American-Iranian meeting in Paris on October 18 and 19. That meeting was organized by Alexander De Marenche [*sic*]. . . . For a long time, Marenche [*sic*] denied anything to do with the meeting."

The takeaway was clear: The Carter administration had outlawed sales of weapons to Iran. Carter had nothing to do with these arms transfers. The flight to and from Nimes was overseen by French intelligence and de Marenches, who had met with Casey during the summer of 1980 and helped arrange the Paris meetings on October 15–20.

Meanwhile, I had not failed to notice that the arms shipments in Salinger's memo bore a striking resemblance to those initiated by the Hashemis. According to a declassified November 12, 1980, FBI memo to Oliver "Buck" Revell, assistant director of the FBI, "Dr. Hashemi and REDACTED are currently engaged in a deal to attempt to obtain repair parts for aircraft, including the F-4, and have held discussions with exporters regarding the purchase of missiles."[36]

All of which raised the question of whether these arms sales might well have represented the payoff to Iran for Casey's October Surprise—or at least the down payment for an ongoing flow of weapons. After all, how many people were violating an embargo by selling F-4 tires to Iran in the fall of 1980? But I still had loads of questions. I needed more corroboration. And I knew some of the answers were in Iran.

Chapter Eighteen
Tehran

IT WAS ABOUT 8:30 IN THE MORNING ON OCTOBER 30, 2014, AT the Melal Hotel in Tehran when my cell phone rang. My translator-fixer was on the line. Like all Western journalists in Iran, I had entered the country with a much sought-after media visa that had one distasteful constraint: I had to be accompanied at all times by a government-approved translator-fixer.

The idea of government supervision by the Islamic Republic was anathema to me, of course—as it is to all journalists. However, after six days in Iran, I realized I had lucked out insofar as my fixer had been able to line up four or five interviews per day for me—a considerable feat given Tehran's horrific traffic and horrendous bureaucracy.

Like dozens of other Western journalists, I had come to Tehran to report on the nuclear negotiations taking place between the United States and Iran. Barack Obama was in his second term as president, and that meant for one brief shining moment the frigid relationship between the United States and the Islamic Republic of Iran had temporarily thawed. Suddenly, it was possible for American journalists to get a media visa to Iran. At the time, I had been covering national security for *Vanity Fair* for more than a decade, and I jumped at this chance.

For the first time since the Islamic Revolution in 1979, there were ongoing face-to-face talks between high-level officials of the two countries—notably Iranian foreign minister Javad Zarif and Secretary of State John Kerry. At the time, the stakes were high enough that the United States had joined forces with the four other permanent members of the UN Security Council—Russia, China, the United Kingdom, and France—as well as Germany, the P5 plus one.[1] Their goal was to reach an agreement that would reduce Iran's nuclear program, in return for which the West would lift economic sanctions. If the negotiations succeeded, a historic rapprochement between Iran and the United States could be in the offing.

Truth be told, I had come to Iran with another agenda. In all the writing about the October Surprise, very little attention had been paid to Iran's role in the conspiracy. I wanted to rectify that, and one of the key people I wanted to interview was Mohsen Rafighdoost, the founding minister of the Islamic Revolutionary Guard Corps (IRGC). In addition to being in charge of logistics for the IRGC at the time of the hostage crisis, Rafighdoost played a key role in arms procurement and likely had oversight of the arms deals at the time—including the Tel-Aviv-Nimes-Tehran deal I was tracking. [2]

The son of a fresh produce merchant at the Tehran market, Rafighdoost first came to prominence in February 1979 when, as head of security for Ayatollah Khomeini, he got in the driver's seat of a Chevy Blazer[3] and drove Khomeini from the airport through the streets of Tehran lined by millions of Iranians hailing the Imam on his triumphant return.[4]

Once Khomeini took power, he appointed Rafighdoost head[5] of the newly founded Revolutionary Guard (IRGC), the nation's premier security force that became a notorious Mafia-like enforcer fighting both domestic and foreign threats to the Islamic Republic. As such he had a key role in arms procurement.

Not long after the Revolution, the Pahlavi Foundation, which held billions of dollars in assets of the Shah, was seized by the new regime and renamed Bonyad-e Mostazafan (Foundation of the Oppressed).* As *Forbes* put it, "Many bonyads seem like straightforward rackets, extorting money from entrepreneurs," who if they refuse to contribute

---

* Bonyads are charitable trusts that control about 20 percent of Iran's GDP and funnel revenues to groups that support the Islamic Republic.

are then accused of not being good Muslims and, possibly, even sent to jail. "The Cosa Nostra meets fundamentalism," the magazine said.[6]

A decade later, after the assets of other wealthy Iranians were confiscated as well, he oversaw what was the successor to the Shah's foundation, and, according to *Forbes*, the largest holding company in the Middle East with four hundred thousand workers and more than $20 billion in assets.

Now, some twenty-five years later, he was a member of Iran's ruling elite, a wealthy, well-known, and powerful figure who was overseeing a multi-billion-dollar cartel. Whenever I mentioned his name, knowledgeable Iranians rolled their eyes and responded with a knowing smile. No one had profited from the Islamic Revolution more than he. He was said to be worth hundreds of millions of dollars himself.[7]

Getting an interview with Rafighdoost was not easy. My fixer had tried repeatedly, but so far had struck out. By this time, I'd been in Iran for six days out of my seven-day visa. I was running out of time.

For the most part, I'd spent the preceding week interviewing various government officials, academics, and economists for *Vanity Fair*. I made the obligatory pit stop at what had been the American embassy, which had been turned into a museum of grievances by Iran against the United States—and a major tourist attraction in Tehran.

To millions of Iranians, the American embassy even after all these years was truly a den of spies—not so much because of the 1979–1980 hostage crisis as it was because of the 1953 coup that overthrew Mossadegh and installed the Shah. After all, this is where the Roosevelt cousins, Kermit Jr. and Archibald Jr., and Miles Copeland had plotted to put together Operation Ajax.

Upon entering, one steps on a doormat reading "Down with the USA," and encounters enormous photographic posters of the 1979 Islamic Revolution showing protesters holding signs reading "No Negotiations, Return the Shah," photos of the American hostages being frog-marched at the embassy, displays of weapons, surveillance equipment, typewriters, and documents—presumably highly classified CIA documents that had been shredded by shredding machines and laboriously reassembled.

No symbol in the entire country more powerfully exemplified Iran's hatred of its puppet masters, enmity that had scarcely faded in the thirty-five years since the Revolution. Yet at the time, Barack Obama in the United States and Iranian president Hassan Rouhani had opened up the possibility of warmer relations. These were the Obama years. There was optimism in the air. Remember that?

One of my first interviews was with Davoud Bavand, an adviser to President Hassan Rouhani, who had become a moderate reformer and who traced his lineage as a supporter of secular democracy back to President Mossadegh.

Bavand welcomed me into his North Tehran home, which was handsomely appointed with fine antiques and Persian art. With his angular features and hawkish nose, the balding, mustachioed Bavand looked every bit the part of an elegant, dignified, and gracious diplomat. He wore a suit and tie—noteworthy in that neckties are considered haram (forbidden) in parts of Iran because they are seen as symbols of Western secularism and therefore are anathema to the Islamic Republic. Thanks to Rouhani, the prospect of change was in the air—only briefly, alas—but at the time that made Bavand's Western attire a bit more acceptable.

Bavand had escaped the fate of many of his colleagues under the Shah, some of whom were imprisoned and even executed as Iran made the transition from a brutal, corrupt, and repressive regime that was secular and pro-West to one which was also brutal, corrupt, and repressive, but theocratic and fiercely anti-American.

But Bavand survived, and, if his sumptuous town house was any indication, flourished. Steeped in the ways of the West, he was acutely sensitive to the high price the Islamic Republic was paying for its isolation from the rest of the world. As spokesman for the National Front, the secular, center-left party founded by Mossadegh, he was firmly behind President Hassan Rouhani's "charm offensive" and his efforts to forge a détente with the United States.

Bavand seemed to have an inborn sense of how far he could test the Islamic fundamentalist regime without crossing the red line—a red line that for many led to prison, and even hanging or the firing squad. Every so often, Bavand challenged those limits. A few months earlier in 2014, Bavand gave a newspaper interview in which he described "eye-for-an-eye" punishment as "inhumane." According to Bavand, the paper was promptly shut down and banned "for spreading lies and insulting Islam." But Bavand escaped punishment.[8]

As my translator and I took our seats in his sitting room, Bavand, in the Iranian fashion, assumed the role of a gracious host serving us tea as honored guests—not merely an official being interviewed by a journalist. He spoke fluent, heavily accented English.[9]

I dutifully asked Bavand about the ongoing negotiations with the Obama administration, but after about thirty minutes, I switched to the October Surprise. During the hostage crisis, he was an aide to President Bani-Sadr, and, along with the president and Foreign Minister Sadegh Ghotbzadeh, he had been among those arguing for the release of the hostages—with no success. After Iraq attacked Iran in September, he said, "We realized we had to do something quickly [to get arms] or we faced disaster."[10]

And what were the obstacles? When he tried to get to the bottom of, he said, "the rumor was that there were negotiations on the part of Reagan that wanted *not* to release the hostages. The rumors were very strong."

At the time, however, in the early days of the Revolution, thousands of komiteh, or revolutionary committees, served as the eyes and ears of the new regime with "many arbitrary arrests, executions and confiscations of property."[11]

Even though it was widely known that talking about the secret deal with the Republicans was dangerous, that hadn't stopped

Ghotbzadeh, who, on September 6, 1980, told Agence France-Presse that he had information proving that the "Reagan camp was trying hard to block a solution of the [hostage] problem."[12] Five days later, Ghotbzadeh went even further and made similar charges in a letter to *Enghelab Eslami* asserting that "we know that the United States Republican Party, in order to win the coming election campaign, is trying hard to delay the solution of the hostage issue until after the United States elections."[13]

And how had Ghotbzadeh found out about Casey's op?

Mustafa Zein, the Lebanese operative who had worked so closely with the CIA's Bob Ames, explained in an email to Parry. When Casey aide Jack Shaw had requested that Zein try to thwart the overture to Arafat, Zein wrote, "[I] went to Paris to see Sadeg Kotbzade [*sic*] and told him in detail of what had happened to me. He made a press statement at the time in Sept 1980, but no one listened to him and later on was sentenced to death."[14]

Two months later, Ghotbzadeh was arrested for speaking out against the Islamic Republican Party.[15] In 1982, after being brutally tortured at Evin Prison, he confessed that he had participated in a plot to kill Khomeini and overthrow the Islamic regime. He was subsequently put to death by a firing squad.[16] "Ghotbzadeh was one of the real heroes in Iran," Jimmy Carter said. "He worked heroically to try to release the hostages."[17]

Like Ghotbzadeh, Bavand had been close to Bani-Sadr, and a proponent of secular democracy. In 2014, it seemed that the regime had moderated somewhat from the early days of the revolution. Decades had passed since the executions of Ghotbzadeh and hundreds of other dissenters. But I wondered how far Bavand would go.

I asked if he knew about the meetings in Madrid and Paris. "Yes," he said.[18] "It was a kind of rumor. You could read between the lines of certain statements and written material, that there was a kind of negotiations at the time on the part of Reagan. The rumors were very strong, but no one could confirm them.

"Of course, the October Surprise happened," he added. "But you'll never prove it." The information was much too closely held, and he had no direct knowledge himself.

For days, I'd been pressing to set up an interview with Rafighdoost with no success. By this time, I knew this would likely be my last chance to interview an Iranian who had been an active participant in the October Surprise. Then, as my last full day in Iran began, I got a phone call urgently telling me to be ready in ten minutes. Mohsen Rafighdoost had agreed to see me. I knew that the man *Forbes* magazine had, in effect, dubbed the Godfather of the Islamic Republic of Iran would be a hostile subject, but I had to try.

The most Westernized neighborhood in the city, North Tehran is Iran's version of Beverly Hills and displays all the contradictions that epitomize Iran. Its main drag, Valiasr Avenue, formerly known as Pahlavi Street, was developed under the Shah to be the Tehran equivalent of what the Champs-Élysées is to Paris, or what Rodeo Drive is to Los Angeles. Even now, under a repressive Islamist regime, it is still lined with department stores, luxury jewelry stores, boutiques selling Rolex watches, chic restaurants, and the like—alongside of which one sees prominently and incongruously displayed banners in memory of the martyrs who lost their lives in the Iran-Iraq War.

In recent years, North Tehran had become the epicenter of a clandestine late-night party scene that belies the repressive ethos of the Islamic Republic. Perhaps as part of the legacy of the Shah, rich kids cruise its streets in Porsches, Mercedes, Lamborghinis, and Maseratis. Its hillsides are dotted with $20 million homes. Indoors, young women wearing six-inch heels doff their hijabs to reveal neon-colored hair, and, at night, ingest bootleg liquor, party drugs, and hallucinogens. It is haram, of course, to watch foreign TV, but if one looks carefully, one can see satellite dishes atop the homes—thanks to Basiji militia who have been bribed to look the other way. There is an old Persian saying, "Whatever goes on between four walls, stays between those walls." Nowhere is it more pertinent.

As it happens, North Tehran is also where Shah Mohammad Reza Pahlavi spent most of his time, in the opulent Niavaran Palace, before Iran's monarchy fell. Today, high-level diplomats and key figures and institutions in the Islamic Republic are based in the neighborhood. Though more sedate and understated than the glitzy party scene nearby, their presence represents even more power and riches. Here too the ancient Persian maxim holds sway—though for very different reasons.

Just after noon, our Peugeot arrived at the bonyad's headquarters on Shariati Street, and my translator and I were escorted into Rafighdoost's office. Rafighdoost was on a tight schedule, we were told. He had thirty minutes for us—no more.

SHORT, BALDING, AND BESPECTACLED, WITH A TRIMMED SALT-and-pepper beard, Rafighdoost was dressed completely in black, in keeping with Shia custom of mourning during the sacred month of Muharram. My translator introduced us, and Rafighdoost greeted me with a firm handshake. Behind him was a portrait of the Supreme Leader, Ayatollah Ali Khameini, who had succeeded Khomeini; a smaller likeness of Maj. Gen. Qasem Soleimani,* the military mastermind who was the leader of the Revolutionary Guard's elite Quds Force; and a beautiful, framed engraving of the word "Allah" in Farsi.

By the time I got to his Tehran office, I still had hundreds of unanswered questions, but I was certain that he was a key figure in what

* On January 3, 2020, Soleimani was assassinated in an American drone strike on orders from President Donald Trump.

had happened. At the time, I had a few shreds of knowledge about the illegal arms shipment on October 24, 1980—eleven days before the US presidential elections.[19] I had been assured that it could not possibly have taken place without Rafighdoost's knowledge. Among other things, I wanted to confirm that they were one and the same. If I could verify that and link the shipments to the Hashemis—Casey's moles!—I figured that would show how the arms pipeline behind the October Surprise began to flow.

With the help of my translator, I introduced myself. I explained that in addition to writing about US policy in the Middle East for *Vanity Fair*, I had written *House of Bush, House of Saud*, and other books that were highly critical of the Saudis, the Bush family, and neoconservatives—all of whom, it could be fairly said, were not in favor in Tehran.

Rafighdoost nodded and smiled. "You are free to ask about whatever you want," he said.[20]

Noting that we were approaching the thirty-fifth anniversary of the Iranian Islamic Revolution, I asked if the nuclear deal might mark a new era in US-Iranian relations. "It's been stated many times that the Supreme Leader said that making the atomic bomb is haram," Rafighdoost replied. "This is not new. Some thirty-three years ago, I talked to Imam Khomeini and he told me making nuclear bombs was haram.[21]

"Thirty years ago," he added, "an ambassador told me you have broken the American hegemony in the Middle East, and for that reason America will be your everlasting enemy."[22]

Of course. The Great Satan. After talking with Rafighdoost for just a few minutes, I could see where this was going, and I didn't like it. I had traveled seven thousand miles to see him, and I wanted more than to hear Rafighdoost parrot the Supreme Leader's diatribe. So, just five minutes or so into our interview, I made a rather unusual break in protocol. I changed the subject and began asking about the October Surprise.

Mind you, this was not a decision I made lightly. Virtually every Iranian I met—government officials included—had been extraordinarily hospitable. But I also knew that, for all the graciousness I enjoyed, there was an unspoken "red line" that one crossed at one's peril. In late July 2014, just three months prior to my arrival in Iran, *Washington Post* reporter Jason Rezaian, an Iranian American, and his wife, Yeganeh Salehi, had been taken into custody by Iranian authorities, with Rezaian being locked up on trumped-up charges of espionage at Iran's infamous Evin Prison. The most notorious prison in Iran, Evin had been the site of countless executions and torture sessions dating back to the Shah, a tradition that had continued under the new regime.

Because he had both American citizenship and an Iranian passport (which meant Iran regarded him as an Iranian national), Rezaian was vulnerable to such charges, and I wasn't—or so my colleagues assured me. In addition, I had confided about my interest in the October Surprise with several Iranian friends, and they felt that raising questions about it now, more than thirty years after the fact, would not put me at risk. There was no one in Iran more knowledgeable than Rafighdoost about vital events that took place more than thirty-five years earlier—and this might be my only chance.

Before I continued, however, I took several photos of Rafighdoost with my iPhone. He projected a certain feral intensity. A profile of Rafighdoost by Robert Kaplan in *The Atlantic* described him as someone who "straddled the line between suave and sleazy. He could almost have passed for a nightclub bouncer."[23] I could see what Kaplan meant.

When I finished taking pictures, I put the phone on the desk in front of me, propped up horizontally in its case. I noticed that the camera function was still on display, and Rafighdoost was perfectly framed in the screen. On the right side of the phone, I could see the words signifying various functions from top to bottom. At the time, in 2014, videotaping was operational on new cell phones like mine, but it was not yet ubiquitous—certainly not in Iran. Without thinking about it in advance, I secretly began to videotape Mohsen Rafighdoost, one of the founders of the powerful and feared Iranian Revolutionary Guard Corps. I felt reasonably sure they would not figure it out. But I wasn't certain.

As founding minister of the Revolutionary Guard, from the earliest days of the Islamic Revolution, Rafighdoost had firsthand knowledge of every substantive arms deal in the entire country in its early years.[24] He lived in a shadow world of duplicity and clandestine arms deals, at a time during the early days of the Iran-Iraq War, when the vast majority of weapons bought by Tehran came from Israel or the United States—even though such transactions amounted to a capital crime in Iran. All of which suggested that Mohsen Rafighdoost was the overlord of all such arms deals, he had to be knowledgeable about the Tel Aviv-Nimes-Tehran flight.

I realized that it was highly unlikely he would spill his guts to me, but I plowed ahead anyway. "I hope you don't mind if I change the subject," I said. "I want to go back in time to 1980."

Then, I proceeded to outline the October Surprise scenario for Rafighdoost. Since he was in charge of Iran's arms trade, I asked if he was aware of any arms sales to Iran through Israel.

Rafighdoost began by knocking down the premise that Israel played any role in the October Surprise. "After the revolution, Khomeini said we do not consider Israel a legitimate state," he said.[25] "The information you provide regarding secret meetings brokered by Israel is totally wrong. There were many secret meetings between Americans and Iranians, but they were not brokered by Israel. There is a possibility that Americans cooperated with Israel, but Iran didn't know that."

I knew he was not telling the truth, but I let it slide and moved on. Sometimes a lie was a great place to start.

What about the Republicans, I asked? Was Iran secretly meeting with Republicans during the summer of 1980? That would nail down at least one essential element of the October Surprise.

For several minutes, there was a frenzied back-and-forth between my interpreter and Rafighdoost in Farsi. I understood nothing. Over the years, I've had considerable experience trying to tease out information from reluctant interview subjects. But in this case, the language barrier—the fact that I had to go through a translator—made that virtually impossible.

Rafighdoost clearly understood English well enough to grasp what I was saying, so by the time my interpreter translated my question into Farsi, he already had a clearly thought-out response. On the other hand, I couldn't understand a word of his Farsi. Consequently, it was impossible to catch him off guard, and as we politely said goodbye, I left not knowing what had really transpired.

Then, it was over. My thirty minutes was up, and, thanks to the language barrier, I had lost control.

As we drove back to my hotel, my translator explained that for a nanosecond, Rafighdoost began to open up. "When we met with the Republicans, and they made an offer . . ." Rafighdoost had said.

With that, my translator had pounced. "So the Republicans *did* make an offer?" he asked.

But Rafighdoost instantly backtracked. "I meant, '*If* the Republicans had made such an offer,'" he said, "Iran would have refused it."

Which had he really meant—*when* or *if*? Had he slipped up?

After I thought about it, I realized no matter how you sliced it, my interview with Rafighdoost had not truly advanced the story. In the end, he had denied everything.

My plane was scheduled to leave early the next afternoon. There was no possibility of extending my visa on such short notice. Time was running out.

AT 8:00 A.M. THE FOLLOWING DAY, MY CELL PHONE RANG. IT was a friend I'd met in Iran who was familiar with my quandary. He said he'd meet me in the hotel's cafe downstairs—with someone I had to meet.

At about 9:00 a.m., I went to the café and saw my friend, accompanied by a man we'll call Hamid.* He was thirty-eight years old, rugged, and balding. As we chatted for a few minutes over coffee, it soon became apparent that Hamid was friendly, knowledgeable, and smart. His English was fluent. And he was steeped in the details of the Iranian hostage crisis in a way that few if any Americans were. So, I recounted at length my interview with Rafighdoost the previous day.

Hamid listened attentively. "Rafighdoost was lying to you," he said.

I wasn't surprised. That was what I wanted to hear—but could he back it up?

"This is what really happened," Hamid said.

With that, he launched into a richly detailed narrative about a plane carrying a shipment of illegal weapons to Iran in October 1980. Hamid did not have all the particulars I needed, but I knew instantly that he was talking about the famous series of flights that constituted one of the most controversial parts of the October Surprise—Iran Air Flight 999, which delivered military equipment from Israel to Iran, from Nimes, on October 24, 1980.

The flights in question were a crucial part of the October Surprise scenario because the military equipment was said to comprise the down payment by the Republicans for the secret deal they made with Iran. This was the flight for which Jacques Montanès had brought the receipts.

---

* To protect his identity, Hamid's name has been changed, as have various identifying details.

According to a report compiled by the Congressional Research Service (CRS), in the appendix of the House task force account, "the complete list of the immediate needs of the Iranian Army was put in the hands of an Israeli diplomat in Paris."[26] Then, on October 23, the report said, a Caravelle jet airliner owned by a French company called Aerotour was chartered to pick up Israeli military equipment.[27] According to Gary Sick's *October Surprise*, the shipment would never have moved forward "without at least tacit approval by French intelligence."[28] Specifically, he was referring to Alain Gagneron de Marolles, who was a principal deputy to de Marenches at the Service de Documentation Extérieure et de Contre-Espionnage (SDECE).[29]

The CRS report added that the plane flew from Paris to Bastia, Corsica, where it waited for a go-ahead from Israel, and then on to Tel Aviv, where it was loaded with 250 retreaded tires for F-4 Phantom fighter jets.

From Tel Aviv, the Caravelle flew to Nimes, a city of 120,000 people in southern France, on October 23, where its cargo was loaded onto a DC-8 that belonged to Cargolux Company and had been charted by SETI. Now, the F4 tires from Israel were loaded onto the new plane, along with spare parts for M60 tanks, an M60 engine, and other materiel. The CRS report noted that the "flight documents had been amended for customs and for purposes of discretion."[30]

The CRS also reported that "Flight authorizations were obtained with the help of the Iranair Company, and the flight was carried out under flight number Iranair 999 [*sic*]."[31]

In other words, once the Aerotour plane landed in Nimes, the cargo was transferred to a DC-8 that appeared to be just another Iranian commercial jet—Iran Air Flight 999, scheduled to go from Nimes to Tehran. But in fact, the payload included the tires for Iranian F-4 fighter jets from the flight that originated in Tel Aviv and other cargo that had been loaded in Nimes.

The report even cited an account in which a French official gave "a green light" for the mission but demanded secrecy. "If you go to

Iran to organize the recruiting of three specialists to put order in the stock of armament, we have nothing against it," a French official told Pierre Gaudinat, specialist in international cargo who helped organize the arms deliveries.[32] "So green light. But no paper. If you asked, they know nothing. They never saw me, and they never told me anything."

But in the end, the task force dismissed the ties to French intelligence and said that the arms shipments had been set in motion simply because they were profitable and that they had nothing to do with Casey and the Republicans.

To the best of my knowledge, no one had investigated these flights from the Iranian perspective, but now, thanks to Hamid, I was learning details about the shipment from the Iranian side. "Israel was the arch enemy of Iran," he said, "but it helped Iran against our common enemies. That was the bottom line. Khomeini was told by his advisers to promote this hypocritical policy of shouting against Israel but secretly making deals with them."

"Iran had people inside Israel overseeing the deal," he added.[33] "I can get you the names."

Given the degree to which Israel had been demonized by the regime, secrecy was paramount. If such an operation was exposed, the offender faced execution.

According to Hamid, the shipment was so sensitive that when it got to France, Mohsen Rafighdoost himself had to be on board personally to oversee it. "Rafighdoost did it," said Hamid. "He was privileged to carry the guns by passenger airline . . . He did it."

Once it took off, the DC-8 had to fly approximately 2,500 miles to Tehran, a five-hour flight that took it over the Mediterranean, Italy, what was then Yugoslavia, over Bulgaria, the Black Sea, and Turkey before reaching its destination in Iran. According to Hamid, the first half of the flight was relatively uneventful. But about three hours after takeoff, as it flew over Turkey, a Turkish air controller spotted the unauthorized flight.

"I'll give you the scene," Hamid said. "The control tower of a Turkish airport radioed the pilot. 'Come down,' he said. 'Land! You are suspicious. You must land! You are not civilian! You are carrying something!'"

With that, according to Hamid, the pilot left the cockpit to tell Rafighdoost what was going on and ask for instructions. Rafighdoost instantly understood that if they landed in Turkey, the entire operation would be exposed. He recoiled.

"Don't land!" he shouted. "Don't land!"

The pilot did as told by Rafighdoost, ignored the Turkish air control tower, and continued on course to Tehran. In the end, Turkey did not fire on the plane. In an hour, they were over Iranian airspace, and from there it was just another hour to Tehran. At 4:00 p.m. on the afternoon of October 24, 1980, Iran Air Flight 999 from Nimes arrived at Mehrabad International Airport in Tehran. Its slightly disguised bill of lading listed 250 tires, one Caterpillar motor, one truck motor, spare parts for ten other motors, and other sundries—all of which was consigned to "Presidency, Republic of Iran, Tehran."

TEHRAN TIME IS EIGHT AND A HALF HOURS AHEAD OF Washington time, which means that at that time, President Carter's day was just getting started. As was often the case, the fate of the hostages in Iran was the top item on his agenda.

Just two days earlier, the White House had received a positive response from Tehran about returning the hostages. Carter felt he was a hair's breadth from finalizing a deal and that if he got another positive response from Iran he would be able to go on national television to announce that the hostages were coming home soon. There were just eleven days before the presidential election, and the return of the hostages might be just the thing to put Carter over the top.

But, at the same meeting, Carter received another piece of news that was far more closely tied to the fate of the hostages than he realized: Israel was notifying the United States that it had sent a shipment of military equipment to Iran.

Just a few months earlier, in April 1980, Israeli prime minister Menachem Begin had given Carter his solemn word that under no circumstances would he allow Israeli arms shipments to Iran or equipment of any kind—"not . . . even shoelaces."[34] Thus, the shipment that Carter was now learning about was a clear violation of the arms embargo.

Hamid's fluid and spontaneous presentation was enormously compelling, but I knew it was all secondhand information and I still had dozens of follow-up questions. How did he know all this? Who were his sources? Would they talk? If they talked, could I use their names, or did they too fear the wrath of Rafighdoost and his colleagues?

By this time, however, it was 10:30. My plane was scheduled to leave in three hours, which meant that I had to leave for the airport in less than an hour. I now had so many people I wanted to reach out to in Iran that I wanted to stay a few extra days. If I could corroborate what Hamid had told me, if I could find a firsthand witness to the payoff for the October Surprise, in effect, I would have truly advanced the story. But this was not simply a matter of changing flights. My visa would expire in just a few hours. There was no way to get an extension fast enough.

I decided to make the most of the little time that was left. I asked Hamid: Was this arms shipment a direct result of meetings the Iranians had with Bill Casey and other Republicans in Paris and Madrid earlier that summer? Did the Israelis who were involved have direct contact with the Republicans as well as Iran? I also needed to make sure that Hamid was talking about the same flight. He said he didn't have all the answers, but he said he knew people who might.

"Rafighdoost wasn't alone," he said.[35] Then he gave me the name and phone number of another man who was on the flight with Rafighdoost. I had never heard of him before, but I soon discovered he was a well-known professional. The only reasonable course was to return to New York and pursue it later. At last, I had a new lead. Given the security concerns of the Islamic Republic of Iran, I also knew that calling him from the United States while he was in Iran would jeopardize his safety, so I would have to figure out a way to reach him while he was in another country.

A considerable period of time passed before I was able to reach out to him. When I finally did, however, I encountered a new insurmountable obstacle: he was dead.

Chapter Nineteen
The End of the Beginning

My Iranian leads had hit a dead end, but the importance of that October 24, 1980, flight stayed with me. It seemed that if I could get on the other side of that flight, the how of the Iranian arms shipments would finally become clear. It was another eight years after my trip to Iran before I came up with another way of tracking the arms shipments from Bill Casey's operatives to Iran: the receipts.

When I interviewed Bani-Sadr in Versailles in 2016, he had given me copies of his documents—the same batch, presumably, that he had given to the task force, Bob Parry, and several other people. When I returned to the United States, I'd had his articles and interviews translated from Farsi to English—but that was it.

Bani-Sadr had also given me a pile of receipts and invoices. Stupidly, perhaps, I had never bothered to have them translated.

In case that didn't sink in, let me repeat: Bani-Sadr had the receipts. He had also given them to the House October Surprise Task Force which had access to professional translation services, which translated *everything* Bani-Sadr had turned over to Congress. And that meant Lee Hamilton's October Surprise Task Force had the translated receipts. The documents had been translated by Ibrahim Pourhadi of the African and Middle Eastern Collection Services.

As I discovered, however, the task force report had omitted any mention of them. Instead, they filed them in cardboard boxes, and left them in the abandoned ladies' room near the tampon dispenser, where Bob Parry discovered them. They were in a folder titled "A Sample of 'Documents' Provided by Abol Hassan Bani-Sadr, Former President of Iran." In addition to Bani-Sadr's columns for his publication, *Enghelab Eslami* (Islamic Revolution), there were newspaper clippings in Farsi, and an order from Iran's Ministry of Defense labeled "Top Secret," with invoices for parts for F-4 fighter jets, Shinook helicopters, an M60 tank, and more. There was also the translation of a note on top of the list, which presumably had been written by one of Bani-Sadr's English-speaking acolytes. "Khomeini allows Iranian officers to buy arms from the Israelis though he considered them Satanic," it read.

But by the time he discovered them, Parry had amassed millions of pages of documents—literally—regarding the October Surprise. So far as I can tell, these were among those he overlooked.

And that meant *no one* had ever bothered to examine the receipts—receipts that recorded arms sales that had been delivered to Iran at a time when Bani-Sadr was president just after the Revolution.

They just didn't bother to look at them.

When I finally found them, it instantly became clear that Bani-Sadr's records clearly tied illegal arms shipments to Iran and Casey's operatives, the Hashemis. More specifically, among the documents submitted to the task force by the former Iranian president was an invoice containing a list of spare parts purchased by Iran and their costs.

The translation noted, "The needed arms were purchased from the United States and Israel. However, it was soon discovered that Iran's Revolutionary Forces were also purchasing arms through other channels. Of course, all these needed arms were purchased in strict secrecy."[1]

It also noted, on page fifteen, that there was a copy of an invoice containing a list of spare parts purchased and their cost. "The spare parts were for C-130 Airplane [*sic*]," the translation said. "On the lower left side, a reproduction of a visiting card of M. A. Hashemi-Bolonian, representative of an Import-Export R.R.C. Co."[2]

And indeed, there was a receipt in Farsi that, of course, was mostly unintelligible to me. But it was accompanied by a barely legible itemized list in English, of spare parts—for valves, props, engines, and radar beam couplers, and the like—amounting to $1,136,766.[3]

As for the names on the invoice, one of them, M. A. Hashemi-Balanian, was too familiar for me to ignore. The Hashemis—Jamshid, especially—frequently used aliases. In fact, even though he was usually identified as Jamshid Hashemi in news reports and both congressional investigations, and later changed his name to James Khan, his real full name was Mohamad Ali Balanian Hashemi.[4] He used it[5] when he checked into the hotel in Madrid. And he used it as a member of the Central Committee,[6] headed by Ayatollah Kani, who had met with Casey at the mid-August meetings in Madrid.

The last name on the business card among Bani-Sadr's receipts was slightly different, however. But Hashemi-Bolonian—that is, Bolonian rather than Balanian—also had to be Jamshid, I figured. When I looked at the business card, I understood the discrepancy immediately because it used an unusual font in which the lowercase *a* looked very much like an *o*. That was how Balanian became Bolonian.

Moreover, when Jamshid—or, rather, Balanian-Hashemi—had first arrived in the United States in 1980, he had set up a company called Import-Export R.R.C. in Stamford, Connecticut, which, Jamshid said, "originally dealt in commodities such as rice and sugar, construction machinery parts and Oriental rugs."[7]

It was hard to believe that there could be an M. A. Hashemi-Bolonian Import-Export R.R.C. in Stamford, Connecticut, and an M. A. Hashemi-Balanian who had set up a company with the same name in the same city. So, it had to be him.

Bani-Sadr's documents also contained articles from *Enghelab Eslami*, which further explained that "RRC Company, Inc. was nominally an import-export company for Iranian carpets, but was really a front for sales of massive amounts of U.S. arms to Iran. The president of RRC Co., [*sic*] Gamshid Hashemi (aka Mohammad Ali Hashemi-Balanian), received letters of credit from the Khomeini regime."[8]

By this time, it was well established that the Hashemis were Casey operatives, so I asked Gary Sick to evaluate the documents. "Jamshid Hashemi's business card on the sheet suggests very strongly that he was involved in the illegal sale of parts for C-130 American cargo planes in Iran's inventory from the days of the Shah, and that he was one of the trusted intermediaries Iran relied on to procure military equipment on the black market," he wrote in a March 2024 email to me. "It indicates almost casually that Iran was receiving shipments of military equipment from Israel during or just after the period of the US presidential election of November 1980—the so-called October Surprise.[9]

"These deliveries were unknown to the Carter White House and would appear to be part of the 'payoff' that William Casey arranged via Israel in return for Iran holding the hostages until after Ronald Reagan became president. Regardless, this is the first documentary evidence of the highly secret Israel-Iran weapons trafficking, contrary to the Carter administration's best efforts to prevent it, and ties it definitively to one of the arms dealers who was 'playing both sides' in Casey's plan to defeat Carter in the 1980 election."[10]

Of course, back in 1980, the Carter administration had no idea that all the Hashemis had been putting these shipments together for Casey. As the presidential campaign neared its end, Reagan and Carter were still running neck and neck in the polls. On October 23, a report in the *New York Times* had offered a ray of hope for Carter. Iranian prime minister Mohammed Ali Rajai, just returned to Tehran from New York, said, "The hostages are not really a problem for us; we are in the process of resolving it."[11]

Similarly, according to Hojatolislam Ashgar Mousavi Khoeiny, a member of Iran's parliamentary commission, the terms for the hostage release could be announced as early as Sunday, October 26. If

Carter agreed to them, he said, the hostages could be freed as early as the following day—Monday, seven days before the election.[12]

At the time, a *New York Times*/CBS poll gave Carter 39 percent, Reagan 38 percent, and third-party candidate John Anderson 9 percent, with 13 percent undecided. It was a virtual dead heat between the major party nominees,[13] and it was reasonable to assume that bringing back the hostages could secure Carter's reelection.

But then, everything went south. Reagan emerged victorious from the October 28 presidential debate, and the Republicans went full throttle in assaulting Carter for "manipulating the crisis to his advantage." Former president Gerald Ford charged that Carter was using the hostages for "purely partisan" reasons.[14] Casey's longtime friend William Safire used his *New York Times* column to attack President Carter just in case he managed to bring the hostages home at the last minute. "Ayatollah Khomeini and his men—after imposing a Year of Shame on their sworn enemy—prefer a weak and manageable U.S. President, and have decided to do everything in their power to determine our election result," Safire wrote. ". . . Why, after holding our diplomats for 51 weeks, are the Iranians dangling their release in front of American voters one week before election? For maximum leverage on Mr. Carter, that's why: to extract an arms and money deal that only a desperate candidate would offer."[15]

All of which meant that Carter's best hope to salvage victory lay seven thousand miles away in Tehran. But when the Majlis resumed debate on October 29, its leisurely deliberations gave every indication they would make no decision before the American elections.[16] On October 30, eighteen members of the Majlis, including four members of its hostage committee, refused to attend the scheduled public session to discuss their release.[17] With no quorum present, they could not move forward.

The Iranians had Carter where they wanted him, and were doing everything possible to humiliate him. And as they ran out the clock, President Jimmy Carter didn't know what to say. On Friday, October

31, in Columbia, South Carolina, he was asked whether the hostages would be released soon. "I hope so," he replied. "I can't predict anything. I don't have a time schedule."[18]

Meanwhile, the Majlis had scheduled a meeting Sunday morning, November 2, just two days before America's presidential election, and the Iranians were expected to produce a specific set of conditions whereby the hostage crisis could be ended.[19]

As Carter's chief of staff Hamilton Jordan wrote in his memoir, if something dramatic happened that day "like the release of the hostages, it would probably allow us to nose Reagan out; a bad signal from the Iranian Parliament would probably mean Reagan's election."[20] In any case, the Carter team was desperate to bring back the hostages.

At 3:45 a.m. on November 2, 1980, Carter, who had been campaigning in Chicago, was awakened by a phone call. The word had come down: The Majlis had finally taken action. Their decision had not yet been translated into English for the president, but it would not be long. Carter rushed back to the White House.

As soon as the presidential chopper landed on the South Lawn, Jimmy Carter hurried down the metal steps to be greeted immediately by National Security Adviser Zbigniew Brzezinski, who handed him the latest communique from Iran. The men went inside and settled into the cabinet room.

By the time he sat down at the oval table, Carter had read the decision of the Iranian parliament.[21] It was quiet in the room. After reading the translation, Carter said that the Majlis had simply restated the same conditions that Khomeini had approved a month earlier.[22]

The president didn't have to say anything more. For all the diplomatic circumlocutions, for all the parliamentary filigree, the communication could be boiled down to two words: no deal.

"The best we can do for the next few days is to indicate our willingness to pursue negotiations," Carter said. It was the resigned response of a man who had almost no options left.[23]

The following day, Pat Caddell, the pollster for the Carter campaign, saw a gigantic political earthquake begin to take place. On Saturday, November 1, three days before the election, Caddell's polls showed Carter in the lead by two or three points. By Monday, November 3, Reagan was ahead by six or seven points.[24] The "undecideds" were stampeding toward Reagan. A nail-biter for Carter had become a sweeping victory for Reagan.

In the end, Reagan won the popular vote by a nearly 10 percent margin, and beat Carter in the Electoral College by a landslide, 489 votes to 49.

IMMEDIATELY AFTER THE ELECTION, REAGAN APPOINTED Casey to be cochair of the transition team with Ed Meese. John Shaheen was thrilled. It meant that his old pal was the pivotal powerbroker in deciding the fate of hundreds of people vying for cabinet-level jobs or anything that would increase their proximity to the most powerful man in the world.

On November 8, four days after the election, John Shaheen called Cyrus Hashemi, on a call recorded by the FBI. "I called [Stanley] Pottinger and told him that if he needed anything from Casey . . . or if Cyrus wants anything in his stuff let me know because, you know, we're one team that works together. And Stan was very appreciative and being a Washington lawyer they live on connections."[25]

Right, Cyrus replied.

"That's their game," Shaheen said.

Then he started talking to Cyrus about Casey. "I told him I was getting into a banking venture with you, and you know, what the hell you might as well have a direct one to one relationship."[26] The banking venture was an apparent reference to Cyrus's attempt to fund Shaheen's bankrupt refinery in Newfoundland.

And that was it. "I'm here if you want me," Shaheen said and signed off.

NOW THAT CASEY WAS IN A POWERFUL POSITION TO DETERmine who got what job in the Reagan administration, there was one person in particular he was concerned about—himself. He wanted to be secretary of state—but it wasn't going to happen.

It did not take a particularly astute observer to see why. The secretary of state was not just a powerful cabinet post. It was a post that called for a mastery of manners, etiquette, formalities. It called for being diplomatic, for presiding over state dinners, for making exactly the right toast at state dinners while attired in black tie.

That wasn't Casey. He mumbled and stumbled and bumbled and spilled food everywhere.[27] And with Nancy Reagan, the fastidious first lady-in-waiting sitting in the wings, aggressively protecting her husband's welfare and public image, it just wasn't going to happen.

Casey talked about it over lunch one day with Richard Allen, who recounted the episode in an oral history interview he gave to the Miller Center at the University of Virginia. "We discussed it and I said, 'Bill, you're not going to be Secretary of State.'

"So, Casey said to me, 'mumble, mumble, mumble Secretary of State.'

"I said, 'Well, you can't be Secretary of State.'

"'Mumble, mumble, mumble.' With that wonderful built-in scrambler of his. I could interpret actually, and did. I said, 'Bill, my view is that you should be DCI.' Director of Central Intelligence."[28]

Before he took the job, however, Casey insisted that Reagan elevate the position to cabinet level. Ultimately, if he wanted to run Reagan's foreign policy—and he did—he'd be able to do it behind the scenes. He also wanted to have complete oversight of intelligence without any interference.[29]

And that was exactly what he got.

FOR PROFESSIONAL MAGICIANS, ONE OF THE KEYS TO GREAT magic is getting the audience to buy into false assumptions—assumptions that they believe to be unquestionably true but that will lead them away from seeing what really happened. If they assume something is true—incontrovertibly true—and they are wrong, then the trick will work and they will be unable to see the truth.

One way they do that is through misdirection. If you really want to understand how a magic trick works, you should do the opposite of what the magician says. When the illusionist says, "Follow my hand," don't. Follow his *other* hand. Chances are, he's intentionally misdirecting you.

And so, like a master illusionist, did Casey. Having created and propagated false assumptions that the Carter administration was cynically manipulating events to bring the hostages home just before November 4, he had sent the press in the wrong direction. It was not a particularly difficult task given that the Republicans had long ago instilled in the American public the assumption that they were tougher than the Democrats. They were the hawks, and the Democrats were the doves. They had been hardliners throughout the Cold War and Vietnam, and now Iran was no exception.

Indeed, one of the Reagan campaign's most frequently told jokes asked, "What's flat and glows in the dark?"

"Tehran, five minutes after Reagan's Inauguration" was the answer.[30]

So it was simple for Reagan, Bush, and Casey and all the campaign surrogates to accuse Carter of weakness, appeasement, and being responsible for America's humiliation.

And if you bought those assumptions, how could you possibly believe the Reagan campaign was secretly arming the people who were chanting, "Death to America!"?

And most Americans had bought those assumption when, on January 20, 1981, Ronald Reagan was to be inaugurated as president of the United States and George H. W. Bush as vice president.

For President Carter, however, this day was about more than the end of his administration. Nothing had affected Carter more intensely as president than the hostage crisis. More than anything, he wanted the hostages released—on his watch.

The day before, Iran and the United States had finally signed a pact known as the Algiers Accords, in which Iran agreed to release the hostages in return for certain legal and monetary concessions. Every *I* had been dotted; every *T* had been crossed. There was nothing left to be done—but the hostages were still in Iran. Day after day, the drumbeat had gone on: America held hostage. The fact that the hostages were still in captivity had come to symbolize the humiliation of America as a pitiful helpless giant. And January 20, 1981, was Day 444, the last day of his presidency.

The president had stayed in the West Wing overnight just in case he was needed to iron out some last-minute hitch. Telexes regarding the unfreezing of Iranian assets and the freeing of the hostages were going back and forth in English, French, and Farsi—and that made for added complexities and interruptions. "I can just see the Iranians delaying for another day, Reagan saying something inflammatory, and our deal going down the drain," Carter said.[31]

Save for an occasional nap on a couch in the Oval Office, on this, the last day of his presidency, he had gone forty-eight hours without sleep.[32]

At 8:28 a.m. Carter had been given word that the planes with the hostages were on the tarmac in Tehran, ready to take off.[33] Reagan was to be sworn in at noon. That left the president waiting anxiously for the next three and a half hours, hoping that the planes would take off. Instead, they just sat there on the tarmac at Tehran's Mehrabad Airport. Carter looked at the grandfather clock in the Oval Office, as the seconds ticked away.[34]

Finally, at about 11:00, President-elect Ronald Reagan and incoming first lady Nancy Reagan came by the White House to socialize and prepare for the ceremonies. As they chatted in the car on the way to the ceremony, Reagan said how much he was looking forward to seeing Bob Hope and Frank Sinatra at the Inaugural. Carter, however, was preoccupied with the fate of the hostages.[35]

The cameras followed the Carters and the Reagans as they took their places on the Inaugural platform erected on the West Front of the White House. George H. W. Bush had already been sworn in as vice president.

At 11:57 a.m., Chief Justice Warren Burger administered the oath of office to Ronald Wilson Reagan.[36] President Reagan then took his place in front of the podium and a crowd of thousands. Jimmy Carter, sat behind Reagan on his left—silent, motionless. The clock had run out on his presidency. At times, his eyes were shut, as if in prayer.

Once he took the podium, Reagan began with an observation that seemed commonplace at the time. "The orderly transfer of authority as called for in the Constitution routinely takes place, as it has for almost two centuries," he said, "and few of us stop to think how unique we really are. In the eyes of many in the world, this every-4-year-ceremony we accept as normal is nothing less than a miracle."[37]

Reagan gave a gracious nod to Carter for "maintaining a political system which guarantees individual liberty to a greater degree than any other."[38] Then, the new president voiced what would become gospel for Reagan conservatism, asserting, "In this present crisis, government is not the solution to our problem; government is the problem."

Reagan couldn't have been more polished. Nothing was amiss. Everything seemed not just orderly but infused with the sheen that only Hollywood can produce. At the same time, one had to wonder what was going on with the hostages. Carter had complied with *all* of Iran's conditions for the hostage release, but they had not been released. Now, he was no longer president. And President Reagan, of course, had never even talked to Iran. He had been giving his Inaugural Address.

Immediately after the speech, Reagan, Jimmy Carter, and a host of dignitaries withdrew to the Capitol Rotunda. Meanwhile, half a world away, just minutes after Reagan finished, that is, at 12:33 and 12:38 p.m. Washington time, two jets took off from Mehrabad Airport in Tehran with all fifty-two hostages on them.[39]

By the time Reagan arrived at the luncheon for congressional leaders in the Capitol's Statuary Hall, he had a special announcement to make. "Some thirty minutes ago," he said, "the planes bearing our prisoners left Iranian air space, and they're now free of Iran."[40]

With that, the audience erupted into excited cheers and applause. Forty-two million people had been watching the Inaugural on TV. Within seconds, the entire country knew about the hostage release. As if by magic, under Reagan, the entire country's mood instantaneously changed. Yellow ribbons—the symbolic display of hope for the safe return of the hostages—were festooned on trees and telephone poles everywhere. There were celebratory parades in New York and Washington. As if scripted by Hollywood, Reagan rode in on his golden steed to rescue the hostages and to replace Carter's malaise with his vision of "a new morning in America." In the end, the nation was too dazzled by Reagan's regal pageantry to ask the right questions. And almost no one in America understood what really happened.

Epilogue

Oddly enough, one of the people who knew the least about what Casey and the Republicans had been up to was one of the first to be clued in. "We were at the bottom of the food chain in terms of knowledge," John Limbert told me.[1]

A former official at the US embassy in Tehran who later served as deputy assistant secretary of state for Iran during the Obama administration, Limbert was one of the fifty-two hostages held captive for the entire 444 days, during which they had little or no access to newspapers, radio, or TV. "The Iranians we knew were at the bottom of the food chain as well. They were nothing more than prison guards."

That, Limbert said, meant that for most of their captivity the hostages didn't have a clue about what was going on. So far as they knew, America had forgotten all about them. But after they were finally released, and landed at New York Stewart International Airport in Orange County, New York, Limbert boarded a bus to nearby West Point, and embraced his wife for the first time in more than a year.[2] "The first thing she told me was 'You were there longer than you needed to be,'" he said. "She meant that the Republicans had negotiated with Iran to keep us longer than necessary. It took about forty years, but I guess now she can say, 'I told you so.'"[3]

By now, it should be clear to all Americans that the October Surprise was not a tinfoil hat conspiracy theory. It happened. Some of its staunchest foes even reversed field and conceded the point. In May 2023, *The New Republic*, once a major antagonist of journalists investigating the October Surprise (including me), determined that the evidence "is now overwhelming" that the "Reagan campaign delayed the release of the Iranian hostages."[4]

Similarly, the evidence is overwhelming that Bill Casey was secretly running a sophisticated intelligence network that made illegal arms deals in return for which Iran detained the hostages until after the election. It's overwhelming that Casey thwarted President Carter's attempts to negotiate a settlement with Iran, that he *was* in Madrid for the July meetings with the Iranians. And Bani-Sadr's receipts show that the Hashemis sent illegal arms shipments to Iran at a time when they were acting on Casey's behalf.

It's not an overstatement to say that this act of treason has played an enormous role in shaping the world we live in, from our domestic politics to our current global crises. In Tehran, the repercussions from the October Surprise still reverberate today thanks to the brutal, repressive theocracy that remains in place. Initially, President Bani-Sadr had been unaware that Ayatollah Khomeini had any role in approving the October Surprise deal, and, shortly after meeting with Pasandideh, he wrote the Supreme Leader, his longtime mentor, in hopes of disrupting any agreement with the Republicans.

"I joined you because I saw you as a man of belief and action," he wrote to Khomeini.[5] "I accepted the post of presidency in order to serve the people according to my belief and spend all my power in defending the principles. However, it has become obvious that you do not want a man of belief and action, but a lackey. The title of presidency is not a status to violate my principles and belief for them. If I am not able to serve, I have no attraction to such titles. If you are looking for a lackey, there are so many lackeys, do not expect such a thing from me. The Shah was not overthrown to be replaced with a worse system."

Afterward, Bani-Sadr met with the Ayatollah and his son, Ahmed, in hopes of a reckoning. "You keep talking about the American hostage deal," Ahmed told Bani-Sadr. "It's done, it's over. Forget about it."[6]

"[Ahmed] said that in front of Khomeini, in front of the Ayatollah," recalled Bani-Sadr, when I spoke with him in 2016.[7] "At that moment, I realized Khomeini himself was behind it. It was the bitterest day of my life. If I had known, I never would have written the letter."

And that meant that the once sacred father-son relationship between Khomeini and Bani-Sadr was over. The hardline mullahs began to consolidate power. Bani-Sadr's supporters were arrested and executed.[8] By early June, Bani-Sadr had directly challenged Khomeini by calling for resistance to dictatorship, an act that was tantamount to treason.[9]

And Khomeini was not going to let his former protégé get away with it. Bani-Sadr was impeached by the Majlis on June 21. Then came the assassination attempts. On one occasion, Bani-Sadr said, two would-be assassins approached him rather sheepishly, guns in hand, and told him they had been ordered to shoot him but didn't want to. Then, they handed their weapons over to Bani-Sadr. "I had to give them their guns back, because if I didn't, they would have been killed," he told me.[10]

Not long afterward, his house was bombed, his office was attacked, and members of his staff were arrested.[11] Bani-Sadr went into hiding. And in July, he fled the country in disguise.

His colleagues who remained in Iran tried to gather documents regarding the conspiracy, but many of them ended up being captured, tortured in Evin Prison, and, ultimately, executed. Among them was Bani-Sadr aide Hussein Navab Safavi.

According to Mahmood Delkhasteh, once Safavi was incarcerated at Evin Prison, an unidentified official came to Safavi and pleaded for him to give up Bani-Sadr in order to save his life. "'My brother, come and say something so you can live. We really don't want to execute you.'"

"I understand what you mean," Safavi is said to have replied, "but I can't do anything against my conscience."

As Delkhasteh told the story, when the official continued to press him specifically about Bani-Sadr, he refused to comply. A few days later, in late 1981, Safavi was executed by a firing squad. According to his cellmate, his last words were "Long live Bani-Sadr."[12]

According to Bani-Sadr, Safavi was just one of many people who were executed because they knew too much about the October Surprise.[13] By the fall, the new Islamic regime had executed more than one hundred people close to Bani-Sadr, including his attorney, Manucher Massoudi. Even political activists, journalists, and others who had supported the overthrowing of the Shah but who now strictly adhered to the new regime's doctrine found out exactly what it meant to cross the red line. In the end, Bani-Sadr's worst fears had been realized in that Iran had overthrown the brutal repressive monarchy of the Shah, but it had been replaced with a brutal repressive theocracy that was just as bad. "I was like a child watching my father slowly turn into an alcoholic," he said of Khomeini.[14] "The drug this time was power."

When Bani-Sadr died in 2021, his obituaries in the *New York Times*, *Washington Post*, and *The Guardian* as well as on Reuters and the BBC, among other media outlets, omitted any reference to his most important utterance regarding American politics—namely, his repeated insistence that the October Surprise was real.

As *The Intercept* noted, one of the few to mention it was the Associated Press, where Parry had worked for so many years, which wrote that Bani-Sadr "gained notoriety after alleging without evidence in a book that Ronald Reagan's campaign colluded with Iranian leaders to hold up the hostage release."[15]

Without evidence.

And that meant more than forty years after the October Surprise, the false narrative put out by *Newsweek*, *The New Republic*, and the congressional investigations still held. Bani-Sadr could not be taken at his word when it came to the October Surprise. Instead, he was viewed with skepticism as an exiled politician with an axe to grind.

In the United States, the repercussions from the October Surprise were different than those in Iran, but equally momentous. Bill Casey's unholy alliance with Iran gave birth to Reaganism and the modern conservative movement. The "Bush" name later became part of no fewer than *five* Republican administrations—two with George H. W. Bush as vice president, one with him as president, and two with his son as president. Cumulatively, those administrations made no fewer than *eight* conservative Supreme Court appointments and led the way to the newly right-wing Court that made sweeping decisions allowing virtually unlimited contributions from corporate donors for political races, limiting voting rights, and criminalizing abortion.

It also cast in stone the perception of Jimmy Carter as a feckless Boy Scout who was so hobbled by his Sunday school morality that he allowed America to be weakened and humiliated by Iran. We will never know, of course, whether Carter could have brought home the hostages had he not been sabotaged by Casey, but if he had, clearly he would be seen very differently today. But now we know that what has been characterized as Carter's ignominious failure was really the Republicans' treachery. It was a treasonous plot that sabotaged his foreign policy strategy. It was the Republicans' willingness to discard all the rules and regulations that made America a constitutional democracy, and their willingness to join forces with the repressive Islamic fundamentalists who took over Iran.

That was Casey's magic trick. His misdirection. In getting Americans to focus on Carter's failure to bring back the hostages, Casey made Carter appear to be a handmaiden to America's humiliation, and in so doing was able to mask his own treasonous complicity with the mullahs of Iran. The problem was not that Carter was too weak to stand up to Khomeini and Iran's militant Islamists. It was that Bill Casey and the Republicans had joined forces with Iran, and Carter didn't even know it.

In the end, the October Surprise casts a long shadow, not only because of the magnitude of its political consequences but also because it has become the blueprint for Republican malfeasance in more than forty years of presidential elections, and part of a decades long legacy of the Democrats' failure to fight back. Starting in 2004, with *House of Bush, House of Saud*, I wrote the first of five books exploring the largely *unseen* assaults on democracy by the Republican Party, how Republican leaders secretly cultivated lucrative relationships with foreign powers for personal riches and political conquests alike, how they conducted covert operations that sabotaged presidential elections, how they discreetly ginned up voter suppression campaigns to prevent African Americans from voting, how they quietly began taking over the judiciary in Texas and Alabama in the nineties as a prelude to taking over the United States Supreme Court in 2020, and much, much more.

In fact, six of the last eight Republican White House victories were won with the help of well-orchestrated campaigns featuring illegal arms deals with foreign powers, disinformation, cyber warfare, voter suppression, or other anti-democratic measures. After the Anna Chennault Affair in 1968, the Watergate scandal in 1972 was a rare episode in which the American people did learn the truth about what was going on in something approaching real time. But it is worth remembering that even though Woodward and Bernstein began covering Watergate in June 1972, five months before the elections, Nixon was reelected by a massive landslide that year and was not forced to resign until 1974 after impeachment hearings had begun. At the time, the Anna Chennault scandal was not widely known, and when it was fully documented it did not resonate nearly so much as Watergate even though its treasonous implications were far more serious.

The third such scandal, in 1980, of course, is the subject of this book. The fourth took place in 2000, when the presidency was determined by the United States Supreme Court's ruling in *Bush v. Gore*, after Democrat Al Gore won the popular vote but lost the Electoral College thanks to voting irregularities in Florida and a handful of court rulings. It is worth remembering that those "irregularities" included the so-called Brooks Brothers riots featuring scores of middle-aged white Republican lawyers led by Roger Stone, among other GOP operatives, in an assault on election canvassers that stopped vote counting in highly Democratic precincts. There were confusingly designed "butterfly ballots" in Palm Beach County in which the names of the candidates were not in the same order as the corresponding punch holes—thereby leading many Al Gore voters to mistakenly cast ballots for third-party candidate Patrick Buchanan.[16] And there was the intervention of Florida secretary of state Katherine Harris, a Republican, who purged 173,000 voters[17] from a "flawed" list of purported felons on Florida's voting roll to sabotage the recount.

Similarly, in 2004, George W. Bush's victory over John Kerry came down to the electoral votes of one state—Ohio—and a contest, in turn, that was riddled with chicanery that involved deliberately disseminating misinformation in Black neighborhoods about when and where to vote, uneven distribution of voting machines, the restricted use of provisional ballots, and much more that disenfranchised hundreds of thousands of primarily Democratic voters.

Prior to Trump, these horrendous assaults on democracy, when and if they were uncovered, were largely dismissed as wacky conspiracy theories, or marginalized in the press. On the rare occasion that the offense in question became a national scandal—à la Watergate in 1972—it was valorized for showing how well the system works. More often, it was buried under piles of disinformation and counter charges as with the October Surprise. Moreover, each time the Republicans went into battle they were aided by the unwitting assistance of Democrats who typically brought a knife to a gunfight and failed to hold the Republicans accountable. The few investigative reporters who were willing to take a deep dive into the weeds usually faced unpleasant consequences for their careers.

During my 2016 interview with Bani-Sadr in Versailles, the Hillary Clinton–Donald Trump presidential race was just entering the home stretch. Thirty-six years had passed since the October Surprise and given the passage of so much time, at the end of our interview, I asked Bani-Sadr if he still thought it was important, if he still thought anyone cared, if anyone still cared.

"You have to write it," he told me.[18] "If not, it will happen again."

It was September 17, 2016, and, at the time, I did not know how right he was. Thirty-seven days later, with considerable help from Russian president Vladimir Putin, Donald Trump was elected president, and a new era of authoritarian populism was born. Along with it came a new paradigm of shameless cynicism that demonized inconvenient truths as fake news, that validated lies as "alternative facts," and demonized anyone who challenged him.

Bani-Sadr's warning. of course, was a variation on Santayana's hoary maxim that those who forget the past will be doomed to repeat it. My journey into the world of the October Surprise taught me that most Americans did not know their past well enough to have forgotten it. To the extent they were presented with indisputable hard, cold facts that threatened their preconceptions, many people simply refused to accept them. Thirty-three years ago, I discovered a secret world that, when exposed to sunlight, was widely dismissed, discredited, and derided. And I cannot get out of my head the notion that the refusal to accept the truth, to acknowledge our history is very much at the root of the problems we face today.

So, after more than three decades, I no longer doubt whether the October Surprise took place. The larger question to me was whether it would remain merely a footnote to history or whether America could accept it, come to terms with it, and confront it forcefully enough to prevent it from happening again. Just as individuals are often deeply in denial of the most elemental but darkest and most problematic parts of their lives, so too can entire countries deny the darkest iniquities that might soil the legacies of their homeland.

In fact, America has a long history of deceits and denials that date back to its founding. And no lies were more elemental than those regarding our original sin, slavery. Proclaiming, in the Declaration of Independence, that "all men are created equal," and that among their inalienable rights are "life, liberty, and the pursuit of happiness," Thomas Jefferson omitted the inconvenient truth that he was not counting any of the slaves he or other plantation owners owned, that he was omitting *all* women, and that he was not even including his own offspring who had been born to Sally Hemings, one of his slaves. After all, they were legally Jefferson's property—not human beings with inalienable rights. As countless scholars, historians, and journalists have shown us, such fictions have been woven inextricably into the fabric of American life since its inception.

But that is not always the case with other countries that have been guilty of heinous crimes. As Susan Neiman shows in *Learning from the Germans*, since World War II ended in 1945, thanks to the rigorous commitment to *vergangenheitsverarbeitung* (a word that means "coming to terms with the past"), Germans on both sides of the Berlin Wall have been taught about the Nazis and the Holocaust.

They learned that their countrymen had murdered millions of people by gassing them in showers and incinerating them in ovens. They learned that the country that brought us Bach and Beethoven also brought us the mass slaughter of Jews, homosexuals, and prisoners of war. They learned that the entire country had bought Hitler's lies. Including their parents.

And, having accepted those ugly truths, Germany outlawed shrines to Hitler, Himmler, Goering, and the rest. As German president Frank-Walter Steinmeier put it, "German history is a broken story, with responsibility for millions of murders and millions of sufferings." That is precisely why, he added, "You can only love this country with a broken heart."[19]

By contrast, the American South to this day still boasts hundreds of monuments honoring Robert E. Lee, Jefferson Davis, and the like. Traitors all, who killed hundreds of thousands of Americans.

I started to become aware of all this when I first visited Germany in 1963. I was fourteen years old at the time, and, by all rights, like other Jewish boys my age, I should have just been bar mitzvahed. But my father opted for a more secular introduction to manhood: He took me to Dachau, the Nazi concentration camp just outside Munich. The sign over the entrance had the same words as the sign at Auschwitz: *Arbeit Macht Frei.* I remember the buildings as being banal, utilitarian, unexceptional, save for one thing: their purpose. What *was* exceptional was that everything had been designed to accomplish mass murder on an industrial scale. There were ovens, gas "showers," a crematorium, and other instruments of mass extermination. Genocide had been industrialized as an instrument of state policy—just as America had once industrialized a different crime against humanity: slavery.

Horrifying as it was to me, there was one other extraordinary aspect to Dachau that I did not appreciate until many years later. By unflinchingly acknowledging its role in such genocidal horrors, by publicly displaying its instruments of mass extermination, Germany was accepting reality.

It accepted history. It accepted responsibility for its crimes. And it did so with the understanding that acknowledging those horrors was essential to preventing them from happening again.

A few weeks after I returned to my home in Dallas, I went on a school trip that offered me a very different kind of history lesson. The subject was Texas history, and as we toured the state, we inevitably came to the Alamo in San Antonio, the Spanish mission that was the site of a pivotal battle in the Texas Revolution, a historic thirteen-day siege in 1836 that took the lives of Davy Crockett, William Travis, Jim Bowie, and more.

Texas history buffs weren't the only Americans to whom these names were familiar. Thanks to a flood of books, popular songs, TV shows, and movies, not to mention merchandise celebrating these icons of the frontier, the cry "Remember the Alamo!" was known across the country. And when my schoolmates and I arrived at the site, we were told all about how the defenders of Texas heroically gave their lives in the battle against the Mexican onslaught.

The only problem was that none of it was true. The real story was that Mexico had just abolished slavery, and the slaveowners of Texas, then a Mexican state, didn't like it. The real story was that Crockett, Bowie, and the rest were not so much patriots fighting for the glory that is Texas as they were fighting to the death so that slave owners and cotton oligarchs would continue to have the "freedom" to own, buy, and sell humans as chattel.[20]

Of course, none of us understood that. Instead, we celebrated the romantic folklore—lies, really—about rugged frontiersmen who, in reality, were brutal slaveowners. I wore a Davy Crockett tee-shirt when I was six. I owned a "Remember the Alamo" lunch box and had a coonskin cap just like Davy. I watched the Disney TV series. I knew the words to "Davy Crockett, King of the Wild Frontier." Only decades later did I realize we had gotten it backwards, that the German equivalent would have been to have an "Arbeit Macht Frei" lunch box.

And, to me, that was America's original sin—denying and distorting our history. When my colleagues and I first took on the October Surprise more than thirty years ago, we became actors in a case study of America's denial of its dark history, its refusal to accept the ugly truth. It was something that had to be addressed.

After all, if those who have the power to change the way the past is perceived remain unchallenged, they will also have the power to shape the future, to determine the outcome of presidential elections, to invade foreign countries, to start huge wars. And at a certain point, when that happens repeatedly, it becomes irreversible. When the truth is profoundly devalued, when the facts are radically distorted on a regular basis, when our history is denied us, then it becomes impossible—really impossible—to stop.

Indeed, now that we have entered a world of post-truth politics in which history and facts have been so astonishingly devalued, it is more important than ever for America to come to terms with the darkest chapters in its history. After all, at this point, it would be folly to assume that this is the end of the line when it comes to malfeasance from the Republican Party. On the contrary, there is every indication that Trump and his MAGA followers are creating a new paradigm of shamelessness and cynicism in which inequities are not just baked into the system, but are protected by a right-wing judiciary, a do-nothing Congress, and a compliant press corps.

How one competes with adversaries who don't play by the rules without bending the rules yourself is a difficult question to answer. But I am certain that rigorous accountability has to be part of it. In the end, Democrats can either learn from this dark, dark history and figure out how to deploy effective countermeasures. Or they will be destroyed by Republican treachery when it is too late.

Acknowledgments

THIS BOOK WOULD NOT HAVE BEEN POSSIBLE WITHOUT THE help of many people.

At Mariner/HarperCollins, Matt Harper has been a terrific editor who oversaw the book at every stage. I am also grateful to Ivy Givens, Maureen Cole, Sarah Falter, Jen McGuire, Dale Rohrbaugh, Kyran Cassidy, Isha Mehmood, and Peter Hubbard.

My literary agent, David Kuhn, at Aevitas Creative Management, and his colleagues, Nate Muscato and Helen Hicks, did a superb job of taking this project from its inception to finding a wonderful home for it at Mariner. Given that this project began in 1991 and started and stopped multiple times along the way, that was no easy task. I can't thank David enough for seeing it through to its completion.

I'm also indebted to my terrific photo editor Cynthia Carris Alonso, tireless fact checker Ben Kalin, and my friend, photographer James Hamilton, for the author's photo. Lynn Collardin and Leo Greenberg also helped with research, and I'm grateful for their assistance.

My reporting for this book began in 1991 when I first wrote about the October Surprise for *Esquire* and continued as I worked on it and related stories for *Newsweek*, the *Washington Post*, the *Village Voice*, and *The New Yorker* over the next year. Parts of this book grew out of those articles and short passages have been adapted from them.

In 2014, I visited Iran where I interviewed Revolutionary Guard founder Mohsen Rafighdoost among other sources and visited the American embassy, or, as the Iranians would have it, the den of spies. I am grateful to the many Iranians who helped me—especially those sources whose privacy I must continue to respect.

In 2016, I interviewed former president Bani-Sadr in Versailles, and set about interviewing his colleagues. I'm indebted to Mahmood

Delkhasteh for setting up the interviews, interpreting, and for his help in subsequent years.

Over the course of more than three decades, there were a number of colleagues to whom I returned repeatedly to compare notes. I am especially grateful to Gary Sick for his time and his pioneering book on the subject. My book also would not exist in its presence form without the landmark work of Bob Parry who I came to regard as a friend and colleague until his death in 2018. His widow Diane Duston was wonderfully generous in providing me access to Bob's archives, which became such an important part of this book.

When I first started on this project in 1991, I often compared notes with Martin Kilian, and continued to do so right up until publication in 2024. Spencer Oliver was enormously helpful in helping me understand what was happening on Capitol Hill with regard to the October Surprise investigation. In Israel, Pazit Ravina proved invaluable in helping me navigate the world of Israeli intelligence. I am also grateful to Garry Emmons for his contributions to this project.

Among the many people who were either interview subjects or gave me assistance, I am indebted to Don Albosta, Richard Allen, Jonathan Alter, David Andelman, Richard Babayan, John Ballentine, Abolhassan Bani-Sadr, Gen. Avraham Bar-Am, John Barry, Davoud Bavand, Chester Paul Beach, Kai Bird, Tom Blanton, Jack Blum, Zbigniew Brzezinski, Lucy Gregg Buckley, Jonathan Chadwick, Susan Clough, William Colby, Mahmood Delkhasteh, Robert Dreyfuss, Tom Dunn, Arif Durrani, Stuart Eizenstat, Erik Furmark, Alexis Gelber, Sean Gervasi, Mel Goodman, Bill Hamilton, Robert Hawley, Moshe Hebrony, Bill Herrmann, Seymour Hersh, Henry Hoberman, Mark Hosenball, Mark Hulbert, Amir Ali Hussein, Bobby Ray Inman, Christopher Isham, Carole Jerome, Albert Jolis, David Kimche, John Limbert, Bob Lystad, Richard Manning, Victor Marchetti, Joel McCleary, Ari Ben-Menashe, Nico Minardos, Rosy Nimrodi, Joseph O'Toole, Nat Parry, Sam Parry, Walter Pincus, Jody Powell, Mohsen Rafighdoost, Elliot Richardson, Mitchell Rogovin, Yehoshua Saguy,

Pierre Salinger, Raji Samghabadi, Bruce Sanford, Saeed Sanjabi, John Sears, Robert Sensi, Tara Sonenshine, Ted Stanger, Ahmad Taghvaii, Evan Thomas, Scott Thompson, Stansfield Turner, Ed Williamson, Jonathan Winer, Bob Woodward.

Many friends and colleagues helped either by contributing in one way or another to the book itself or through much-needed moral support. Most of all, I'm indebted to Kim Dempster for her warmth and support and for putting up with my absences while I was writing. I'd also like to thank all our pals in Shelter Island, including Jonathan Russo and Deborah Grayson for the use of their gazebo as a temporary writing facility.

Other friends and family members who have been supportive during this long journey include: John Anderson, Gabriel Benincasa, Sidney Blumenthal, Andy Cohen, Alan Heilbron and Kerry Malawista, Robert Kaufelt and Nina Planck, Susanna Kaysen and John Daniels, Michael Mailer, Don and Marji Mendelsohn, Jamie Robins, Felicia Rosshandler, James Sheldon and Karen Brooks Hopkins, Jeff Stein, Neal Stevens, Arthur Tannenbaum, Paco Underhill. Finally, thanks to my extended family including Chris, Shanti, Thomas, Marley and Miles; Jimmy, Marie-Claude; Adam, Mel, Noah, Rose, and Otis; Matthew and Jacelyn; Romy-Michelle and Gregg.

Cast of Characters

Robert Ames. The Near East Director of the CIA, and the eponymous spy in Kai Bird's *The Good Spy*, Ames built a secret network of valuable contacts in the Middle East that included ties to Palestine Liberation Organization (PLO) chief Yasser Arafat. Ames's outreach to Arafat through Lebanese businessman Mustafa Zein was one of the most promising channels pursued by the Carter administration during the Iran hostage crisis—but Bill Casey and his operatives did everything they could to disrupt it.

Abolhassan Bani-Sadr. The first president of Iran after the Islamic Revolution, Bani-Sadr called for the release of the hostages soon after their capture but did not have the power to carry it out. After being betrayed by Ayatollah Khomeini, his former mentor, Bani-Sadr was impeached, targeted for assassination, and ultimately fled to France where he lived in exile until his death in 2021. President Bani-Sadr provided the House task force with relevant documents regarding arms sales to Iran, but many of them were discarded by the task force and have not come to light until now.

Ari Ben-Menashe. A rogue operative/arms dealer from Israeli Military Intelligence, Ben-Menashe was a problematic source who said he was part of the Israeli team that provided security and logistical support at key meetings of the October Surprise in Paris. *Newsweek*, *The New Republic*, and the *Wall Street Journal* tried to discredit Ben-Menashe as "a low-level translator." But in 1992, Israeli intelligence official Moshe Hevrony told me that "Ben-Menashe served directly under me. . . . He had access to very, very sensitive material." Many of Ben-Menashe's assertions about the secret arms trade between Israel and Iran were corroborated by other sources.

George H. W. Bush. As an incumbent president running for reelection, Bush became an even bigger target for journalists than Casey when investigators started looking into the October Surprise in 1991. Nevertheless, Bush categorically denied allegations that he attended the Paris meetings in October 1980 where the hostage deal was said to have been finalized. Key questions about his role in any conspiracy remain unanswered.

Jimmy Carter. President Carter's hopes for reelection went up in smoke on April 24, 1980, when the attempt to rescue the hostages known as Operation Eagle Claw failed and resulted in the deaths of eight US servicemen. Throughout the remainder of the election season, Carter's attempts to win the return of the hostages were repeatedly thwarted by Casey's operatives.

William J. Casey. A dazzlingly brilliant spy who orchestrated the penetration of Nazi Germany by American spies in World War II, Casey trained his sights on the Carter administration in 1980 with the help of a secret intelligence network he had cultivated over the years. Using cutouts to communicate with arms dealers, Israeli intelligence officials, Iranian operatives, Middle East leaders, and the like, Casey and his team set up meetings in Madrid and Paris with Iranian leaders with the intent of selling arms to Iran, in return for which the Islamic Republic prolonged the incarceration of the fifty-two American hostages until Reagan's inauguration.

John Connally. Former Texas governor and failed GOP presidential candidate, John Connally was tasked by Casey to lobby Middle Eastern leaders to tell Iran to keep the hostages imprisoned until after the 1980 election. In 2023, Ben Barnes, a close friend of Connally's who accompanied him on their 1980 mission, came forward to reveal Connally's role in the October Surprise.

Miles Copeland Jr. A former member of the OSS and CIA who had been instrumental in the Operation Ajax, the CIA's 1953 coup in Iran, Copeland was appalled that Jimmy Carter had "lost" Iran and did everything he could to make sure Carter wasn't reelected. In April 1980, Copeland wrote a piece in the *Washington Star* putting forth the idea of implementing a covert operation to rescue the hostages. As a result, Carter officials suspected he had breached security of their top-secret mission.

Alexandre de Marenches. The legendary head of the Service de Documentation Extérieure et de Contre-Espionnage (SDECE), the French counterpart of the CIA, de Marenches was a longtime friend of Bill Casey's and was said to have provided logistical support in Paris for the October Surprise. According to David Andelman, who cowrote *The Fourth World War: Diplomacy and Espionage in the Age of Terrorism* with de Marenches, the French spymaster told him he had helped set up meetings between Casey and Iranian officials in Paris in October 1980.

Lee Hamilton. As head of the House of Representatives' October Surprise Task Force, Congressman Hamilton (D-IN) proved to be a lapdog when the investigation needed a pit bull. Under his aegis, the task force left some of the most compelling documents regarding the October Surprise in an abandoned ladies' room where they were later discovered by Bob Parry.

Cyrus Hashemi. With homes in London, Paris, and Wilton, Connecticut, Cyrus traveled the world on the supersonic Concorde and presented himself to Carter administration officials as a sophisticated Iranian businessman who ran a small merchant bank and had ties to key figures in Iran who could help negotiate the release of the hostages. However, he and his brother were also double agents allied with Bill Casey and John Shaheen. According to FBI wiretaps, the Hashemis were secretly engaged in illegal arms deals with Iran at the time.

Jamshid Hashemi. Cyrus's older brother—or half brother, by one account—Jamshid ended up working with his sibling as a double agent for Casey after the latter paid him an unexpected visit at the Mayflower Hotel in Washington. When Cyrus died in London in 1986 just two days after being diagnosed with a rare form of leukemia, Jamshid said he believed his brother had been murdered "by the CIA and Mossad" to silence him. He became an important primary source regarding the meetings in late July in Madrid with Casey and Mehdi Karroubi.

Mehdi Karroubi. As a highly placed member of the Majlis and a longtime student of Ayatollah Khomeini, Karroubi was selected by the Supreme Leader to negotiate with William Casey in Madrid in July 1980. When Casey made it clear the Republicans wanted the hostage release delayed until after the election, Karroubi said he thought progress was finally being made. "I think," he told the Iranians in the room, "we are now opening a new era and we are now dealing with someone who knows how to do business."

Ayatollah Ruhollah Khomeini. The leader of Iran's Islamic Revolution, Khomeini returned from Paris to Tehran in 1979 and transformed it into the Islamic theocracy he ruled until his death ten years later. Khomeini's betrayal of President Bani-Sadr, who was once his protégé, ended any hopes of secular democracy in Iran and helped Casey execute the October Surprise.

Henry Kissinger. Former secretary of state Kissinger who served as chair of the Chase Manhattan Bank's International Advisory Committee, and, along with Chase CEO David Rockefeller Jr.; Archibald Roosevelt Jr., a longtime CIA officer who had become head of international relations at Chase; and Joseph V. Reed, the Chase vice president and assistant to Rockefeller, was a member of the so-called Rockefeller Group which successfully pressured Jimmy Carter into admitting Shah Reza Pahlavi to the United States for medical care. In doing so, they triggered the takeover of the American embassy and subsequent hostage crisis.

JACQUES MONTANÈS. A pilot who ran a company called SETI that was allegedly tied to French intelligence, Montanès delivered documentary evidence to ABC News's Pierre Salinger that revealed how and when the arms flow began from Israel to France to Iran in the aftermath of the Paris meetings.

SHAH MOHAMMAD REZA PAHLAVI. After the 1953 CIA-led coup in Iran that overthrew Prime Minister Mohammad Mossadegh, Shah Reza Pahlavi ruled Iran as an American puppet who brutally repressed dissidents with the help of SAVAK, his CIA created intelligence force. After he was toppled in the Islamic Revolution, the Shah's arrival in the United States in 1979 for medical treatment led to demonstrations that stormed the American embassy in Tehran, seized control over it, and ignited the hostage crisis.

MAYNARD PARKER. At *Newsweek*, editor in chief Maynard Parker and Pentagon correspondent John Barry launched an investigation into the October Surprise that created a phony alibi for Bill Casey. *Newsweek*'s work, along with that of Steven Emerson in *The New Republic* and other publications, helped forge the conventional wisdom that the October Surprise was a hoax.

BOB PARRY. The winner of the George Polk Award for his work in 1984 on the Iran-Contra scandal, Parry did more than any single reporter to unravel the October Surprise. In 2011, Parry destroyed Casey's alibis for the October Surprise when he uncovered a memorandum from the White House that noted Casey was in Madrid "for purposes unknown" in July 1980. Parry investigated the October Surprise for *Newsweek*, PBS's *Frontline*, his consortiumnews.com website, and several books including *Trick or Treason: The October Surprise Mystery* and *The October Surprise X-Files*. In 2015, he was awarded the I. F. Stone Medal for Journalistic Independence by Harvard University's Nieman Foundation.

Reza Pasandideh. Early in the hostage crisis, Cyrus Hashemi, working on behalf of the Carter administration reached out to Pasandideh, the nephew of Ayatollah Khomeini, who finally sat down with Carter representatives in Madrid in early July 1980. But soon afterward, Pasandideh told President Bani-Sadr that the Islamic Republic had to make a deal with the Republicans, not the Democrats.

Mohsen Rafighdoost. Just after the Islamic Revolution, Khomeini appointed Rafighdoost head of the newly founded Revolutionary Guard (IRGC), the nation's premier security force fighting both domestic and foreign threats to the Islamic Republic. As such, Rafighdoost had a key role in arms procurement, and allegedly accompanied an illegal arms shipment to Iran on October 24, 1980, just eleven days before the US presidential elections.

Ronald Reagan. Where Jimmy Carter was often criticized for micromanaging his staff, Ronald Reagan saw the big picture, and eschewed details when it came to his relationship with Casey. "My problem with Bill was that I didn't understand him at meetings," Reagan once said. "Now, you can ask a person to repeat himself once. You can ask him twice. But you can't ask him a third time. You start to sound rude. So, I'd just nod my head, but I didn't know what he was actually saying."

Elliot Richardson. A Boston Brahmin who was straight out of central casting as a scion of the Eastern Establishment, Richardson made his most enduring mark on history when, as Richard Nixon's attorney general, he emerged as the moral hero of Watergate by refusing Nixon's order to fire the special prosecutor leading the investigation. "Like everyone else in Washington, I have the attitude that one shouldn't put anything past Bill Casey," he told me. "If it happened, it was despicable. Compared to the October Surprise, Watergate was an innocent child's frolic.

Yehoshua Saguy. Head of Israeli Military Intelligence, Saguy kept in touch with Casey regularly before and during the Iranian hostage crisis in 1979 and 1980.

Pierre Salinger. As an ABC News correspondent in Paris, Pierre Salinger, onetime press secretary to President John F. Kennedy, received a bagful of documents from Jacques Montanès in 1981 that revealed how and when the arms flow began from Israel to Iran in the aftermath of the Paris meetings and under the guidance of French intelligence chief Alexandre de Marenches.

Salinger's report on ABC's *World News Tonight* on August 21, 1981, noted that "the bill of lading for the plane, which flew from Nimes, France, to Tehran, was completely falsified with the tacit knowledge of French government officials. It described the tank motors as tractor and truck motors, the M-60 tank spare parts as parts for trucks and the F-4 tires as those on compressors." At the time of Salinger's report, the idea that the Republicans had pulled a treasonous October Surprise had never even been discussed in mainstream media. There was no context, and, as result, no follow-up—for ten years.

Robert Sensi. A onetime manager for Bahrain's Gulf Air and Kuwait Airways, Sensi later worked for Casey in the CIA. In 1980, he was a fixer for Casey who said he helped set up the second set of meetings in Madrid to facilitate the October Surprise. Did the October Surprise happen? "Absolutely. Unequivocally," he told me.

John Shaheen. Casey's best friend, John Shaheen was a maverick oilman who bonded with Casey in the Office of Strategic Services in World War II and served as Casey's chief cutout in the October Surprise. FBI wiretaps documented his communications with the Hashemis in 1980 when they were overseeing illicit arms transfers to Iran.

Jack Shaw. A former associate of Casey's from the Nixon administration, Shaw helped Casey raise funds for the 1980 Reagan-Bush campaign. In the summer of 1980, he secretly intervened with Palestinian operative Mustafa Zein in hopes of getting PLO chairman Yasser Arafat to drop his efforts to win the early return of the hostages from Iran.

Gary Sick. During the 1980 hostage crisis, Sick served as point man on Iran for the Carter administration's National Security Council. Initially, he dismissed evidence about the conspiracy as a coincidence, but after doing more research he told me, "You take events you know very well and strip off a layer and suddenly there is a whole different world. . . . Things happened for different reasons than you thought. There is another world. A whole different reality." The author of *October Surprise,* Sick runs Gulf/2000, a Columbia University–based Internet forum on the Persian Gulf.

Stansfield Turner. As Jimmy Carter's DCI, Turner eviscerated the CIA's clandestine arm by eliminating 820 operatives in what was known as the Halloween Massacre, and in doing so alienated hundreds of CIA agents. Susan Clough, who served as Carter's personal secretary in the White House, told Carter "the problem with Stansfield Turner was so serious that it would not go away or be resolved without his guidance. It had to be dealt with, directly or indirectly, by the president. In the CIA, disloyalty was potentially far more destructive than in any other department. It was a problem that could get out of control and leave a legacy other presidents would have to deal with."

Mustafa Zein. Lebanese businessman Zein provided the CIA's Robert Ames with ties to the Palestinian Liberation Organization in hopes that PLO chief Yasser Arafat would negotiate with Iran to release the hostages. However, Casey operative Jack Shaw intervened in an effort to stop Zein. In addition, Zein, in a letter to Parry and in his unpublished memoirs, asserted that the catastrophic failure of Operation Eagle Claw to rescue the fifty-two hostages was the result of intentional sabotage.

Notes

Chapter One: Blood in the Water

1. Zbigniew Brzezinski, *Power and Principle: Memoirs of the National Security Adviser 1977–1981* (London: Weidenfeld and Nicolson, 1983), 499.
2. Hamilton Jordan, *Crisis: The Last Year of Carter's Presidency* (New York: G. P. Putnam's Sons, 1982), 255.
3. George C. Larson, "Extreme Machine," *Smithsonian Magazine*, November 1998.
4. "Amnesty International Annual Report 1974–1975," Amnesty International.
5. *The Iran Hostage Crisis: A Chronology of Daily Developments*, Committee on Foreign Affairs U.S. House of Representatives by the Foreign Affairs and National Defense Division, Congressional Research Service Library of Congress, March 1981.
6. "Toasts of the President and the Shah at a State Dinner in Tehran, Iran," The American Presidency Project, December 31, 1977.
7. *A Chronology of Daily Developments*.
8. Ibid.
9. William K. Stevens, "Shah's Son Greets His Relatives in Tight Security in West Texas," *New York Times*, January 17, 1979.
10. *A Chronology of Daily Developments*.
11. Ervand Abrahamian, *Tortured Confessions* (Berkeley: University of California Press, 1999), 106.
12. *Hostages*, episode three, Show of Force/HBO, 2022.
13. Mark Hulbert, *Interlock: the Untold Story of American Banks, Oil Interests, the Shah's Money, Debts, and the Astounding Connections Between Them* (New York: Richardson & Snyder, 1982), 50–51.
14. David D. Kirkpatrick, "How a Chase Bank Chairman Helped the Deposed Shah of Iran Enter the U.S.," *New York Times*, December 29, 2019.
15. Hulbert, *Interlock*, 68.
16. Ibid., 85.
17. Kirkpatrick, "How a Chase Bank Chairman Helped the Deposed Shah of Iran Enter the U.S."
18. Henry A. Kissinger, "Kissinger on the Controversy over the Shah," *Washington Post*, November 29, 1979.
19. Terence Smith, "Why Carter Admitted the Shah," *New York Times*, May 17, 1981.
20. Kai Bird, *The Outlier: The Unfinished Business of Jimmy Carter* (New York: Crown, 2021), 399.
21. Rosalynn Carter, *First Lady from Plains* (Little Rock: University of Arkansas Press, 1994), 292.
22. Kai Bird, *The Chairman: John J McCloy & The Making of the American Establishment* (New York: Simon & Schuster, 1992), 772.
23. Jonathan Alter, *His Very Best: Jimmy Carter, a Life* (New York: Simon & Schuster, 2020), 509.

24. Smith, "Why Carter Admitted the Shah."
25. Ibid.
26. Josh Levs, "A Summary of Sanctions Against Iran," CNN, January 23, 2012.
27. Alter, *His Very Best*, 2.
28. Donnie Radcliffe, "For Carter—Relatively Speaking," *Washington Post*, December 1, 1979.
29. "Film Discussion: *Desert One* Discussion, Part One," Jimmy Carter Presidential Library, May 21, 2021.
30. Alter, *His Very Best*, 520.
31. Bird, *The Outlier*, 493.
32. "Summary of Conclusions of a Special Coordination Committee Meeting," November 5, 1979, *Foreign Relations of the United States, 1977–1980, Volume XI, Part 1, Iran: Hostage Crisis, November 1979–September 1980.*
33. U.S. Energy Information Administration, "The Strait of Hormuz Is The World's Most Important Oil Transit Chokepoint," *Today in Energy*, January 4, 2012.
34. David Crist, *The Twilight War: The Secret History of America's Thirty-Year Conflict with Iran* (New York: Penguin Publishing Group, 2012), 1.
35. Seymour M. Hersh, "Huge C.I.A. Operation Reported in U.S. Against Antiwar Forces, Other Dissidents in Nixon Years," *New York Times*, December 22, 1974.
36. James Risen, *The Last Honest Man the CIA, the FBI, the Mafia, and the Kennedys—and One Senator's Fight to Save Democracy* (New York: Little, Brown and Company, 2023), 306.
37. J. Dana Stuster, "Mapped: The 7 Governments the U.S. Has Overthrown," *Foreign Policy*, August 20, 2013.
38. Christopher Andrew, *For the President's Eyes Only: Secret Intelligence and the American Presidency from Washington to Bush* (New York: HarperCollins, 1995), 434.
39. Risen, *The Last Honest Man*, 360.
40. Benjamin F. Schemmer, "The Intelligence Community's Case Against Turner," *Washington Post*, April 7, 1979.
41. George F. Will, "Reaping the Whirlwind," *Newsweek*, January 21, 1980.
42. Joe Trento, *Prelude to Terror: The Rogue CIA and the Legacy of America's Private Intelligence Network* (New York: Carroll & Graf, 2005), 61.
43. Author interview with Susan Clough, 1991.
44. Ibid.
45. Ibid.
46. Ibid.
47. Stephen Kinzer, *All the Shah's Men: An American Coup and the Roots of Middle East Terror* (Milwaukee, WI: Trade Paper Press, 2008), 123.
48. Robert Stone, "Taken Hostage: The Making of an American Enemy," PBS/*American Experience*, 2022.
49. Kermit Roosevelt, *Countercoup: The Struggle for the Control of Iran* (New York: McGraw-Hill, 1979), 85–87.
50. "Iran: The People Take Over," *Time*, August 31, 1953.
51. Carl Bernstein, "The CIA and the Media," *Rolling Stone*, October 20, 1977.

52. Peter Grose, *Gentleman Spy: The Life of Allen Dulles* (New York: Houghton Mifflin Company, 1994), 416.
53. David Binder, "Northrop Cites Undercover Role," *New York Times*, June 7, 1975.
54. Michael T. Klare, "Military Madness," *New Internationalist*, September 2, 1980.
55. "The Select Committee to Study Governmental Operations with Respect to Intelligence Activities, Foreign and Military Intelligence," Church Committee Report, no. 94-755, 94th Cong., 2d Sess. (Washington, DC: United States Congress, 1976), 111.
56. Roosevelt, *Countercoup.*
57. James Risen, "Secrets of History: The C.I.A. in Iran—A Special Report; How a Plot Convulsed Iran in '53 (and in '79)," *New York Times*, April 16, 2000.
58. "CIA Confirms Role in 1953 Iran Coup," *National Security Archive*, August 19, 2013.
59. Bridey Heing, "Operation Ajax," *Lapham's Quarterly*, November 26, 2018.
60. Kai Bird, *The Outlier*, 493.
61. Jessica Taylor, "The Last Candidate to Skip the Final Iowa Debate? Ronald Reagan," NPR, January 28, 2016.
62. Joseph Persico, *Casey: The Lives and Secrets of William J. Casey: From the OSS to the CIA* (New York: Viking, 1990), 179.
63. Lee Byrd, "Carter Draws Huffs, Hurrahs and Hindsight over Iran from Rivals," Associated Press, April 8, 1980.
64. Bird, *The Outlier.*
65. Mark Bowden, "The Desert One Debacle," *The Atlantic*, May 2006.
66. Edward T. Russell, "Crisis in Iran: Operation EAGLE CLAW," *Short of War: Major USAF Contingency Operations 1947–1997*, Air Force Historical Research Agency, 1983.
67. *Hostages*, episode three, Show of Force/HBO, 2022.
68. Warren Christopher et al., *American Hostages in Iran: The Conduct of a Crisis* (New Haven, CT: Yale University Press, 1985), 390.
69. Author interview with Susan Clough, 2023.
70. John M. Goshko, "Vance Formally Resigns, Citing Raid Opposition," *Washington Post*, April 29, 1980.
71. Col. Charlie A. Beckwith, *Delta Force* (New York: Harcourt Brace Javanovich, 1983), 10.
72. Bird, *The Outlier*, 530.
73. Jordan, *Crisis*, 253
74. Alter, *His Very Best*, 566.
75. "After Action Report," *Foreign Relations of the United States, 1977–1980, Volume XI, Part 1, Iran: Hostage Crisis, November 1979–September 1980.*
76. Bowden, "The Desert One Debacle."
77. Russell, "Crisis in Iran: Operation EAGLE CLAW."
78. Jimmy Carter, *Keeping Faith: Memoirs of a President* (New York: Bantam Books, 1982), 111.
79. Stuart E. Eizenstat, *President Carter: The White House Years* (New York: St. Martin's Publishing Group, 2018), 821.

Chapter Two: Dark Secrets

1. R. J. Reinhart, "George H. W. Bush Retrospective," Gallup, December 1, 2018.
2. Author interview with Jody Powell, 1991.
3. Author interview with Hodding Carter, 1991.
4. "Joint Report of the Task Force to Investigate Certain Allegations Concerning the Holding of American Hostages by Iran in 1980," [House Task Force Report], 542.
5. "The 'October Surprise' Allegations and the Circumstances Surrounding the Release of the American Hostages Held in Iran," Report to the Special Counsel to Senator Terry Sanford and Senator James M. Jeffords of the Committee on Foreign Relations, United States Senate, [Senate Report], 88.
6. House Task Force Report, 36–37.
7. Gary Sick, "The Election Story of the Decade," *New York Times*, April 15, 1991.
8. Ibid.
9. Ibid.
10. Frank Zucker, "Letter to the Editor: October Surprise—Rusher Neglected to Mention Some Important Sources," *Seattle Times*, May 10, 1991.
11. "Alleged Reagan-Iran Deal Sparks Carter Ire," *Chicago Tribune*, April 26, 1991.
12. Richard L. Berke, "Inquiry Is Ordered on 1980 Campaign," *New York Times*, August 6, 1991.
13. Adam Clymer, "End Hostage Deal 'Rumors,' Bush Asks," *New York Times*, May 4, 1991.
14. Senate Report, 15.
15. Seymour M. Hersh, *Reporter: A Memoir* (New York: Knopf, 2018), 271–72.
16. "Robert MacNeil, Jim Lehrer Guests: Walter Levy, Henry Precht, Thomas Ricks, Joseph Kraft," *PBS NewsHour*, November 2, 1978.
17. "Press Ban Imposed, Lifted," *Facts on File World News Digest*, October 20, 1978.
18. Flora Lewis, "Exiled Holy Man Hints He'll Call for War in Iran," *New York Times*, November 7, 1978.
19. Angus Deming et al., "The Khomeini Enigma," *Newsweek*, January 29, 1979.
20. Sick, "The Election Story of the Decade."
21. Ibid.
22. Author interview with Bob Woodward, 1991.
23. Mark Hosenball, "October Surprise! Redux! The Latest Version of the 1980 'Hostage-Deal' Story Is Still Full of Holes," *Washington Post*, April 21, 1991.
24. Sick, *October Surprise*, 83.
25. Ibid., 82.
26. Craig Unger, "October Surprise," *Esquire*, October 1, 1991.
27. *Nightline* transcript, ABC News, June 20, 1991.
28. *American Experience:* "Taken Hostage: The Making of an American Enemy," PBS, November 14, 2022.
29. Author interview with Gary Sick, 1991.
30. Ibid.

31. Ibid.
32. Unger, "October Surprise."
33. *Scouting the Future: The Public Speeches of William J. Casey* (Gateway Books, 1989), 80.
34. Author interview with John Sears, 1991.
35. Author interview with Scott Thompson, 1991.
36. Ibid.

Chapter Three: Mumbles

1. Eli Rosenberg, "'Olliemania': The Stage-Worthy Scandal That Starred Oliver North as a Congressional Witness," *Washington Post*, May 8, 2018.
2. Bob Woodward, *Veil: The Secret Wars of the CIA* (New York: Simon & Schuster, 1987), 492–93.
3. Dan Morgan, "Senate Staff Report Finds Casey's Iran Testimony Misleading, Incomplete," *Washington Post*, January 20, 1987.
4. Woodward, *Veil*, 493–94.
5. Persico, *Casey*, 545–46.
6. Ibid., 550.
7. Ibid.
8. Esther B. Fein, "C.I.A. Director Suffers Seizure; Testimony Is Off," *New York Times*, December 16, 1986.
9. Woodward, *Veil*, 504.
10. Keith Schneider, "The White House Crisis: Surgery for a Central Figure; Tumor Is Removed from Casey's Brain," *New York Times*, December 19, 1980.
11. Woodward, *Veil*, 507.
12. Tim Weiner, *Legacy of Ashes* (New York: Knopf Doubleday Publishing Group, 2007), 376.
13. Chris Whipple, *The Spymasters: How the CIA Directors Shape History and the Future* (New York: Scribner, 2020), 110.
14. Scott Glabe, "The Original Privatization of Intelligence: Iran-Contra Revisited," *American Intelligence Journal*, Volume 28, 2010, 114.
15. Whipple, *The Spymasters*, 21.
16. Persico, *Casey*, 122.
17. Weiner, *Legacy of Ashes*, 540.
18. Persico, *Casey*, 571.
19. Ibid., 86.
20. Ibid., 53.
21. Ibid., 54.
22. Ibid., 56.
23. Raymond E. Spinzia, "Society Chameleons: Long Island's Gentlemen Spies," *Nassau County Historical Society Journal*, 2000, 55.
24. Persico, *Casey*, 56.
25. Spinzia, "Society Chameleons," 55.

26. Persico, *Casey*, 56–57.
27. *Scouting the Future, the Public Speeches of William J. Casey* (Washington, DC: Regnery Gateway, 1989), 216.
28. Persico, *Casey*, 57.
29. Douglas Waller, *Disciples: The World War II Missions of the CIA Directors Who Fought for Wild Bill Donovan* (New York: Simon & Schuster, 2015), 85.
30. David Maker Abshire, *Saving the Reagan Presidency: Trust Is the Coin of the Realm* (College Station: Texas A&M University Press, 2005), 57.
31. Ibid.
32. Persico, *Casey*, 51.
33. Ibid., 70.
34. Waller, *Disciples*, 290.
35. Persico, *Casey*, 71.
36. Waller, *Disciples*, 189.
37. Ibid., 293.
38. Ibid., 293.
39. Author interview with Albert Jolis, 1991.
40. Weiner, *Legacy of Ashes*, 540.
41. Persico, *Casey*, 85.
42. Rhoda Koenig, "Basket Casey," *New York*, October 15, 1990.
43. Persico, *Casey*, 93.
44. William Safire, "Essay, Cassey at the Source?" *New York Times*, December 15, 1986.
45. Persico, *Casey*, 99.
46. Author interview with Ari Ben-Menashe, 1991.
47. William Safire, "The Moscow Summit," *New York Times*, July 2, 1972.
48. Persico, *Casey*, 210.
49. Ibid., 172.
50. Murray S. Waas and Craig Unger, "In the Loop: Bush's Secret Mission," *The New Yorker*, October 25, 1992.
51. Persico, *Casey*, 175.
52. William J. Casey, letter to Tom Casey, November 1, 1979.
53. Persico, *Casey*, 174.
54. Author interview with Robert Sensi, 2024.
55. Haynes Johnson, "Casey Circumvented the CIA in '85 Assassination Attempt," *Washington Post*, September 26, 1987.
56. Lou Cannon, "Reagan's New Campaign Chief: So Far, So Good," *Washington Post*, March 17, 1980.

Chapter Four: The Secrets Men Die For

1. Author interview with Elliot Richardson, 1991.
2. Sick, *October Surprise*, 53.
3. Senate Report, 48.

4. Robert Parry interview with Elliot Richardson, 1992.
5. Ibid.
6. Ibid.
7. Ibid.
8. Ibid.
9. Ibid.
10. William C. Rempel, "Panels Probing Mysterious Death of Iran Affair Figure," *Los Angeles Times*, June 13, 1987.
11. Ibid.
12. Unger, "October Surprise."
13. Parry interview with Elliot Richardson.
14. Affidavit of Ari Ben-Menashe, United States Bankruptcy Court for the District of Columbia, February17, 1990.
15. Author interview with Gary Sick, 1991.
16. John Cassidy, "James Comey and Donald Trump Go to War," *The New Yorker*, April 13, 2018.
17. Author interview with Ari Ben-Menashe, 1991.
18. *McFarlane v. Esquire Magazine*, United States Court of Appeals, District of Columbia Circuit, January 30, 1996.
19. Author interview with Ari Ben-Menashe, 1991.
20. Richard Norton-Taylor and Andrew Meldrum, "Zimbabwe Plot Video 'A Smear,'" *The Guardian*, February 13, 2002.
21. Author interview with Victor Marchetti, 1991.
22. Author interview with Chris Isham, 1991.
23. Author interview with Raji Samghabadi, 1991.
24. Author interview with Avraham Bar'Am, 1992.
25. Author interview with Elliot Richardson, 1991.
26. Author interview with Richard Babayan. 1991.
27. "Drugs, Law Enforcement, and Foreign Policy: A Report," Subcommittee on Terrorism, Narcotics, and International Operations of the Committee on Foreign Relations, 110th Congress, 2nd Session, December 1988.
28. Oswald Le Winter, *More Atoms of Memory* (Englewood, CO: Howling Dog Press, 2006), Inside Flap.
29. "Overwhelming Evidence Debunks October Surprise Myth," Congressional Record, House of Representatives, February 24, 1992.
30. Author interview with Martin Kilian, 2023.
31. House Task Force Report, 156.
32. House Task Force Report, 96–97.
33. House Task Force Report, 25.
34. Sick, "The Election Story of the Decade."
35. Bob Woodward and Carl Bernstein, *All the President's Men* (New York: Simon & Schuster, 1999), 79.
36. Joint Task Force Report, 155.

37. Author interview with Milt Bearden, 1991.
38. Author interview with Martin Kilian, 2023.
39. TOI Staff, "Palestinians Hail Bush as 'The Only US President to Stand Up to Israel,'" *Times of Israel*, December 2, 2018.
40. Author interview with Gary Sick, 1991.
41. Author interview with Shimon Peres, 1991.
42. Simon Henderson, "Russian Oil to Transit Israel: The Trans-Israel Pipeline is Reborn," Washington Institute for Near East Policy, November 17, 2003.
43. "Hitler 'Diary' Postscript: The Scandal Stalks Stern," *New York Times*, May 25, 1983.
44. Sally McGrane, "Diary of the Hitler Hoax," *The New Yorker*, April 25, 2013.
45. Kim Masters, "What Killed Danny Casolaro?" *Washington Post*, August 32, 1991.
46. Ron Rosenbaum, "The Strange Death of Danny Casolaro," *Vanity Fair*, December 1991.
47. Richard L. Fricker, "The INSLAW Octopus," *Wired*, January 1, 1993.
48. Rosenbaum, "The Strange Death of Danny Casolaro."
49. Author interview with Elliot Richardson, 1991.
50. Elliot L. Richardson, "A High-Tech Watergate," *New York Times*, October 21, 1991.
51. Jeffrey A. Frank, "The INSLAW File," *Washington Post*, June 14, 1992.
52. Masters, "What Killed Danny Casolaro?"
53. B. Drummond Ayres Jr., "As U.S. Battles Computer Company, Writer Takes Vision of Evil to Grave," *New York Times*, September 3, 1991.
54. Keith Botsford, "Danny and the Octopus," *The Independent* (London), January 25, 1992.
55. "U.S. Senator Says Murdered Journalist Was Working on BCCI Case," UPI, August 8, 1991.
56. Senator John Kerry and Senator Hank Brown, "The BCCI Affair: A Report to the Committee on Foreign Relations," United States Senate, December 1992.
57. Peter Truell and Larry Gurwin, *False Profits. The Inside Story of BCCI, The World's Most Corrupt Financial Empire* (Boston: Houghton, Mifflin Company, 1992).
58. David Sirota and Jonathan Baskin, "Follow the Money," *Washington Monthly*, September 4, 2004.
59. "U.S. Senator Says Murdered Journalist Was Working on BCCI Case," UPI, August 8, 1991.
60. Robert Parry, "October Surprise X-Files (Part 3: Bill Casey's Iranian)," *Consortium News*, 1995.
61. "BCCI and October Surprise Task Force," House Banking Committee, not dated.
62. Ephraim Kahana, *Historical Dictionary of Israeli Intelligence* (Scarecrow Press, 2006), 210–12.
63. TOI Staff, "Israeli Counterterror Chief's Son Blames US for His 1988 Assassination," *Times of Israel*, May 31, 2014.
64. Murray S. Waas and Craig Unger, "In the Loop: Bush's Secret Mission," *The New Yorker*, November 2, 1992.

65. Michael Ross, "Probe Ordered of Alleged 1980 Hostages Deal," *Los Angeles Times*, August 6, 1991.

Chapter Five: Pretty Poison

1. Associated Press, "2 Acquitted of Trying to Sell Military Cargo Planes to Iran," *Washington Post*, November 29, 1990.
2. Robin Pogrebin, "Maynard Parker, the Editor of *Newsweek* Is Dead at 58," *New York Times*, October 17, 1998.
3. Author interview with Ari Ben-Menashe, 1991.
4. *Newsweek*'s internal memos, 1991.
5. Flora Lewis, "The Wiles of Teheran," *New York Times*, August 3, 1987.
6. Alfonso Chardy, "CIA Knew in 1981 of Iran Arms Sale," *Miami Herald*, August 9, 1987.
7. Marshall Wilson, "The Almost Vanunu," *Consortium News*, February 19, 2013.
8. Seymour M. Hersh, "U.S. Said to Have Allowed Israel to Sell Arms to Iran," *New York Times*, December 8, 1991.
9. Ari Ben-Menashe, *Profits of War: Inside the Secret U.S.—Israeli Arms Network* (New York: Sheridan Square Publications, 1992), 29.
10. Steven R. Weisman, "For America, A Painful Reawakening," *New York Times*, May 17, 1981.
11. Author interview with Ari Ben-Menashe, 1991.
12. Ibid.
13. Joint Task Force Report, 226.
14. Sick, *October Surprise*, 72.
15. Jeffrey Benkoe, "Planes for Hostages Scheme Exposed," *Jerusalem Post*, March 26, 1990.
16. Author interview with Ari Ben-Menashe, 2023.
17. Author interview with Jonathan Alter, 2023
18. Mary Alma Welch, "Hersh Wins Apology from British Papers," *Washington Post*, August 19, 1994.
19. Jack McKinney, "A Question Never Asked: Did Reagan Cut Deal with Iran to Win in '80?" *Philadelphia Inquirer*, August 3, 1987.
20. Karlyn Baker, "Famous Long Ago Barbara Honneger," *Washington Post*, June 21, 1987.
21. Parry, *Trick or Treason*, 309.
22. Maurice Carroll, "Right to Life Leaders Say Choice of Bush Bars Backing of Reagan," *New York Times*, July 30, 1980.
23. Author interview with Jonathan Chadwick, 1991.
24. Jonathan Chadwick, "Letter to the Editor: When Casey Could Have Met Iranians in '80," *New York Times*, December 5, 1991.
25. Author interview with Jonathan Chadwick, 1991.
26. Joint Task Force Report, 89.
27. Author interview with Jonathan Chadwick, 1991.

28. Ted Stanger's *Newsweek* File, 1991
29. Ibid.
30. John Barry et al., "One Man, Many Tales," *Newsweek*, November 3, 1991.

Chapter Six: The Hand That Feeds You

1. John Barry, "Making of a Myth," *Newsweek*, November 10, 1991.
2. John Barry, "A Case of Confused Identity?" *Newsweek*, November 18, 1991.
3. Reed Irvine and Joe Goulden, "ABC's moral lip service," *Washington Times*, September 28, 1991.
4. Steven Emerson and Jesse Furman, "The Conspiracy That Wasn't," *The New Republic*, November 18, 1991.
5. David Klion, "Everybody Hates Marty," *The Baffler*, September 13, 2023.
6. Eric Alterman, "My Marty Peretz Problem—And Ours," *The American Prospect*, June 18, 2007.
7. Sridhar Pappu, "Post-Gore Marty Re-Refurbishing *The New Republic*," *The Observer*, February 24, 2003.
8. Christopher Madison, "It's Wild-Goose Season Again," *National Journal*, November 16, 1991.
9. Jonah Goldberg, "Baghhad Delenda Est, Part Two," *National Review*, April 23, 2002.
10. Jonathan Kwitny, "Tale of Intrigue: How an Italian Ex-Spy Who Also Helped U.S. Landed in Prison Here," *Wall Street Journal*, August 7, 1985.
11. John Canham-Clyne, "October Reprisals," *Fairness & Accuracy in Reporting*, November 1, 1993.
12. Ibid.
13. Author interview with Evan Thomas, 2023.
14. Author interview with Bob Woodward, 1991.
15. Author interview with Michael Isikoff, 1992.
16. "The Top 100 Works of Journalism of the Century," Arthur L. Carter Journalism Institute, New York University, March 1999.
17. Ervand Abrahamian, *A History of Modern Iran* (New York: Cambridge University Press, 2008), 124.
18. Henry A Kissinger, "Dealing with a New Russia," *Newsweek*, September 2, 1991.
19. Katharine Graham, *Personal History* (New York: Vintage Books, 1998), 617.
20. John Barry, "Casey at the Bat," Newsweekmemories.org (undated).
21. Author interview with John Barry, 2023.
22. Robert Parry, "White House Reportedly Gave Advice to Contra Fund Raisers," Associated Press, June 10, 1985.
23. Robert Parry and Brian Barger, "Contras Funded by Cocaine Trafficking," Associated Press, December 21, 1985.
24. Associated Press staff, "Nicaraguan Rebels Linked to Cocaine Trafficking," *Galveston Daily News*, December 21, 1985.
25. Robert Parry, "Fooling America," speech given in Santa Monica, CA, March 28, 1993.
26. Paul Goepfert, "American Held by Nicaragua," *Chicago Tribune*, October 8, 1986.

27. Author interview with Robert Parry, 2016.
28. Ibid.
29. Ibid.
30. Ibid.
31. Letter from Robert C. McFarlane to Terry McDonell, October 10, 1991.
32. Maureen Dowd, "The White House Crisis; McFarlane Suicide Attempt," *New York Times*, March 2, 1987.

Chapter Seven: My White Whale

1. Press Conference with Speaker of the House of Representatives Tom Foley (D-WA), *Federal News Service*, October 23, 1991.
2. "BCCI, the CIA and Foreign Intelligence," A Report to the Committee on Foreign Relations United States Senate by Senator John Kerry and Senator Hank Brown, December 1992.
3. "GOP Tactics Delay 'October Surprise' Vote Until 1992," *National Journal*, December 2, 1991.
4. Elana Varon, "Sanford to Begin Probe of October Surprise," *States News Service*, February 18, 1992.
5. "Democrats' Hostage Probe Is Ploy to Smear Bush," *Columbus Dispatch*, February 7, 1992.
6. Craig Unger, "The Trouble with Ari," *Village Voice*, July 1992.
7. Pazit Ravina, *Da'var*, date unknown.
8. "Israeli General Resigns from Army," *New York Times*, August 15, 1983.
9. Author interview with Yehoshua Saguy, 1992.
10. Sick, *October Surprise*, 179.
11. Craig Unger, "The FBI's Mystery Tapes," *Washington Post*, May 17, 1992.
12. Ibid.
13. Neil A. Lewis, "Panel Rejects Theory Bush Met with Iranians in Paris in '80," *New York Times*, July 2, 1992.
14. Ibid.
15. "Senate Report Finds No 'October Surprise' Deal," *National Journal*, November 23, 1992.
16. Neil A. Lewis, "Casey's Widow Hails Hostage Theory's Rejection," *New York Times*, January 14, 1993.
17. House Joint Task Force Report, 5.
18. Neil A, Lewis, "House Inquiry Finds No Evidence of Deal on Hostages in 1980," *New York Times*, January 13, 1993.
19. Ruth Sinai, "Bipartisan Probe Clears 1980 Reagan Campaign of Hostage Deal with Iran," Associated Press, January 13, 1993.

Chapter Eight: The Alibi Club

1. Author interview with Spencer Oliver, 2023.
2. Author interview with Walter Pincus, 2023.
3. David Johnston, "Lawmaker Says Reagan Officials Misled Panel on North and Rebels," *New York Times*, February 23, 1989.

4. Parry, *Trick or Treason*, 278–79.
5. Robert Parry, *American Dispatches: A Robert Parry Reader* (Bloomington, IN: iUniverse, 2022), 176.
6. "The Powerful Washington Insiders Hired by BCCI," Associated Press, November 25, 1991.
7. Parry, *Trick or Treason*, 298.
8. "Not Exactly Up in Arms," *National Journal*, May 25, 1991.
9. Senate Report, 10
10. Senate Report, 9.
11. Senate Report, 14.
12. Senate Report, 25.
13. Senate Report, 15.
14. Ibid.
15. Senate Joint Report, 50.
16. House Task Force Report, 89.
17. Senate Report, 59.
18. House Joint Task Force Report, 85.
19. Craig Unger, *Boss Rove: Inside Karl Rove's Secret Kingdom of Power* (New York: Scribner, 2012), 89.
20. Unger, *House of Bush, House of Saud*, 494.
21. Justin Sherin, "The Confessions of @dick_nixon," *Vox*, October 8, 2015.
22. House Joint Task Force Report, 85.
23. House Joint Task Force Report, 86.
24. Robert Parry, "The Looking-Glass 'Surprise,'" *Washington Post*, December 5, 1992.
25. Ibid.
26. House Joint Task Force Report, 86.
27. Senate Report, 73.
28. Senate Report, 63.
29. Parry, *Trick or Treason*, 307–11.
30. House Joint Task Force Report, 85.
31. House Joint Task Force Report, 86.
32. House Joint Task Force Report, 87.
33. Parry, *Trick or Treason*, 309.
34. House Joint Task Force Report, 87.
35. Ibid.
36. Ibid.
37. Sick, "The Election Story of the Decade."
38. B. Drummond Ayres Jr., "Bush, Confident of Winning, Is Satisfied in No.2 Role," *New York Times*, October 5, 1980.
39. House Joint Task Force Report, 172–73.
40. Ibid.
41. House Joint Task Force Report, 173.

42. Author interview with Spencer Oliver, 2023.
43. Ibid.
44. Ibid.
45. Parry, *Trick or Treason*, 184.
46. Ibid.
47. Author interview with Spencer Oliver, 2023.
48. House Joint Task Force Report, 154.
49. Robert Parry, "Real-Life 'National Treasure'—in Reverse," *Consortium News*, May 6, 2005.
50. Ibid.
51. Ibid.
52. House Joint Task Force Report, 170.
53. Ibid.

Chapter Nine: The X-Files

1. Author interview with Diane Duston, 2023.
2. Parry, *American Dispatches*, 177.
3. Ibid., 176.
4. Author interview with David Andelman, 2024.
5. Alexandre de Marenches, *The Evil Empire: The Third World War Now* (London: Sidgwick & Jackson, 1988), 142.
6. Ibid.
7. House Joint Task Force Report, 167.
8. Author interview with David Andelman, 2024.
9. Ibid.
10. House Joint Task Force Report, 167.
11. House Joint Task Force Report, 78.
12. Ibid.
13. Parry, *American Dispatches*, 178.
14. Robert Parry, *The October Surprise X-Files: The Hidden Origins of the Reagan-Bush Era* (Arlington, VA: The Media Consortium, 1996), 13.
15. Robert Parry, "October Surprise X-Files (Part I)," Russia's Report, *Consortium News*, 1995.
16. Ibid.
17. Ibid.
18. Robert Parry, "Accusation of October Surprise 'Lying,'" *Consortium News*, August 5, 2010.
19. Robert Parry, *The X Files*, 13.
20. Author interview with Diane Duston, 2024.
21. Thomas Frick, "Unconventional Wisdom," *LA Weekly*, September 12, 1996.
22. Author interview with Diane Duston, 2024.
23. Author interview with Sam Parry, 2023.
24. Author interview with Diane Duston, 2024.

25. Author interview with Sam Parry, 2023.
26. Robert Parry, "Inside the October Surprise Cover-up," *Consortium News,* July 12, 2011.
27. Author interview with Bob Parry, 2013.
28. Author interview with Paul Beach, 2023.
29. Ibid.
30. Ibid.
31. Paul Beach, "Memorandum for Record: Subject: Meeting with Ed Williamson—October Surprise," November 4, 1991.
32. Bird, *The Outlier,* 562.
33. Robert Parry, "Second Thoughts on October Surprise," *Consortium News,* June 8, 2013.
34. Ibid.
35. Author interview with Abolhassan Bani-Sadr, 2016.
36. Ibid.

Chapter Ten: Casey's Network

1. Waas and Unger, "In the Loop: Bush's Secret Mission," *The New Yorker,* October 25, 1992.
2. Defendant's Reply Brief, United States District Court for the District of Columbia, Civil Action No. 9200711 (TAF) April 7, 1994,
3. Laurie Asseo, "Supreme Court Turns Away McFarlane Suit Against Esquire," Associated Press, October 7, 1996.
4. Marissa Gerny, "The Speech Act Defends the First Amendment: A Visible and Targeted Response to Libel Tourism," *Seton Hall Legislative Journal,* 2012.
5. Adrienne Edgar, "A Defector's Story," *New York Times,* May 19, 1991.
6. Robert Friedman, *The Nation,* May 15, 1005, quoted in John Sugg, "Steven Emerson's Crusade," FAIR (Fairness & Accuracy in Reporting), January 1, 1999.
7. Steven Emerson interview, C-SPAN, April 16, 2013.
8. "No Legal Action over Fox News for 'Totally Muslim' Birmingham Comments," ITV, January 12, 2015.
9. Wajahat Ali et al., "Fear, Inc.: The Roots of the Islamophobia Network in America," Center for American Progress, August 2011.
10. John Sugg, "Steven Emerson's Crusade," FAIR, January 1, 1999.
11. Donald M. Rothberg, "Reagan Criticizes Carter's Handling of Iran Situation," Associated Press, April 30, 1980.
12. "U.N. Commissioner Glum on Hostage Outlook," Associated Press, March 27, 1980.
13. Rothberg, "Reagan Criticizes Carter's Handling of Iran Situation."
14. Maureen Santini, "Carter TV Performance Raises GOP Ire and Network Concern," Associated Press, September 19, 1980.
15. House Joint Task Force Report, 188.
16. House Task Force Report, 187–88.
17. Robert Parry, "Original October Surprise (Part 3)," *Consortium News,* October 29, 2006.

18. Author interview with Richard Allen, 2024.
19. Ibid.
20. Author interview with Richard Allen, 2024.
21. Ibid.
22. Ibid.
23. Author interview with David Andelman, 2024.
24. Trento, *Prelude to Terror*, 102.
25. Miles Copeland, *Game Player: The Confessions of the CIA's Original Political Operative* (London: Aurum Press, 1989), 239.
26. Ibid.
27. Author interview with Erik Furmark, 2023.
28. Ibid.
29. Ibid.
30. Bird, *The Good Spy*, 244.
31. Larry Kolb, *America at Night* (New York: Riverhead Books, 2007), 25.
32. Lee Hockstader, "Ex-Kuwait Airways Official Gets 6 Months for Theft," *Washington Post*, July 2, 1988.
33. Ibid.
34. Larry Kolb, *America at Night* (New York: Riverhead Books, 2007), 25.
35. Author interview with Robert Sensi, 2024.
36. Ibid.
37. Ibid.
38. Author interview with Richard Manning, 1992.
39. House Joint Task Force Report, 95.
40. Robert Parry and Martin Kilian videotaped interview with Jamshid Hashemi.
41. Henry Mitchell, "British Lace and Grace," *Washington Post*, February 28, 1981.
42. Jill Gregorie, "A Look Back: Whatever Happened to Airport Insurance Vending Machines?" *Insurance Business*, May 27, 2015.
43. "Pioneer of Airport Vending-Machine Insurance Dies," *Los Angeles Times*, November 5, 1985.
44. "John Shaheen—Quiet Multi-Millionaire and One of the World's Biggest Borrowers," *Montreal Gazette*, August 3, 1973.
45. John C. Crosbie, *No Holds Barred: My Life in Politics* (Toronto: McClelland & Stewart, 1997), 120.
46. Crosbie, *No Holds Barred*, 120.
47. Ibid., 123.
48. William Borders, "Shaheen Dedicates Canada Refinery," *New York Times*, October 11, 1973.
49. Jenny Higgins and Melanie Martin, "The Come by Chance Oil Refinery," *Heritage Newfoundland & Labrador*, 2006.
50. Senate Report, 45.
51. Author interview with Richard Manning, 1992.
52. Ibid.

53. Robert Parry, "October Surprise: Finally, Time for the Truth," *Consortium News*, 1997.
54. Robert Parry, videotaped interview with Jamshid Hashemi.
55. Author interview with Richard Manning, 1992.

Chapter Eleven: Double Agents

1. Robert Parry interview with Elliot Richardson, 1992.
2. Sick, *October Surprise*, 52.
3. Memorandum of interview with Stanley Pottinger, December 3, 1979.
4. House Task Force Report, 37.
5. Senate Report, 39–40.
6. Christopher et al., *American Hostages in Iran*, 107.
7. "Memorandum from Gary Sick of the National Security Council Staff to the President's Assistant for National Security Affairs (Brzezinski)," January 9, 1980.
8. House Task Force Report, 37.
9. Robert Parry interview with Jamshid Hashemi, Parry Archives.
10. House Task Force Report, 940.
11. Robert Parry interview with Jamshid Hashemi, Parry Archives.
12. Ibid.
13. House Task Force Report, 37.
14. Ibid.
15. Harry A. Penich, "Memorandum of Interview Stanley Pottinger," May 12, 1992.
16. House Task Force Report, 37.
17. "State/TNR Morning Summary," July 31, 1980.
18. House Task Force Report, 38.
19. Senate Report, 39.
20. House Task Force Report, 37.
21. House Task Force Report, 38.
22. Ibid.
23. "Memorandum from Gary Sick to Brzezinski," January 9, 1980.
24. "Jimmy Carter Public Approval (Gallup data)," The American Presidency Project.
25. Parry videotaped interview Jamshid Hashemi.
26. Author interview with Erik Furmark, 2023.
27. Parry, *Trick or Treason*, 81.
28. House Task Force Report, 104.
29. Sick, *October Surprise*, 77.
30. Senate Report, 52.
31. Videotaped interview with Jamshid Hashemi.
32. Ibid.
33. Robert Parry, *Secrecy & Privilege: Rise of the Bush Dynasty from Watergate to Iraq*, 112.

Chapter Twelve: Eagle Claw

1. Draft Letter from the White House Chief of Staff (Jordan) to Iranian president Abolhassan Bani-Sadr, March 13, 1980.
2. Memo Sick to Brzezinski, March 19, 1980.
3. Ibid.
4. Jack W. Germond and Jules Witcover, *Blue Smoke and Mirrors: How Reagan Won and Why Carter Lost the Election of 1980* (New York: Viking Press, 1981), 157.
5. "Minutes of a National Security Council Meeting, April 7, 1980, 9–11:30 a.m.," *Foreign Relations of the United States, 1977-1980, Volume XI, Part 1, Iran: Hostage Crisis, November 1979–September 1980.*
6. "Editorial Note," *Foreign Relations of the United States, 1977–1980, Volume XI, Part 1, Iran: Hostage Crisis, November 1979–September 1980.*
7. "Minutes of a National Security Council Meeting, April 11, 1980, 11:30 a.m.–1:19 p.m.," *Foreign Relations of the United States, 1977–1980, Volume XI, Part 1, Iran: Hostage Crisis, November 1979–September 1980.*
8. Author interview with Ari Ben-Menashe, 1991.
9. "Israel's 'Spymaster' David Kimche Dies Aged 82," BBC, March 9, 2010.
10. Author interview with Ari Ben-Menashe, 1991.
11. Parry, *Trick or Treason*, 48.
12. Ibid., 49.
13. Unger, "October Surprise."
14. Parry, *Trick or Treason*, 51.
15. Author interview with Ari Ben-Menashe, 1991.
16. Robert Parry interview with Ari Ben-Menashe, May 22, 1991.
17. House Task Force Report, 120.
18. House Task Force Report, 162.
19. House Task Force Report, 121.
20. Parry, *Trick or Treason*, 51.
21. Copeland, *The Game Player*, 257.
22. Ibid., 258
23. Ibid., 259.
24. Ibid., 258.
25. Parry, *Trick or Treason*, 53.
26. Ibid., 52.
27. Adam Entous, "Last Man Standing," *The New Yorker*, February 3, 2020; John K. Cooley, "Public Favors Action on Iran; US Seeks Mideast Bases; Majority in Polls Back Blockade or Rescue Attempt," *Christian Science Monitor*, April 21, 1980.
28. Martin Schram and Edward Walsh, "Behind the Scenes in Planning the Hostage Rescue Attempt," *Washington Post*, April 25, 1980.
29. Author interview with Stansfield Turner, 1991.
30. Sick, October Surprise, 24.
31. Author interview with Robert Sensi, 2024

32. Author interview with Joel McCleary, 2023
33. Michael Barber, "Obituary: Brigadier Tim Landon," *The Guardian*, August 27, 2007.
34. Brett Popplewell, "Life of the White Sultan Shrouded in Controversy," *Globe and Mail*, July 14, 2007.
35. Barber, "Landon Obituary."
36. Author interview with Joel McCleary, 2024.
37. Ibid.
38. Popplewell, "Life of the White Sultan Shrouded in Controversy."
39. Barber, "Landon Obituary."
40. Dewa Mavhinga, "Robert Mugabe Leaves Behind Legacy of Abuse," Human Rights Watch, September 6, 2019.
41. Joel McCleary bio, International Campaign for Tibet.
42. Author interview with Joel McCleary, 2024.
43. Ibid.
44. Ibid.
45. Ibid.
46. David Corn, *Blond Ghost* (New York: Simon & Schuster, 1994), 177.
47. Leslie Cockburn, *Out of Control: The Story of the Reagan Administration's Secret War in Nicaragua, the Illegal Arms Pipeline, and the Contra Drug* (London: Bloomsbury Publishing, 1988), 102.
48. Corn, *Blond Ghost*, 330.
49. Trento, *Prelude to Terror*, 8–9.
50. Parry, "Accusation of October Surprise 'Lying.'"
51. Author interview with Joel McCleary, 2024.
52. Ibid.
53. Tabby Refael, "America held Hostage, 40 Years Ago," *Jewish Journal*, November 13, 2019.
54. David Ignatius, "The Secret History of U.S.-PLO Terror Talks," *Washington Post*, December 3, 1988.
55. Bird, *The Good Spy*, 243.
56. Augustus Richard Norton, "The Irreplaceable Spy," *Lobe Log*, June 11, 2014.
57. Bird, *The Good Spy*, 75–76.
58. Mustafa Zein, unpublished memoir, 269.
59. Ibid.
60. Ibid., 270.
61. Ibid.
62. Mustafa Zein letter to Robert Parry, July 10, 2014.
63. Ibid.
64. David Vergun, "U.S. Remember Service Members Killed in Beirut Bombings 40 Years Ago," *U.S. Department of Defense News*, October 24, 2023.
65. Gordon Thomas, *Journey into Madness: Medical Torture and the Mind Controllers* (London: Bantam Press, 1988), 88–89.

66. Tom Clancy with General Carl Stiner, *Shadow Warriors: Inside the special Forces* (New York: G. P. Putnam's Sons, 2002), 261.
67. Mustafa Zein letter to Robert Parry, July 10, 2014.
68. Mustafa Zein, unpublished memoirs, 274.
69. Author interview with Kai Bird, 2023.

Chapter Thirteen: Asymmetry

1. "Briefing Memorandum from the Acting Assistant Secretary of State for Near Eastern and South Asian Affairs (Constable) to the Deputy Secretary of State (Christopher)," *Foreign Relations of the United States, 1977–1980, Volume XI, Part 1, Iran: Hostage Crisis, November 1979–September 1980*, May 24, 1980.
2. Ibid.
3. "Summary of Conclusions of a Policy Review Committee Meeting," *Foreign Relations of the United States, 1977–1980, Volume XI, Part 1, Iran: Hostage Crisis, November 1979–September 1980*, May 8, 1980.
4. Efraim Karsh, *The Iran–Iraq War: 1980–1988* (Oxford, UK: Osprey Publishing, 2002), 1–8, 12–16, 19–82.
5. Sick, *October Surprise*, 79.
6. Robert Parry interview with Jamshid Hashemi, Parry Archives.
7. Senate Report, 40.
8. *Encyclopedia Britannica,* Ruhollah Khomeini: Iranian religiousleader. https://www.britannica.com/biography/Ruhollah-Khomeini.
9. Penich, "Memorandum of Interview with Stanley Pottinger."
10. Senate Report, 40.
11. Ibid.
12. Ibid.
13. House Task Force Report, 57.
14. Not for attribution.
15. Not for attribution.
16. Not for attribution.
17. House Task Force Report, 38.
18. Not for attribution.
19. Not for attribution.
20. House Task Force Report, 37.
21. Senate Report, 40.
22. House Task Force Report, 37.
23. Senate Report, 40.
24. House Task Force Report, 38.
25. Memorandum from Secretary of State Muskie to President Carter, Washington, DC, July 3, 1980.
26. Senate Report, 41.
27. House Task Force Report, 38.

28. Senate Report, 41.
29. Memorandum from Secretary of State Muskie to President Carter, July 3, 1980.
30. Author interview with Abolhassan Bani-Sadr, 2016.
31. Senate Report, 42.

Chapter Fourteen: Overdrive

1. Author interview with Mahmood Delkhasteh, 2016.
2. Author interview with Abolhassan Bani-Sadr, 2016.
3. Ibid.
4. Ibid.
5. Ibid.
6. Levant Correspondent, "Iran; Out with Them All," *The Economist*, July 5, 1980.
7. Written follow-up interview with Abolhassan Bani-Sadr, 2016.
8. Author interview with Abolhassan Bani-Sadr, 2016.
9. Ibid.
10. Ibid.
11. Ibid.
12. Kate Hewitt and Richard Nephew, "How the Iran Hostages Crisis Shaped the US Approach to Sanctions," *Brookings*, March 12, 2019.
13. Author interview with Abolhassan Bani-Sadr, 2016.
14. House Task Force Report, 409.
15. Author interview with Abolhassan Bani-Sadr, 2016.
16. Ibid.
17. Ibid.
18. House Task Force Report, 413.
19. Author interview with Abolhassan Bani-Sadr, 2016.
20. Not for attribution.
21. Author interview with Abolhassan Bani-Sadr, 2016.
22. Not for attribution.

Chapter Fifteen: Interference

1. "Memorandum from Gary Sick of the National Security Council Staff to the President's Assistant for National Security Affairs (Brzezinski)," *Foreign Relations of the United States, 1977–1980, Volume XI, Part 1, Iran: Hostage Crisis, November 1979–September 1980, January 9, 1980.*
2. Author interview with Kai Bird, 2023
3. Bird *The Good Spy*, 242.
4. Bird, *The Good Spy*, 243. Kindle Edition.
5. https://history.state.gov/historicaldocuments/frus1977-80v11p1/d95.
6. Bird, *The Good Spy*, 244.
7. Ibid.
8. Ibid.
9. Ibid., 244–45.

10. Mustafa Zein letter to Robert Parry, July 10, 2014.
11. Bird, *The Good Spy*, 245. Kindle Edition.
12. Bird, *The Good Spy*, 245.
13. Ibid., 246.
14. Ibid.
15. Abbie Hoffman and Jonathan Silvers, "An Election Held Hostage," *Rolling Stone*, October 1988.
16. Ibid.
17. Morgan Strong, "Arafat & the Original 'October Surprise,'" *Consortium News*, November 2, 2004.
18. Jonathan Alter, Gary Sick, Kai Bird, and Stuart Eizenstat, "It's All but Settled: The Reagan Campaign Delayed the Release of the Iranian Hostages," *The New Republic*, May 3, 2023.
19. Robert Parry, "Lost History: Arafat Confirms GOP 'October Surprise' Bid," *Consortium News*, 1997.
20. William Safire, "The Way We Leave Now: 9-15-02: On Language; Perp Walk," *New York Times*, September 15, 2002.
21. Jules Witcover, *The Year the Dream Died* (New York: Warner Books, 1997), 418.
22. Anna Chennault, *The Education of Anna* (New York: Times Books, 1980), 176.
23. Ibid., 190–91.
24. Ken Hughes, *Chasing Shadows: The Nixon Tapes, the Chennault Affair, and the Origins of Watergate* (Charlottesville: University of Virginia Press, 2014), 22–23.
25. Author interview with Richard Allen, 2024.
26. Hughes, *Chasing Shadows*, 38.
27. Ibid., 39.
28. Ibid., 46.
29. Gene Roberts, "Thieu Says Saigon Cannot Join Paris Talks Under Present Plan," *New York Times*, November 2, 1968.
30. Robert B. Semple Jr., "Nixon Is Willing to Go to Saigon," *New York Times*, November 4, 1968.
31. Martin Kettle, "Nixon 'Wrecked Early Peace in Vietnam," *The Guardian*, August 8, 2000.
32. Lawrence O'Donnell, *Playing with Fire: The 1968 Election and the Transformation of American Politics* (New York: Penguin, 2017), 399–400.
33. John A. Farrell, "Anna Chennault: The Secret Go-Between Who Helped Tip the 1968 Election," Politico, December 30, 2018.
34. Seymour M. Hersh, *The Price of Power: Kissinger in the Nixon White House* (New York: Summit Books, 1983), 21.
35. Stephen E. Ambrose, *Nixon: The Triumph of a Politician 1962–1972* (New York: Simon & Schuster, 1989).
36. Roger Morris, "Just Like Old Times, Except . . . ; Richard Nixon: He Can Go to China as Envoy *Extraordinaire*, but the World Today Is Less Amenable to His Grand Diplomacy," *Los Angeles Times*, November 11, 1989.
37. Robert "KC" Johnson, "Did Nixon Commit Treason in 1968? What the New LBJ Tapes Reveal," History News Network.
38. Author interview with Richard Allen, 2024.

39. Files of William J. Casey, Hoover Institute, Stanford University, Boc 204, Folder 7.
40. Adrienne Edgar, "A Defector's Story," *New York Times*, May 19, 1991.
41. Peter Baker, "A Four-Decade Secret: One Man's Story of Sabotaging Carter's Re-election," *New York Times*, March 18, 2023.
42. William J. Casey's personal papers, Hoover Institute.
43. Baker, "A Four-Decade Secret."
44. "Saudis Join Connally to Buy Bank," *New York Times*, August 22, 1977.
45. Baker, "A Four-Decade Secret."
46. Ibid.
47. Ibid.
48. H. W. Brands, *Reagan: The Life* (New York: Anchor Books, 2016), 235.
49. "H. W. Brands on Ben Barnes's 'Revelation' About the Iran Hostage Crisis," HNN, March 20, 2023.
50. Baker, "A Four-Decade Secret."
51. Ibid.
52. Ibid.

Chapter Sixteen: The Wire

1. Parry, *Secrecy and Privilege*, 113.
2. Author interview with Robert Sensi, 2024.
3. Ibid.
4. Ibid.
5. Ibid.
6. Ibid.
7. Ibid.
8. Ibid.
9. Ibid.
10. Felicity Barringer and Donald P. Baker, "Anti-Khomenini Iranian Slain at Bethesda Home," *Washington Post*, July 23, 1980.
11. House Task Force Report, 18.
12. Ibid.
13. Ibid.
14. "Affidavit for a Search Warrant, First Gulf Bank, 9 West 57th Street, 38th Floor," United States District Court for SDNY.
15. Senate Report, 54.
16. Craig Unger, "The FBI's Mystery Tapes," *Washington Post*, May 16, 1992.
17. House Task Force Report, 103.
18. Robert Parry, "Original October Surprise (Part 3)," *Consortium News*, October 29, 2006.
19. Memorandum from Ted Planzos to E. Lawrence Barcella, September 19, 1992.
20. Ibid.
21. "Gallup Presidential Election Trial-Heat Trends, 1936–2008," Gallup.
22. Ibid.

23. Sick, *October Surprise*, 157.
24. Ibid., 156.
25. Senate Report, 35.
26. Sick, *October Surprise*, 132.
27. Ibid., 133.
28. David B. Ottoway, "Iraqi-Iranian Clash Endangers Oil to West," *Washington Post*, September 22, 1980.
29. Sick, *October Surprise*, 130.
30. Zbigniew Brzezinski, *Power and Principle: Memoirs of the National Security Adviser 1977–1981* (London: Weidenfeld and Nicolson, 1983), 504.
31. Sick, *October Surprise*, 156.
32. Lou Cannon, "Casey Operated an 'Intelligence' System in 1980," *Washington Post*, July 1, 1983.
33. Ibid.
34. "Bush Fears 'October Surprise' from Carter Campaign," Associated Press, October 2, 1980.
35. Persico, *Casey*, 195.
36. "Unauthorized Transfers of Nonpublic Information During the 1980 Presidential Election," Report Prepared by the Subcommittee on Human Resources of the Committee on Post Office and Civil Service, House of Representatives, May 17, 1984, 49.
37. Ibid.
38. House Task Force Report, 186.
39. Leslie H. Gelb, "Reagan Aides Describe Operation to Gather Inside Data on Carter," *New York Times*, July 7, 1983.
40. Parry Archives, B13F02.pdf, Exhibit 470324.
41. Albosta Report, Part 2, 1490.
42. Lydia Saad, "Late Upsets Are Rare, but Have Happened," Gallup, October 27, 2008.
43. Ann Blackman, "Hostage Crisis Poses Dilemma for Reagan," Associated Press, October 24, 1980.
44. Ibid.
45. Howard Kurtz, "Reagan '80 Campaign Sought Data on US Probe of Billy Carter," *Washington Post*, May 24, 1984.
46. Sick, *October Surprise*, 24.
47. Albosta Report, Part 1, 36.
48. Jack Lesar, "A Former Ronald Reagan Campaign Official Charged Thursday Administration . . . ," United Press International, July, 7, 1983.
49. Albosta Report, Part 1, 39.
50. Albosta Report, Part 2, 1606–12.
51. Albosta Report, Part 1, 35.
52. Albosta Report, Part 1, 3.
53. Albosta Report, Part 1, 111.
54. Stuart E. Eizenstat, *President Carter* (New York: St. Martin's Publishing Group, 2018) 906.

55. Laurence I. Barrett, *Gambling with History: Ronald Reagan in the White House* (New York: Penguin Books, 1983), 383.
56. Albosta Report, Part 1, 102.
57. Albosta Report, Part 1, 100.
58. Sworn affidavit of James A. Baker III, Albosta Report, Part 2, 1086.
59. Not for attribution.
60. Albosta Report, Part 1, 124–30.
61. Godfrey Sperling Jr., "Reagan Win on Tuesday Seems Likely Unless Dramatic Shift Occurs," *Christian Science Monitor*, October 31, 1980.
62. "Cyrus Hashemi Chronology: March 1980 to September 1981," Parry Archives, FBI tapes, File B13B13F01.
63. Classified memo, February 24, 1981.
64. Ibid.
65. Ibid.
66. Ibid.
67. Sick, *October Surprise*, 88.
68. Robert Parry interview with Jamshid Hashemi, 1992.
69. Ibid.
70. Ibid.
71. Parry, "October Surprise X-Files (Part 3)."
72. "Memo to Director," undated, Parry Archives, FBI documents.
73. Sick, *October Surprise*, 156.
74. Sick, "Election Story of the Decade."
75. Sick, *October Surprise*, 129.
76. Bernard D. Nossiter, "Mideast's Stability at Stake, U.S. Says," *New York Times*, October 24, 1980.
77. "A Chronology of Majlis's Handling of Hostage Issue," Parry archives.
78. House Task Force Report, 424.
79. Robert Parry interview with Jamshid Hashemi, 1992.
80. FBI wiretaps summaries, Parry archives.
81. Ibid.
82. FBI wiretaps summaries.

Chapter Seventeen: Paris

1. Author interview with Ari Ben-Menashe, 1991.
2. House Task Force Report, 84.
3. Sick, *October Surprise*, 143.
4. Author interview with Ari Ben-Menashe, 1991.
5. Ibid.
6. Ibid.
7. Ibid.
8. Ibid.

9. Author interview with Jody Powell, 1991.
10. Statement from Pierre Salinger, Parry archives.
11. Robert Parry, "Lost History (Part 4): Pierre Salinger & a 1980 Taboo," *Consortium News*, 1996.
12. Salinger letter to Parry.
13. *World News Tonight*, ABC News, August 21, 1981.
14. Ibid.
15. Ibid.
16. Parry, "Lost History (Part 4): Pierre Salinger & a 1980 Taboo."
17. House Task Force Report, 82.
18. House Task Force Report, 80.
19. House Task Force Report, 82.
20. House Task Force Report, 220.
21. Parry, "Lost History (Part 4): Pierre Salinger & a 1980 Taboo."
22. Censored excerpt from Pierre Salinger book, Parry Archives.
23. House Task Force Report, 216.
24. Sick, *October Surprise*, 110.
25. Ibid.
26. Ibid.
27. Ibid., 112.
28. Ibid.
29. House Task Force Report, 219.
30. House Task Force Report, 228.
31. House Task Force Report, 219.
32. Ibid.
33. Author interview with Gary Sick, 2024.
34. Peter Bergen, "When Passenger Jets Mysteriously Disappear," CNN, March 11, 2014.
35. Salinger memo to Robert Parry.
36. FBI memo to Oliver "Buck" Revell, undated.

Chapter Eighteen: Tehran

1. Shlomo Brom, "Nuclear Negotiations with Iran," *American Progress*, November 17, 2014.
2. "Former General Reveals IRGC's Role in US Embassy Takeover," *Iran International*, August 19, 2023.
3. Robert D. Kaplan, "A Bazaari's World," *The Atlantic*, March 1996.
4. "Millionaire Mullahs," *Forbes*, June 21, 2003.
5. Sick, *October Surprise*, 85.
6. "Millionaire Mullahs," *Forbes*.
7. Kaplan, "A Bazaari's World."
8. Author interview with Davoud Bavand, 2014.

9. Ibid.
10. Ibid.
11. Shaul Bakhash, *The Reign of the Ayatollahs: Iran and the Islamic Revolution* (New York: Basic Books, 1986), 211.
12. House Task Force Report, 80.
13. Ibid.
14. Zein letter to Parry, July 10, 2014, Parry archives.
15. "Ghotbzadeh, Iran Hostage Crisis Figure, Executed," *New York Times*, September 17, 1982.
16. Semira N. Nikou, "Timeline of Iran's Political Events," *The Iran Primer*, August 10, 2021.
17. A. D. Horne, "Iran Executes Ghotbzadeah, Who Sought to Negotiate on Hostage," *Washington Post*, September 17, 1982.
18. Author interview with Davoud Bavand, 2016.
19. Sick, *October Surprise*, 166–67.
20. Author interview with Mohsen Rafighdoost, 2014.
21. Ibid.
22. Ibid.
23. Kaplan, "A Bazaari's World."
24. Ibid.
25. Author interview with Mohsen Rafighdoost, 2014.
26. House Task Force Report, 848.
27. House Task Force Report, 849.
28. Sick, *October Surprise*, 110.
29. House Task Force Report, 168.
30. House Task Force Report, 849.
31. Ibid.
32. House Task Force Report, 217.
33. Interview in Tehran, 2014.
34. Gary Sick testimony before the House Task Force, November 22, 1992.
35. Interview in Tehran, 2014.

Chapter Nineteen: The End of the Beginning

1. Translated article from Enghelab Eslami, September 18, 1980.
2. Ibid.
3. Ibid.
4. Senate Report, 48.
5. Ibid.
6. House Task Force Report, 75
7. Kenneth R. Timmerman, "Fanning the Flames: Guns, Greed & Geopolitics in the Gulf War," *The Iran Brief*, 1986.
8. Translation of Portions of Articles from *Enghelab Eslami*, Parry archives

9. Email from Gary Sick to Author, 2024.
10. Ibid.
11. Bernard Gwertzman, "Teheran Indicates It Is Moving Closer to Hostage Decision," *New York Times*, October 23, 1980.
12. Ibid.
13. Godfrey Sperling Jr., *Christian Science Monitor*, October 24, 1980.
14. "Carter Heads for Final Campaign Blitz," Associated Press, October 29, 1980.
15. William Safire, "The Ayatollah Votes," *New York Times*, October 27, 1980.
16. "Majlis to Vote on Release Terms in Public Session Thursday," Associated Press, October 29, 1980.
17. ABC News Transcripts, October 30, 1980.
18. "Carter Won't Predict Hostage Developments," Associated Press, October 31, 1980.
19. Jordan, *Crisis*, 361–62.
20. Sick, *October Surprise*, 174.
21. Unger, "October Surprise."
22. Alter, *His Very Best: Jimmy Carter, a Life*, 592.
23. Unger, "October Surprise."
24. "1980 Presidential Election Remarks With Reporters on the Results of the Election," The American Presidency Project, November 5, 1980.
25. FBI wiretaps, Parry Archive.
26. Ibid.
27. Weiner, *Legacy of Ashes: The History of the CIA*, 540.
28. "Richard Allen Oral History," UVA Miller Center.
29. Jonathan Beaty and S. C. Gwynne, *The Outlaw Bank: A Wild Ride into the Secret Heart of BCCI* (New York: Random House, 1993), 304.
30. Abbie Hoffman and Jonathan Silvers, "An Election Held Hostage."
31. Mark Bowden, *Guests of the Ayatollah: The First Battle in America's War with Militant Islam* (New York: Atlantic Monthly Press, 2006), 583.
32. Alter, *His Very Best: Jimmy Carter, a Life*, 604.
33. Bird, *The Outlier*, 595.
34. Carter, *Keeping Faith*, 3.
35. Gordon Thomas, *Journey into Madness: The True Story of Secret CIA Mind Control and Medical Abuse* (New York: Bantam, 1989), 312.
36. Steven R. Weisman, "Reagan Takes Oath as 40th President; Promises an 'Era of National Renewal,'" *New York Times*, January 20, 1981.
37. Reagan Inaugural Address 1981, Ronald Reagan Presidential Library & Museum.
38. Ibid.
39. Lars-Erik Nelson and David J. Oestreicher, "Iranian Hostage Crisis Comes to an End in 1981," *Daily News*, January 20, 1981.
40. Weisman, "Reagan Takes Oath as 40th President."

Epilogue

1. Author interview with John Limbert, 2024

2. Ibid.
3. Ibid.
4. Jonathan Alter, Gary Sick, and Stuart Eizenstat, "It's All but Settled: The Reagan Campaign Delayed the Release of the Iranian Hostages," *The New Republic*, May 3, 2023.
5. Mahmood Delkhasteh, "Lost History of Iran's 1981 Coup," *Consortium News*, June 21, 2016.
6. Author interview with Abolhassan Bani-Sadr, 2016.
7. Ibid.
8. Trevor Mostyn, "Abolhassan Bani-Sadr obituary," *The Guardian*, October 11, 2021.
9. Ibid.
10. Author interview with Abolhassan Bani-Sadr, 2016.
11. Delkhasteh, "Lost History of Iran's 1981 Coup."
12. Author interview with Mahmood Delkhasteh, 2016.
13. Author interview with Abolhassan Bani-Sadr, 2016.
14. Associated Press, "Abolhassan Bani-Sadr; Iran's First President After Islamic Revolution, Dies at 88," *Washington Post*, October 9, 2021.
15. Jon Schwarz, "Obits Black Out Claims That Reagan Conspired to Keep Hostages in Iran Until After 1980 Election," *The Intercept*, October 11, 2021.
16. Nate Cohn, "Revisiting Florida 2000 and the Butterfly Effect," *New York Times*, March 31, 2024.
17. Gregory Palast, "Florida's Flawed 'Voter-cleansing' Program," Salon, December 4, 2000.
18. Author interview with Abolhassan Bani-Sadr, 2016.
19. Josué Michels, "'You Can Only Love Germany with a Broken Heart," *The Trumpet*, May 12, 2020.
20. Bryan Burrough, Chris Tomlinson, and Jason Stanford, *Forget the Alamo: The Rise and Fall of an American Myth* (New York: Penguin Press, 2021).

Index

About MARINER BOOKS

Mariner Books traces its beginnings to 1832 when William Ticknor cofounded the Old Corner Bookstore in Boston, from which he would run the legendary firm Ticknor and Fields, publisher of Ralph Waldo Emerson, Harriet Beecher Stowe, Nathaniel Hawthorne, and Henry David Thoreau. Following Ticknor's death, Henry Oscar Houghton acquired Ticknor and Fields and, in 1880, formed Houghton Mifflin, which later merged with venerable Harcourt Publishing to form Houghton Mifflin Harcourt. HarperCollins purchased HMH's trade publishing business in 2021 and reestablished their storied lists and editorial team under the name Mariner Books.

Uniting the legacies of Houghton Mifflin, Harcourt Brace, and Ticknor and Fields, Mariner Books continues one of the great traditions in American bookselling. Our imprints have introduced an incomparable roster of enduring classics, including Hawthorne's *The Scarlet Letter*, Thoreau's *Walden*, Willa Cather's *O Pioneers!*, Virginia Woolf's *To the Lighthouse*, W.E.B. Du Bois's *Black Reconstruction*, J.R.R. Tolkien's *The Lord of the Rings*, Carson McCullers's *The Heart Is a Lonely Hunter*, Ann Petry's *The Narrows*, George Orwell's *Animal Farm* and *Nineteen Eighty-Four*, Rachel Carson's *Silent Spring*, Margaret Walker's *Jubilee*, Italo Calvino's *Invisible Cities*, Alice Walker's *The Color Purple*, Margaret Atwood's *The Handmaid's Tale*, Tim O'Brien's *The Things They Carried*, Philip Roth's *The Plot Against America*, Jhumpa Lahiri's *Interpreter of Maladies*, and many others. Today Mariner Books remains proudly committed to the craft of fine publishing established nearly two centuries ago at the Old Corner Bookstore.